MUSICAL DESIGN
IN AESCHYLEAN THEATER

MUSICAL DESIGN
IN AESCHYLEAN THEATER

WILLIAM C. SCOTT

PUBLISHED FOR DARTMOUTH COLLEGE
BY UNIVERSITY PRESS OF NEW ENGLAND
HANOVER AND LONDON, 1984

UNIVERSITY PRESS OF NEW ENGLAND

Brandeis University   University of New Hampshire
Brown University   University of Rhode Island
Clark University   Tufts University
Dartmouth College   University of Vermont

LIBRARY OF CONGRESS CATALOGING IN PUBLICATION DATA

Scott, William C. (William Clyde), 1937–
Musical design in Aeschylean theater.

Bibliography: p.
Includes index.
1. Music, Greek and Roman—History and criticism.   2. Aeschylus—Dramatic production.   3. Aeschylus—Stage history.
4. Greek drama—Incidental music—History and criticism.
5. Drama—Chorus (Greek drama).   I Title.
ML169.S37   1984   782.8'3'0938   83-40560
ISBN 0-87451-291-3

FOR MARY LYONS

. . . those ill-fated figures, the Furies . . . We tried every possible manner of presenting them. We put them on the stage, and they looked like uninvited guests who had strayed in from a fancy dress ball. We concealed them behind gauze, and they suggested a still out of a Walt Disney film. We made them dimmer, and they looked like shrubbery just outside the window. I have seen other experiments tried: I have seen them signalling from across the garden, or swarming on to the stage like a football team, and they are never right. They never succeed in being either Greek goddesses or modern spooks. But their failure is merely a symptom of the failure to adjust the ancient with the modern.

T. S. Eliot, *On Poetry and Poets*

CONTENTS

PREFACE

Aeschylus was a dramatic poet interested primarily in giving form to ideas. As such, he is among the world's great dramatists in having written plays that communicate thoughts through the forms of theater: the properly spoken word, the expressive movement, the significant positioning of the actors, the design of the costumes, and the music and the dance of the chorus. Yet to modern readers and revivifiers of classical drama, the chorus seems to pose an insuperable obstacle not only to understanding but also to staging. The chorus, which might be irreverently described as those twelve idle ladies of Thebes, seems always to embarrass modern theatergoers and at times even to have embarrassed the playwrights themselves. G. H. Gellie, in his book on Sophocles, sums up the general puzzlement among scholars: "Even if we perform our Greek plays in the open air and thereby avoid some of the staging difficulties, there seems to be no way to put across the words of a Greek choral ode that will on the one hand preserve some of the Greekness and on the other hand induce the proper sentiments and emotions in a modern audience."[1] Directors are chary of attempting to stage the extended choral songs, and readers in translation are frustrated by the chorus's long chains of words. Our lack of knowledge about the chorus seems so nearly total that it is difficult not to resign ourselves simply to reading Greek plays silently and in solitude. Yet it is clear that tragic choruses occupied the audience's attention for a significant proportion of the play, provided much of the drama's color and movement, filled the huge space of the orchestra, and, in the case of Aeschylus' *Oresteia*, set forth the major generalizing statements that both illuminate the action and set it in a framework.

This study examines closely the words, shape, structure, and placement of the choral songs in Aeschylean drama, especially in the *Oresteia*, to delineate the role of the chorus in the production. Although it is impossible to recapture the dance and music of the original productions, the choral odes of the *Oresteia* provide clues to the effect the dramatist created in his choruses. Moreover, although the scant surviving evidence about music in Greek tragedy does not allow philological proof, the consistency of design in successive odes strongly supports philological probability. What conclusions we can draw about the role of the chorus in the *Oresteia*—and a very large role it is—will serve also as a starting point for a survey of the contribution of the choruses in other plays. This book, it is hoped, will help scholars, directors, and playwrights to develop further their own conceptions and to examine other ancient plays in which there has been little success in staging the chorus.

For readers in translation, the introduction presents the basic meters found in the choral odes of the *Oresteia*. It explains how to annotate a text to reveal the underlying musical design of the play and then to bring the tightly organized metrical forms to life in a contemporary production. The first chapter offers evidence that Aeschylus himself was aware of the importance of music for the proper staging of his dramas. Chapter 2 discusses in detail the scansion patterns and the design of each ode in the *Oresteia*. Once discerned, the repeated metrical configurations yield important clues to production —especially when they seem to reinforce the developing themes of the play and contribute significantly to the resolution of those themes at the end of the trilogy. In Chapter 3 I have tried to incorporate the conclusions about musical design into a broad interpretation of the trilogy. The final chapter identifies features of similar design in the other plays of Aeschylus; as a result the analysis of choral songs in the *Oresteia* becomes an important key to defining an Aeschylean musical style, which stands in significant contrast to the techniques of Sophocles and Euripides.

To satisfy the close demands of the scholar while maintaining the interest of the director, I have presented the evidence in notes when the argument becomes technical. This approach will, I hope, unburden the text and make the book easier to read for those who do not know Greek. I have used the text of Aeschylus edited by D. Page (Oxford 1972) throughout, discussing in notes any passages where I disagree with him. My translations of every Greek text are admittedly free but, I trust, responsible.

I have been supported in writing this book by grants from Dartmouth College and the Marion and Jasper Whiting Foundation. The librarians of Baker Library at Dartmouth College have shown more than usual ingenuity in locating books and manuscripts; the faculty and librarians of Stanford University were gracious hosts and willing helpers during a year's sabbatical.

Many friends have aided me in completing this study. Rod Alexander, Peter Arnott, H. G. Edinger, B. H. Fowler, C. J. Herington, E. G. Hill, Joanna Hitchcock, N. A. Kindelan, David Konstan, H. Y. McCulloch, William Mullen, J. L. Steffensen, Jr., J. T. Svendsen, and Oliver Taplin were faithful guides as the book took shape. Catherine Frasier has again devotedly typed numerous versions of my manuscript; Ann Hawthorne has been a skilled and loyal editor. To the many other friends and colleagues who read sections of the manuscript carefully and patiently and who have offered generous criticism, I offer my grateful appreciation.

My wife has been an unfailing source of aid and encouragement as well as the mainstay of my home. It is a pleasure to dedicate this book to her.

INTRODUCTION FOR
READERS IN TRANSLATION
Vital Tools for Staging a Greek Choral Song

> Greek lyric metres are a subject which reduces many a
> classical scholar to despair; one in which he sees little
> profit and no certainty, its approaches defended by a
> veritable battery of metrical apparatus, and by a kind
> of Foreign Legion of music-symbols. . . . he is in-
> clined to resent them as interlopers, which they are
> not, or to suspect them as being only another way
> of talking nonsense, which very often they are. The
> whole thing, as a Regius Professor has said, is like
> Black Magic.
>
> *H.D.F. Kitto*

Despite H. D. F. Kitto's eloquent expression of
frustration with regard to choral songs,[1] not only
classicists but also readers in translation can quite
readily learn how to hear scansion patterns. The metrical
schemes presented in this section provide both a key to cre-
ative stage direction of the *Oresteia* and an impetus to more
representative and lively productions of all Greek dramas.
The rhythmic patterns are too important to be ignored and
too simple to be a continuing cause of lasting confusion and
frustration. The first two stanzas of the Hymn to Zeus (*Ag.*
160–75), a major section of the long first ode in the *Oresteia*,
are presented on the next two pages as an example of the metrical analysis described below. Using this model the scansion
patterns presented in Chapter 2 for all the odes of the *Oresteia*
can be quickly and easily transcribed into a reader's translation.

STROPHE (*AG*. 160–67)   Scansion Pattern

Ζεὺς ὅστις ποτ' ἐστίν, εἰ τόδ' αὐ-   str/ant — — — ◡ — ◡ — ◡ —
[Zeus hostis pot' estin, ei tod' au-]   ♩ ♩   ♩ ♪ ♩ ♪ ♩ ♪ ♩
Zeus: whatever he may be, if this name

τῶι φίλον κεκλημένωι,   — ◡ — ◡ — ◡ —
[tōi philon keklēmenōi]   ♩ ♪ ♩ ♪ ♩ ♪ ♩
pleases him in invocation,

τοῦτό νιν προσεννέπω·   — ◡ — ◡ — ◡ —
[touto nin prosennepō]   ♩ ♪ ♩ ♪ ♩ ♪ ♩
thus I call upon him.

οὐκ ἔχω προσεικάσαι   — ◡ — ◡ — ◡ —
[ouk echō proseikasai]   ♩ ♪ ♩ ♪ ♩ ♪ ♩
I have pondered everything

πάντ' ἐπισταθμώμενος   — ◡ — ◡ — ◡ —
[pant' epistathmōmenos]   ♩ ♪ ♩ ♪ ♩ ♪ ♩
yet I cannot find a way,

πλὴν Διός, εἰ τὸ μάταν   — ◡◡ — ◡◡ —
ἀπὸ φροντίδος ἄχθος   ♩ ♪♪ ♩ ♪♪ ♩
[plēn Dios, ei to matan   ◡◡ — ◡◡ — —
apo phrontidos achthos]   ♪♪ ♩ ♪♪ ♩ ♩
only Zeus, to cast this
dead weight of ignorance

χρὴ βαλεῖν ἐτητύμως·   — ◡ — ◡ — ◡ —
[chrē balein etētymōs]   ♩ ♪ ♩ ♪ ♩ ♪ ♩
finally from out my brain.

	Name of Meter
ANTISTROPHE (168–175)	

οὐδ' ὅστις πάροιθεν ἦν μέγας,
[oud' hostis paroithen ēn megas]
He who in time long ago was great,

sp + lec

παμμάχωι θράσει βρύων,
[pammachōi thrasei bryōn]
throbbing with gigantic strength,

lec

οὐδὲ λέξεται πρὶν ὤν·
[oude lexetai prin ōn]
shall be as if he never were, unspoken.

lec

τεύξεται φρενῶν τὸ πᾶν
[teuxetai phrenōn to pan]
you will not have failed the truth.

lec

κτῆρος οἴχεται τυχών·
[ktēros oichetai tychōn]
his master, and is gone.

lec

Ζῆνα δέ τις προφρόνως ἐπινίκια κλάζων
[Zēna de tis prophronōs epinikia klazōn]
Cry aloud without fear the victory of Zeus,

da

τεύξεται φρενῶν τὸ πᾶν
[teuxetai phrenōn to pan]
you will not have failed the truth.

lec

The first steps are to obtain as accurate a translation as possible and to read it carefully. Although Aeschylean Greek is elusive and complex in both grammar and content, there are several good translations available, as well as books discussing the development of the chorus's thought throughout the trilogy.[2] Chapter 3 of this book also provides such a discussion. The Lattimore translation is used in the example and is the easiest for a reader in translation to use throughout this study because the line numbers in his text correspond so closely to the standard Greek edition.

To appreciate the sound and rhythmical qualities of each line one should acquire a Greek text of the play and learn the twenty-four letters of the Greek alphabet which are given at the start of any standard grammar. Their pronunciation is straightforward; there are no "hidden" syllables as in French. Therefore, a transliteration of each line of Greek, shown in brackets in the example, is entirely optional. It is simply another way of showing how the line is pronounced.

In the righthand margin of both texts, the reader should enter the scansion pattern of each Greek line. One way to discern the rhythm is to drum it out on a tabletop. It is immediately evident how tightly the words and rhythms are joined: there is one syllable for each mark. This scansion pattern will only have to be noted once for each set of stanzas because the normal form of Greek choral song is strophic; that is, the meter of the first stanza (the strophe) is immediately repeated with different words in the next stanza (the antistrophe). Thus the structure of the normal tragic ode is in strophic pairs: aa, bb, cc, etc. In the example, the scansion pattern is given only once in the second column because—as usual—it is the same for both strophe (160–67) and antistrophe (168–75).

In the lefthand margin of both texts, the reader should enter the abbreviated names of the meters used in each line. For the Hymn to Zeus, these abbreviations appear in the fourth column. These terms are important because small standard units are often joined in varying order to form a full line. Below are the five basic meters, along with their related forms, that occur most frequently in the *Oresteia*.

Iambic (◡–◡–), with its syncopated forms   ia
   the cretic (–◡–)   cr
   and the bacchiac (◡––)   ba
Trochaic (–◡–◡), with its derived forms   troch
   the lecythion (–◡–◡–◡–)   lec
   and the ithyphallic (–◡–◡––)   ith
Dactylic (–◡◡), with its substituted form   da
   the spondee (––)   sp
Anapaest (◡◡– ◡◡– ◡◡– ◡◡–), with the   anap
   associated paroemiac (◡◡– ◡◡– ◡◡– –)
   and monometer (◡◡– ◡◡–)
Dochmiac (◡––◡–), a complex unit   doch
   allowing numerous variations on the
   basic form (◡̮◡◡◡̮◡◡̮◡̮◡◡̮)

The less common meters are:

Aeolic: the choriamb (–◡◡–),   ch
   the glyconic (◡̮◡̮–◡◡–◡–),   glyc
   and the associated pherecratean (◡̮◡̮–◡◡––) pher
Ionic (◡◡–– ◡◡––),   ion
   with the anaclast (◡◡–◡ –◡––) as an   anac
   associated form
Alcaic decasyllable (–◡◡–◡◡–◡––)
Enoplion (◡̮–◡◡–◡––)
Hipponacteum (◡◡̮–◡◡–◡––)
Ibycaean (–◡◡–◡◡–◡–)
Molossus (–––)   mol
Praxillean (–◡◡–◡◡–◡◡–◡––)

At first glance, even the list of the five major meters may appear formidable. In fact, however, to discern the basic musical design of the *Oresteia* it is necessary only to be able to hear the difference between the iambic and trochaic patterns and to identify the anapaest and dochmiac. Thus, in the example the trochaic in its derived form, the lecythion, predominates. Only the first foot and the one long line in the strophe/antistrophe have spondees or dactyls.

Beneath the scansion pattern for each line of the Hymn to Zeus is an approximation of the metrical scheme in quarter notes and eighth notes. Although it is doubtful that the rhythms of Greek meter were equivalent to those of modern musical notation, this form most clearly illustrates the differences in rhythm in sequential passages. Therefore, either at this point or when recording the scansion patterns earlier, the reader may enter in the translation this simple scheme supplementing the scansion patterns.

After adding this information to the translation, the reader can perform the analysis necessary to create music and a dance pattern for the choral odes. Because no translation successfully reproduces the metrical patterns of the Greek original—the cadence and structure of Greek are very different from those of English—the reader should consult the margin of the text for the names of the meters, especially to note where a longer section of a stanza is built from the same basic rhythm. This analysis will produce large sections of anapaestic, iambic, and trochaic meters. From this organization of metrically similar sections, it should be possible to see the general musical design of whole sections of an ode. For example, the parodos of the *Agamemnon* can quickly be analysed into units as follows:

strophe / antistrophe	(104–39)	da
epode	(140–59)	da
str/ant	(160–75)	troch
str/ant	(176–91)	troch
str/ant	(192–217)	ia
str/ant	(218–37)	ia
str/ant	(238–57)	ia

After this ode-by-ode analysis, a comparison of the clustering of similar metrical patterns throughout all the odes will reveal where in the play certain metrical forms are conjoined with similar thoughts or motifs.

With this clear and useful representation of the musical design, the reader or director can then devise patterns of music and dance that will signal to the audience the recurrence of these motifs throughout the production. Whether the music chosen for a production be shepherd's pipe or Shostakovich, the use of a musical line and dance pattern in one ode should prepare the audience to hear that line and to see that pattern when they appear in a later one. A shift in rhythm in a neighboring stanza can be represented by a change in melody, instrumentation, or musical tone of the accompaniment; the repetition of a rhythm can be signaled by a repetition of the earlier musical line and mode. In this way the music develops as a support for the dramatic themes. Finally, both the music and the dance should make clear, through repetition and rounded units, the basic, balanced form of strophe echoed by antistrophe, so that there will be a strong effect at those places where there is no repetition. Because the absence of a balancing stanza may indicate an intent to impress or surprise the audience, wherever unbalanced forms—traditionally called epodes, mesodes, and astropha—occur, the musical pattern should likewise occur only once.

This approach necessarily involves imposing an external musical form on the text; but the imaginative reader or aspiring director can at least be certain that the original production had musical accompaniment and that the restoration of music to the choral odes is serving concepts of stagecraft that Aeschylus deemed vital. The playwright has provided encouragement for such an endeavor by using many images of music-making and by incorporating in the *Oresteia* several scenes that cannot be realized without aural and visual stage effects. An awareness of the full musical design will bring a new dimension to the long odes of the chorus, enabling reader, director, and audience to appreciate their complexity in both thought and form.

MUSICAL DESIGN

IN AESCHYLEAN THEATER

CHAPTER I

THE IMPORTANCE OF MUSIC AND
DANCE IN THE *ORESTEIA*

Since Aeschylus' own time, assessments of the man and his surviving works have variously clouded and illuminated our understanding of his accomplishments as a dramatist.[1] To his contemporaries he was a devoted Athenian citizen and spokesman during the brave years of the democracy, possessed of all the aspirations and fears of his fellow men. The cry of the Greek sailors rowing against the enemy warships in the *Persians* springs undeniably from the heart of a patriotic man who debated, questioned, and defended the ideals of the democracy both in daily life and on the battlefield. Although he is remembered today for his dramatic achievements, his reported epitaph mentions only his service at Marathon:

> Under this monument lies Aeschylus the Athenian,
>   Euphorion's son, who died in the wheatlands of Gela. The grove
> of Marathon with its glories can speak of his valor in battle.
>   The long-haired Persian remembers and can speak of it too.[2]
>
> *(trans. by Richmond Lattimore)*

And at the end of the fifth century, when Aristophanes in *The Frogs* depicted a contest in the underworld between Aeschylus and Euripides to determine which poet would be resurrected in order to save Athens by educating its citizens, the earlier poet won the contest not because of his stagecraft, but because of his moral teachings and conservative values.

Later critics supported Aristophanes' estimation of Aeschylus as a revered but not popular poet,[3] largely because of his penchant for weighty and dignified verses. The author of the anonymous *Life* states that Aeschylus sought "the grand style, making use of onomatopoeic coinages, epithets, metaphors, and every available device to lend weight to his verse."[4] Simonides is reported to have bested him in elegiac competition because Aeschylus' compositions lacked the fineness or subtlety required for that mode.[5] These generally unfavorable and often quite acid assessments reflect the fact that Aeschylus' style differed radically from what later critics considered to be the norm for ancient writing.[6] Today Aeschylus is commonly credited with a vibrant, pictorial mind that searched his own experience intensively for images with which his characters might express themselves strongly and effectively.[7] Critical debate continues about the theological basis of Aeschylean drama. Although it is evident that Aeschylus was concerned with the nature of Zeus's relationship with the other gods of Greek religion, disagreement persists about the degree of sophistication which can be assigned to an early thinker and about the meaning of the harsh actions of Zeus portrayed in the *Oresteia* and *Prometheus Bound*.[8]

Despite this variety of perspectives, all critics of Aeschylus have agreed that he deserves high regard as a dramatic innovator. The anonymous *Life* pays tribute to his influence on the development of the theater:

> Whoever thinks that Sophocles was the more perfect writer of tragedy, thinks correctly, but let him consider that it was much more difficult to bring tragedy to such a point of greatness after Thespis, Phrynichus, and Choerilus than to arrive at the perfection of Sophocles after Aeschylus.[9]

Ancient commentators drawing on earlier sources speak frequently of his personal involvement in the technical production of his plays.[10] He enhanced the visual effectiveness of the performance by increasing the number of actors, by decorating his sets splendidly, by using mechanical devices, by introducing extraordinary characters such as ghosts, the Erinyes, and even Lyssa (Madness),[11] and by highlighting special features of the players' masks.[12] According to Athenaeus,

Aeschylus not only invented that beauty and dignity of dress which hierophants and torchbearers imitate when they put on their vestments, but also originated many dance figures and assigned them to the members of his chorus. For Chamaeleon says that Aeschylus was the first to design steps for his choruses, employing no dancing masters, but devising for himself the figures of the dances, and in general taking upon himself the entire management of the tragedy.[13]

In support of such statements there is ample evidence in his surviving plays of Aeschylus' interest in writing texts that required effective staging if they were to be understood fully. Designers of sets, props, costumes, and masks find scenes of tremendous richness; buildings and monuments, varied stage levels, strong colors,[14] and striking masks[15] are important elements in the plays. Aeschylus' choral odes and the episodes in which motion and gesture convey much of the meaning open obvious opportunities for imaginative directors and choreographers.[16] Actors find demanding and rewarding roles; the lines of Eteocles and Clytemnestra especially require actors not only with a strong voice and presence, but also with subtlety. In regard to all the basic areas of technical production Aeschylus wrote plays that are preeminently theatrical—they must be seen on the stage or in the mind's eye to be appreciated fully as masterpieces of dramatic writing.

Evidence about the theater in Aeschylus' time is too scanty and unreliable to permit reconstruction of an original production. It is obvious that certain devices of modern theatrical technology were unavailable: he could not plunge the theater into darkness or lower a series of suspended backdrops for quick changes of scene. Some general information is available on the types of music in Aeschylus' day, but there is no way to be sure that he did not depart from this norm, especially in such choral songs as that of the terrified women at the beginning of the *Seven against Thebes*.[17] Although there was at least one book in the fifth century on stage painting, no reliable reports on this form survive from contemporary

co-workers or spectators who actually saw a production supervised by Aeschylus.[18] Vase paintings depicting costumes
and staging are necessarily static representations of a three-
dimensional and kinetic medium.[19] There were professional
actors in Aeschylus' time, but little is known of their training
or the predominant style of acting; and what statements there
are may well be derived from later practice.[20] Even the few
nuggets of information about actual productions, such as the
traumatic reaction of the audience to the entrance of the
Furies, are suspiciously similar to exaggerated reviews of audience reaction through the ages;[21] quite possibly they are not
reports of the premier performance but of later, more spectacular productions.[22] It seems that the best evidence for the
staging of Aeschylean drama must come from the text of
the plays themselves. Often they too can tell us nothing of
the actual first performance, but they do convey in the most
direct available way the intent of the dramatist in writing
each scene. By joining an accurate assessment of that intent to
our general knowledge of the Greek theater—granting always that Aeschylus was an innovative playwright who used
all the theatrical resources available to him in staging his plays
—modern scholars and directors can come close to describing how the playwright combined actors, props, and sets to
communicate the total dramatic conception of each scene.

One thing we do know about the theater of fifth-century
Athens: the Athenians considered the chorus so significant a
part of the performance of tragedies that they allocated public
monies for training and equipping choruses for the productions during the state festivals; the poet was left to recruit his
own actors. The Athenians' view of the importance of the
chorus provides justification for better defining its role. Yet
the choruses have been fairly regarded as the most difficult
features of the ancient drama for modern producers to re-
create and for modern scholars to assess. There are strongly
divergent opinions about the function of the choruses in the
plays, about the meaning and relevance of the words in the
choral odes—especially as the concerns of the chorus become

more abstract—and about the staging of the choruses. Non-impressionistic solutions to such problems are elusive in the best of circumstances, but given the loss of the music and the dance patterns, scholars fall back on philological method; yet studies of drama have consistently shown that stage productions—and particularly those incorporating music—must be interpreted from a different vantage.[23] The tools of literary study, which are useful for works that depend for their effect only on the written word, become rather crude instruments when applied to art forms that acquire life only through music, dance, and public performance.

Music and sound were undeniably important elements of production for all the playwrights of the Greek theater, but especially for Aeschylus. His surviving plays contain a larger proportion of rhythmic choral song than do those of either Sophocles or Euripides.[24] Because music and rhythm are directly related to the movement and pattern of the choral dance, and also to the movements of individual dancers, such as Cassandra and Io, this high proportion of musical lines reveals the playwright's constant striving to capture his spectators' eyes as well as ears. The several characters who refuse to speak for whole scenes, Aeschylus' famed "silent characters" are yet another indication of his tendency to employ the aural and visual aspects of production within the logic of his dramas.[25] Consequently, any director who designs a production in which music, sound, and dance are not prominent means of communicating the development of the dramatic idea cannot claim to have re-created Aeschylean drama.

Given that sound and motion are basic elements in a production, learning about ancient dramatic music is a frustratingly difficult task. Secondary sources of varying reliability make casual references to Aeschylus' interest in music and dance, but few offer precise information about their use in an ancient production or about their intended effect. So deficient is our knowledge of ancient staging that we must be grudgingly thankful even for that silly anecdote about the entrance of the chorus in the *Eumenides*, which so frightened the audience that children fainted and women miscarried.[26] This story undoubtedly arose from a production that employed frightening costumes and masks, but it also provides an indication that music, dance, and gesture strongly reinforced the illusion of fear conveyed by the basic costume.[27] In addition to scattered reports about productions, there are more general ancient treatises on music, but these deal mostly with the theory of music and the structure of the scales.[28] Some critics have tried to trace the few surviving fragments of ancient music back to the fifth century and to re-create choral music and rhythm, but so little is known about the notational system that reliable conclusions about dramatic music seem beyond reach.[29] Information on dancing seems to come from sources equally distant from the original performance.[30]

Yet if we can accept a less ambitious goal than an actual re-creation of the original production, it is possible to describe at least the aims of the playwright in designing the odes for his chorus. The scansion patterns, which underlie every stanza of tragic lyric, provide evidence of strophic and nonstrophic forms, of variation in meters, of degrees of resolution, and of the joining of specific meters to individual themes. Developing a workable theory based on a consistent interpretation of this evidence is preferable to the tolerance of individualistic impressionism; at the very least such a theory can challenge others to find a better one that explains more fully the consistencies and patterns revealed on the scansion charts. An additional encouragement for such exploration is the major role of sound-making or music-making in certain Aeschylean scenes. Just as verbal metaphors can be used to deepen characterization or to illuminate the plot by providing penetratingly apt comparisons and ironically truthful insights,[31] so also the repetition of actions and movements can serve as visual or aural metaphors commenting on the role or motives of characters.[32] Perhaps the clearest example of the use of sound as a metaphor-in-action is the Cassandra scene in the *Agamemnon* (1035–1330). At the beginning of this scene the chorus speaks in iambic trimeters while Cassandra addresses them in dochmiacs, a musical response. Her first speeches are more sound than music, comprised of shrieks and wails characterized by the chorus as the cries of a mourner (1075). Later they ask why she continues to interrupt her song by ill-omened cries and shrill, high-pitched notes (1150–55). Her initial failure to respond to Clytemnestra leads the chorus to decide that Cassandra cannot speak or understand Greek. When she does begin to speak, communication is so slight that she does not seem even to hear the chorus's words. Yet when she sings:

> Where have you led me? To what house?

the chorus answers:

> To the house of the Atreidae. If you don't realize that, I'll tell you. And you won't call this a lie.

And Cassandra immediately corrects them:

> No, it is a house that hates the gods, a house that knows many stories of the slaughtering of kin, evil behead-ings[33]—it is a slaughterhouse for men and a floor spattered with blood.

In the interchange (1087–92) it is clear that Cassandra and the chorus have begun to communicate with one another but are thinking on different levels. It is appropriate in the development of this scene that the chorus, which tries to confine its answers and responses to factual statements about the present state of affairs, begins by speaking; and equally appropriate that the prophetess, who sees both the past history of the house and its future, sings. The contrast is good theater, for it shows that Cassandra is attempting to convey her complex vision of the Atreid house whereas the elders want to express themselves only in simple, rational statements.[34]

The elders' reply to Cassandra's imagistic description of the house of Atreus shows that they realize that she knows the history of the family:

> It seems that the stranger is keen-scented like a hunting
> dog; she is looking where she will discover bloodshed.
>
> (1093–94)

At this moment a struggle begins. The members of the chorus do not want to understand the clear implications of Cassandra's musical prophecy while she persistently reminds them of the past and foresees additional bloody events in the future. She continues to sing, and they continue to speak, grudgingly recognizing the facts of the past but expressing unwillingness or inability to make sense of her visions.[35] Yet the forebodings expressed by the chorus in its song at 975–1034 cannot remain hidden before such a constant attack, and the elders begin to acknowledge their anxiety at 1119:

> What is this Erinys which you urge to raise its voice
> over the house? Your word does not cheer me. To my
> heart rushed the pale drop of blood that arrives as the
> light of life sinks low for those killed by the spear.
> Doom comes swiftly.

At this moment they begin to sing with Cassandra. The change from speech to song is gradual but deliberate. At 1119 they speak two iambic lines and then sing three lines of dochmiac, the predominant meter in Cassandra's song, followed by a lyric iambic closing. After Cassandra responds, they reply in the same form: two iambic lines followed by corresponding dochmiacs and a lyric iambic ending. Almost without noticing, they have begun to sing corresponding strophes in the same meter as Cassandra and to imitate, or at least to show the influence of, her excited movements. From this point through 1178, where Cassandra begins to speak in iambics, they sing corresponding strophic stanzas in dochmiacs.

In response to their movement from speech to music, Cassandra diminishes the musical component of her lines. At 1136 she has two lines of dochmiac and then two lines of iambic trimeter. The elders sing their response in dochmiacs, and Cassandra repeats the previous combined pattern of music and speech, continuing the shift from song to speech. Finally, she abandons song altogether, saying: "I will instruct you no more in riddles" (1183). At this point her prophecy becomes much less imagistic, and both priestess and chorus try to communicate clearly through speech. She asks the old men whether she is wrong in asserting that this house has had a gruesome past, and they question her about her previous life. For such a give-and-take conversation, speech is the more appropriate dramatic form.[36]

Thus, two contrasting postures are developed simultaneously in this scene. The members of the chorus at 975–1034 have confessed their confusion and frustration in pondering future events in the house of Atreus and are willing to turn their minds to other matters; but, as Cassandra awakens their deepest concerns, they become anguished in contemplating the forces that are converging on the house of Atreus: the fate of their king, the fears of the Trojan princess, and perhaps ultimately the future of their city and the threat to their own lives. Meanwhile Cassandra becomes increasingly aware of her situation. At first, she is so involved in her inner thoughts that she does not hear Clytemnestra. Then she breaks into a torrent of cries, a mixture of rage and sorrow, still in a trance of anger at Apollo her destroyer. As she moves to speech she becomes increasingly explicit, culminating in the prosaic and factual statement: "I say that you will see the death of Agamemnon" (1246). The act of music-making not only accompanies the developing thoughts of the characters but in itself conveys the conflict in their attitudes far more directly and forcefully than the words of the text.[37]

Even though we cannot hope to recapture with any precision the rhythm, melody, phrasing, and dynamics of the music that Aeschylus composed for this scene and others, it is possible by careful analysis of meter and form to discern the effects that he hoped to achieve. It should even be possible for a contemporary director to re-create the dramatic design of the scene as originally staged by the playwright. Scenes in which music and sound play a determining role include the invocation scene and exodos of the *Persians*, the parodos and exodos of the *Seven against Thebes*, the scene in which the suppliant maidens resist and are saved from the Egyptian, and the opening monologue and the Io scene of *Prometheus Bound*. But aural and visual effects are employed to the limit of their potential in the *Oresteia*; thus it is not surprising that the number of lines in which sound and music are mentioned in the *Oresteia*, either as actual events on the stage or as metaphors, is much higher than in the other four plays. In the *Oresteia* Aeschylus seems to have wanted these words to recur with sufficient frequency and force that the audience would find it difficult to ignore the effect he was trying to create through sound and music-making.[38]

In the trilogy Aeschylus organizes most of the words of music or sound around six motifs:

> Prophets and portents
> Sounds of victims
> The speeches of Clytemnestra
> Song elements within the drama
> People who are singing the wrong song
> Sounds of cities

PROPHETS AND PORTENTS

Prophetic statements and portents in the *Oresteia* are often described by words describing sounds.[39] The clearest example occurs in the third stasimon, at *Ag.* 975–1034, where the chorus hears a prophetic song that comes unbidden from within. The apprehensions of the old men about the return of Agamemnon compel their *thymoi* (hearts) to sing the dirge of the Erinyes as a death hymn without the accompaniment of the lyre.[40] Although they express the hope that their expectation will not be fulfilled, they admit their inability to articulate their feelings clearly and unambiguously at the end of the ode when they find that their "prophetic hearts" only mutter darkly. Then Cassandra sings her prophecy, but the chorus members regard her as the singer of the wrong song. When she addresses Apollo in music that is not suited for the god, they compare her song to a lament (*Ag.* 1072–79). As she sings a tuneless tune and shrieks in a shrill and piercing melody, she is likened to the nightingale Procne, who groans rather than sings the sweet song that is expected (*Ag.* 1142– 45 and 1153–54). Later Clytemnestra characterizes Cassandra as the swan who has sung her final death lament (*Ag.* 1444– 46). The chorus likes neither the content of Cassandra's prophecy nor the way in which she sings it. To them her music, interrupted by shrieks and cries, seems harsh and unpleasant. Later, in the *Choephoroi*, the chorus of slave women is sent from the house bearing their libations because Clytemnestra shrieks in terror during the night and the prophets of the house have "cried out" that the dead are bitterly angry at their murderers (*Ch.* 32–41). Orestes sees that Clytemnestra's cry when she awakens from her dream about the snake is prophetic both for her and for him (*Ch.* 535–50).

In each case prophecies of future events are described by words of sound or music. Because the future is so bleak in the first two plays of the trilogy, the music associated with prophecy is unwanted, inappropriate, the kind of music one would stifle. In fact it is scarcely music because of the constant presence of uncertainty or fear, portrayed in groans or shrieks.

There are several less developed examples. When the elders of the chorus first enter the orchestra in the *Agamemnon*, they want to "cry out" (*throein*) the augury given to Agamemnon and Menelaus by the omen of the eagles and the hare; they state that they possess the persuasiveness of song (*Ag.* 104 and 106). At first they describe Calchas as having spoken his interpretation; later, however, they report that he shouted it out or shrieked it (*apeklanxen*—*Ag.* 125 and 156); likewise, that he *eklanxen* to the kings the cause of the winds from Strymon (201).[41] In a later episode, the prophets in the house of Menelaus groan as they foresee the desperation of their master (*Ag.* 408).

In the *Eumenides* the music of the Furies in their "Binding

Song" is called "lyreless" (*aphormiktos*, 332 and 345), thus recalling the music "without a lyre" and the "tuneless tune"
from the *Agamemnon* (990 and 1142). But following their
conversion, their prophecy of a vague and troubled future
fades before the firm assurances of Athena. With the aid of
the new Eumenides, men look forward to living in a blessed
and prosperous land. Appropriately, the whole community
sings this expectation, joining in harmony to shout out and to
sing with vigor the music that is in their hearts (*ololyxate nun
epi molpais*—1043 and 1047).

SOUNDS OF VICTIMS, ESPECIALLY CHILDREN

Almost the first event described in the parodos of the *Agamemnon* is a religious sacrifice, intended to appease Artemis
so that she will still the contrary winds from the river Strymon (*Ag.* 228–47). Because the sacrifice requires the general's daughter as victim, he becomes the murderer of his
own child. The holy and joyous ceremony to mark the sailing
of a great fleet becomes a ritual so perverse that the leaders
throw their scepters to the ground in tears, and the chorus
recoils from describing it:

> What happened then I did not see nor do I tell; but the
> arts of Calchas do not lack fulfillment.   (*Ag.* 248–49)

Because the ritual prescribes careful attention to accompanying sound and music, Iphigenia is gagged so that there will be
no defiling sound. The chorus points the contrast further by
telling how she used to sing at the banquets of her father and
his friends as they prayed for blessing; now at Aulis she is
again a participant in a religious rite with her father and his
comrades, but no song is allowed at this ceremony. The still-
ing of the song that accompanies the sacrifice is as incongru-
ous as the religious service at which the father must kill his
daughter; but, of course, her only song would be a curse on
her own family.[42]

The desire to silence Iphigenia's song is similar to the elders' reaction to the unpleasant music of Cassandra, another young girl. They protest her shrieks and cries because they believe she is singing the wrong type of song when she calls upon the god Apollo. They cannot gag her, but they do wish that she would stop singing such grating music (*Ag.* 1072–79).

In this trilogy children do not sing and dance; rather, they cry out because they are the victims of a perverse world. At *Ag.* 1095–97 Cassandra reveals some of her vision: children weeping over their own slaughter, their own cooked flesh eaten by their father. When Clytemnestra claims that she can hear the sounds coming from the captured city of Troy, she says that she can hear the wails of children fallen upon the corpses of their fathers (*Ag.* 326–28).

The *Choephoroi* offers the most stunning example of children making sounds of sorrow instead of joy. In the long kommos, which the chorus calls a hymn (475), Orestes and Electra reaffirm that the murder of Clytemnestra is necessary. At line 315 Orestes asks what he can do to reach his father since he can do no more than sing a lament—fully admitting that this is a joyful task for him. The chorus, answering that laments for the dead are effective in seeking out the guilty man, encourages him not to feel so impotent in continuing his song. Electra then begins to sing the lament in earnest: "Your two children groan in a dirge over your tomb" (334–35). The chorus responds that joy may indeed arise from such songs on the day when these children are able to cease singing such dirges and to return to their house accompanied by a song of triumph. But their song is funereal, the type of music that everyone in the play wants to see ended; yet it is all that these children can find to sing—and singing it brings them their only joy. At 500–3 Electra calls upon her father to hear the cries of his two young children sitting at his tomb.

In each of these examples innocent young people are victims. They try to sing but find that their song is unwanted, and they are stopped from singing or told to sing another type of song. The singers themselves do not even like the music they are making but feel unable to find another song because of the perverseness of their world. Only among members of a lost generation would a young girl be put in the paradoxical situation of singing her own dirge (*Ag.* 1322–30).[43]

At the end of the trilogy the processional chorus is composed of children in addition to women, the male jurors, and other members of the community. As they assemble to escort the new favoring deities to their shrine, they sing for the first time in the trilogy—not as victims, but as members of the larger community that will inhabit the new world.

THE SPEECHES OF CLYTEMNESTRA

As the dominant character in the *Agamemnon* Clytemnestra speaks more vigorously than others; thus it is fitting that her speeches are described by words of sound and music.[44] The most common sound word identified with Clytemnestra in the *Agamemnon* is the *ololygmos*, a cry of emotional release and often of triumphant joy.[45] When the watchman sees the torch signal, he immediately calls for Clytemnestra to raise the *ololygmos* (28). Later she says that she has been crying out triumphantly because of the beacon and has stirred the whole town to these jubilant sounds (587–97). Cassandra also comments on the *ololygmos* that Clytemnestra, like a general at the moment of victory, raised in joy at her husband's return (1236).

Twice Clytemnestra's speeches are described by the word *laskein*—"shout" or "cry out" (614 and 1426–7). In a forceful image the chorus announces that Clytemnestra stands vaunting over the bodies "like a hated raven that chants its hymn tunelessly" (1472–4). Clytemnestra even quashes sounds from others as she bans the sound of tears from the funeral that she is planning for Agamemnon, a funeral of joy without the customary sounds associated with death (1554).

In addition, of the major characters in the trilogy Clytemnestra is most inclined to perceive situations in terms of sound. When she reports the fall of Troy, she claims to hear the cries of the victors and the vanquished (321–25). As the queen stands over the body of Cassandra, she compares her to the swan that has sung its last song (1444–5). She says that the messengers, who told false tales of Agamemnon's death, cried out their news (*Ag.* 865).

For Clytemnestra music and sound become sinister tools in twisting the situation in Argos to suit her own desires. Her cry of joy is taken up by the townspeople as a cry of relief and happiness at the return of Agamemnon, but few realize the true reason for Clytemnestra's happiness at Agamemnon's return. Her cries of victory are sincere but warped; she is celebrating only her personal happiness at being able to kill her husband herself rather than hearing of his death at the hands of another on the battlefield. But there is a final irony; as Clytemnestra sings her gloating song of triumph over the slain Agamemnon at the end of the play, she does not realize that her days of singing are over and that she has deluded herself in finding joy in such a murder. The deep and destructive perverseness of the universe in the *Agamemnon* is revealed when even the confident Clytemnestra must admit that she did not know what she was doing in exulting at the cold and brutal murder of husband (1654–61).

In the *Choephoroi*, sound words continue to characterize Clytemnestra, but they are words like "shriek" and "wail" (*Ch.* 535 and 926). Her confidence has failed and her conscious employment of irony is gone. She still seems powerful but is in reality only a hard shell concealing a guilt-ridden mind. The sound words describing her speech in the *Choephoroi* reveal a broken woman who has learned to live with the somber consequences that she has brought upon herself. In the last play Clytemnestra does not sing, nor are any singing words used about her. She is completely involved in her grim and relentless pursuit of blood-revenge on her son. When the Furies finally accept the new mode of determining justice, Clytemnestra is defeated and the music of peace, harmony, and blessing, which closes the play, prevails.

In the *Oresteia* there are numerous examples of and allusions to different types of songs.[46] The refrain *ailinon, ailinon eipe* ("sing sorrow, sorrow"), for example, is repeated three times in the parodos. Although its exact derivation is unknown, this is a standard musical phrase rooted in an earlier song or ritual.[47] This introduction of a traditional song adds to the words of the chorus an allusion whose associations enrich the connotations of the passage.[48] Similar explicit introductions of song elements are:

Ag. 146—the chorus sings a paean;

Ag. 174—the chorus talks of the man who shouts a cry of victory to Zeus;

Ag. 28—the watchman calls for an *ololygmos*;

Ag. 1072–3 and 1076–7—Cassandra sings a portion of a *threnos*;[49]

Ag. 1448—a ritual lament in many elements;[50]

Ch. 305–478—the kommos contains elements of a *threnos anakleterios*;[51]

Eum. 307–96—the Furies sing a cult hymn;

Eum. 1043 and 1047—the *ololyge* is shouted.[52]

Twice there are references to types of songs as means of expressing one's feelings. When the messenger from Troy talks about the man who comes to report a disaster, he says that he sings the paean of the Erinyes (645). Such a paean is a contradiction in terms and shows Aeschylus playing on the associations of the song form.[53] In the *Choephoroi* the chorus looks for the day when Clytemnestra and Aegisthus will be dead so that they can sing loudly a "song of freedom for the house, the women's song when the wind is fair, and not the shrill song of mourning" (819–24; cf. *Ch.* 342–4).[54]

Several times Aeschylus identifies the nature and content of a choral ode as an established song form.[55] At the beginning of the first stasimon of the *Agamenmon* the chorus states its intention to sing a song of thanks to the gods (351–54). At

Choephoroi 150–1 Electra commands the chorus to sing a paean for the dead. In the *Eumenides* the Furies define their song as a "Binding Song" and during the course of singing call it the hymn of the Erinyes (306, 331, 344). Later in the play the Eumenides ask Athena to help in choosing the content of their hymn so that they may sing a series of blessings for Athens (902). Finally, the trilogy ends with a processional hymn sung by the representatives of the townspeople of Athens, raising the *ololyge* as they escort the new goddesses to their home (1033–47). Because this procession resembles the Panathenaic Processions,[56] undoubtedly the music would have alluded to the real event. The most complex musical form in the trilogy is the kommos in the *Choephoroi*, a long song with parts interchanged among Electra, Orestes, and the chorus. It is not as much a debate prior to a decision as a confirmation of Orestes' spirit. His fear and helplessness at the start of the kommos are dispelled, and new resolve is apparent at its conclusion. This reaffirmation of purpose is well suited to the ritual aspect of this long ode, which the chorus calls a hymn (475) as well as a dirge and lament (423–4).[57]

Also worthy of mention are the repeated ephymnia in the chorus's response to Clytemnestra toward the end of the *Agamemnon*, the repeated sections in the Binding Song, and the Erinyes' repeated outbursts against Athena and her city in the *Eumenides*. These repetitions may allude to musical forms taken from religious ritual.[58]

PEOPLE WHO ARE SINGING THE WRONG SONG

Several characters in the trilogy find that they are singing the wrong song—sometimes unwillingly.[59] Whenever the watchman wants to sing or hum, he finds that he cries. Although he does not plan this kind of song, conditions within the house make it impossible for him to sing (16–19). The chorus at 979 keeps hearing an unpleasant and unwanted song from within, yet they cannot stifle it.

There are, however, characters who purposefully sing a

song that does not fit the context. The chorus is shocked when Cassandra begins to sing words of lamentation in addressing Apollo (1072–79), yet Cassandra knows exactly what she is doing in addressing the god who has brought her to her death. Clytemnestra, having assumed the role of a priestess saying the proper words over a successfully completed sacrifice, vaunts over the dead bodies of Agamemnon and Cassandra in what the chorus describes as a tuneless hymn (1472–74). Being fully conscious of the tone of her words, she knows that they are unacceptable to the chorus. Ironically, she herself will change her tone when she finds herself unable to defend the justice of her act. At 1186–93 Cassandra talks about the chorus that never leaves the house of Atreus, a chorus that sings in unison but not in harmony, a band of revelers who drink human blood and sing of the primal sin of the house. The Argive elders do not want to hear about this kind of singing, but they must grudgingly admit that Cassandra has hit the mark.[60]

In one instance in the *Agamemnon* a group begins to sing one song but consciously learns to sing another upon realizing that the first song was wrong. The citizens of Troy celebrated the marriage of Paris and Helen with a loud wedding song. When they discovered the true nature of this marriage, they learned a new type of music, a loud lament calling Paris evil-wed (699–716).

In the *Choephoroi* the question of will is crucial. Orestes, Electra, and the chorus all want to sing a joyous song of triumph but in their helplessness feel able to sing only songs of sorrow. Although Orestes finds his only joy in singing a funeral lament for his father (320–22), the chorus looks forward to the end of laments, when Orestes will enter his house as king accompanied by a song of triumph (340–44). The chorus initially moans in sorrow for Orestes and Clytemnestra as he leads her into the house to kill her, but this lament quickly changes to triumphant music as they define the pattern of justice being reinforced by Orestes' act (931–52). Given the twisted motivations in the *Choephoroi*, the characters learn that the song that sounds wrong may in fact be right in view of the whole situation. Orestes is driven mad after he has committed the murders and cannot sing the awaited song of victory:

> Now I praise him; now at last I am present to groan in lament for him, as I address this robe that killed my father. Yet I grieve for the deed and the suffering and for the whole race—my victory is an unenviable pollution.
>
> (1014–17)
>
> Fear is ready to sing and dance in anger before my heart.
>
> (1024–25)

The whole system of justice and blood-revenge is so confused that there is little chance for the songs of joy that the characters in this play anticipated. Just as Clytemnestra in the *Agamemnon* was brought to reevaluate her corrupt victory, so now Orestes learns that the acts of men to achieve lasting justice will fail until some major changes occur both in society and in the relationship between men and gods.

In the *Eumenides* the gods emerge as the protagonists in their pursuit of justice. The opposition of single-minded gods brings clarity into the confusion that has characterized the previous plays. The songs that are sung—the Binding Song, the curses and blessings for Athens—are each frank, direct, and suitable to the occasion. At the end of the trilogy the processional hymn of blessing sung by the citizens of Athens is undeniably appropriate; finally there is an opportunity for the lasting prosperity and inner peace that allow the wholehearted singing of a hymn of joy.[61]

SOUNDS OF CITIES

There is a small category of sound words that describe cities. The clearest example is Clytemnestra's perception of Troy in defeat. She first hears the sounds of the victors and the vanquished, especially the cries of children (*Ag.* 320–29). The chorus, singing of Troy at *Ag.* 699–716, speaks of the mar-

riage hymn that is ended, Troy now being a city of many laments. Several times Argos is characterized by the sounds of
sorrow that its citizens utter. As the city thinks of its soldiers
who have gone to Troy, they moan and mutter (*Ag.* 445 and
449); when the herald asks if those at home have missed the
soldiers, the elders reply that they groaned from a dark spirit
(*Ag.* 546). Cassandra prophesies that there is some sort of
horrible plot against Agamemnon, and the chorus admits
that the whole city shouts out these things (*Ag.* 1106), yet
when Clytemnestra talks about the sounds that she can hear
in Argos, she reports only the shout of the *ololygmos* (*Ag.*
595). This theme has its final statement in the processional at
the end of the trilogy, when the whole city joins in raising a
hymn to the newly adopted goddesses.

The clustering of key words such as those for sound and
music is typical of Aeschylean style, but even more convincing in establishing these words in the design of the trilogy is
the artful use of sound and music themselves within the action of the play. Several recent studies of Aeschylean language have shown how often words and images emerge on
the stage as physical objects or become key elements in the
development of the plot. Words for net or snare prelude the
actual appearance of the robe at the end of the *Choephoroi*,
when Orestes and the chorus spread it wide to be seen for
what it is; the imagery of animals applied to men becomes
visible when the Furies enter pursuing Orestes like dogs
tracking their quarry (*Eum.* 244–53). In the same way each of
the motifs described by musical words has a place within the
visual and aural design of the staged play. The shouts and
cries of prophets cause the beginning action of the *Choephoroi*
as Clytemnestra screams in the night at her dream visions,
and Cassandra, the prophetess, is driven to shrieks and outcries as she views her future. Electra and Orestes are children
who wail around their father's tomb, and allusions to the vic-
timized children of Thyestes keep them always present in the
background. Men join the choruses in singing hymns and la-

ments on stage. But the crowning event in which all these motifs are gathered and reoriented in the resolution of the trilogy is the final "Panathenaic" procession: the citizens of the city—no longer victims but united in their view of a better future, trusting in the words and deeds of their fellow man, and in harmonious concert—march off the stage in a spectacular musical finale.

Although today's texts of the play are mute, the fact remains that music and sound were indispensable features of fifth-century Athenian theater. The large orchestra area was reserved to the chorus, and music and sound were continuous during the choral songs and were controlling factors in the patterning of choral dances. Without responsible yet imaginative use of the odes to contribute to the total dramatic effect, elements vital to the understanding and appreciation of the plays are lost, and the texts of the strophes and antistrophes become difficult and tedious interruptions to the stage action. Aeschylean drama, particularly the *Oresteia*, is highly musical; lyric accompanied by music and dance occupies a major portion of the trilogy. Although the actual notes and rhythms of the choral odes are lost, evidence with which to reconstruct the basic scheme of the musical design survives in the meters, in the variations and repetitions of musical forms, in the structure of the odes, and in the characterization of the choruses. Aeschylus' organized use and theatrical development of words and images for sound and music offer encouragement for critics and directors to recapture through actual music the effects that the playwright sought.

CHAPTER 2

CHORAL METER AND MUSICAL
FORM IN THE *ORESTEIA*

In a discussion of opera, Edward Cone comments:

In any opera, we may find that the musical and the verbal messages seem to reinforce or to contradict each other; but whether the one or the other, we must always rely on the music as our guide toward an understanding of the composer's conception of the text. It is this conception, not the bare text itself, that is authoritative in defining the ultimate meaning of the work.[1]

Although it is probable that the ancient tragedians also supported their texts with music so artfully that the whole was greater than its parts, dramatic choruses remain frustrating for both readers and contemporary directors. Some copies of the plays included musical notation, but it had probably disappeared by the time of the edition that Aristophanes of Byzantium (ca. 257–180 B.C.) made for an age of readers rather than performers.[2] Nevertheless the words of the songs survive, and the colometry of Alexandrian and Byzantine critics indicates how the metrical phrases appeared on the page.[3]

Previous study of choral metrics in Greek tragedy has yielded far more in the way of what cannot be assumed or stated confidently about music and dance in ancient times than positive results. It is immediately evident that all the actual notes of Greek dramatic music have disappeared.[4] The comments about ancient music by Plato, Plutarch, and several other writers are very generalized, of questionable authority, and often yield little more than a basic acquaintance with the modes and theories of Greek music.[5] There is no information about the specific music used in any one tragedy, and for every general statement about music by an ancient author the number of exceptions to be found in surviving dramas would probably fill a book many times larger than each play itself. In addition to the loss of the actual scales and melodies of tragic music it is almost impossible to make firm assumptions about the rhythm.[6] The easiest assumption in defining rules for rhythm would be that one long is equal to two shorts: expressed musically, one quarter note is equal to two eighth notes. If this equation could be strictly applied throughout the choral meters of drama, then undoubtedly there would be a foundation for defining significant differences in rhythm. But unfortunately this basic assumption is not sufficiently precise. The initial short syllable of an iambic foot can become a long syllable by substitution (⌣‒ ⌣‒); in exceptional cases that long syllable can be replaced by two shorts (⌣⌣‒⌣‒).[7] Thus one short becomes equal in time to two shorts; expressed in musical terms, one eighth note has come to equal two eighth notes. Furthermore, such resolution can occur in the first, second, and fourth position in an iambic metron, producing a large range of rhythmical possibilities (⌣⌣⌣⌣ ⌣⌣⌣). Suddenly the precision that seems so clear when Greek lyric meters are transcribed into modern musical symbols vanishes. Syncopated meters offer even further difficulty because each contains a value, a short syllable, that has been suppressed (⌣‒·‒ or ·‒⌣‒). Whether the chorus sang a syncopated line as though there was something missing—indicated by a brief pause in the flow of music—or whether syncopation is merely an analytical tool employed by later metricians to regularize certain shorter forms of a basic meter, is unknown.[8] Although a series of many successive short syllables requires faster delivery than a succession of long syllables, most lyric meters fall between these two configurations, and it is a much safer course to admit our ignorance than to hazard guesses on rhythm.

Amid this welter of uncertainty there are two precious and certain facts about dramatic meters. First, dramatic lyric, even in its most confusing configurations, is generally reducible to a certain limited group of standard and basic forms.[9] There will always be lines that elude even the most ingenious metrician, but these are distinctly in the minority. For the majority of lines in dramatic choruses there is a recognizable standard metrical form as a base, and if this line cannot actually be sung, it can at least be represented on paper in schematized form. Second, there is a characteristic phenomenon called responsion. The metrical pattern of each foot in the antistrophe is identical to the corresponding foot in the strophe. For textual critics responsion means that, however mutilated the manuscript may be, there are at least two chances to recover the scansion. For the poet the close responsion between strophe and antistrophe meant that the same rhythm occurred twice, and this fact allows the strong suspicion that the same music was sung twice and that the dance pattern was probably similar if not the same in each stanza. Several sets of corresponding lines contain close echoes in structure and sound; the clearest is *Persians* 550–52, metrically corresponding to 560–62.

Ξέρξης μὲν ἄγαγεν, ποποῖ,
Ξέρξης δ᾽ ἀπώλεσεν, τοτοῖ,
Ξέρξης δὲ πάντ᾽ ἐπέσπε δυσφρόνως

νᾶες μὲν ἄγαγον, ποποῖ,
νᾶες δ᾽ ἀπώλεσαν, τοτοῖ,
νᾶες πανωλέθροισιν ἐμβολαῖς·

Thus the inferior poet could be pleased that he had only half as many melodies to write, whereas the master tragedian could seek to enrich his scene in several ways, knowing that the audience would have heard the rhythm and probably the music twice in succession even though the words were different.

Two of the fundamental assumptions of this study are that the music of the strophe was repeated during the antistrophe and that the dance pattern was similar if not precisely the same. Such an assumption is not denied by any available evidence and is reinforced by the statements of the critic Dionysius of Halicarnassus in the first century B.C.[10] But more important, the metrical design of the *Oresteia* can be explained in ways that accord with Aeschylean technique in terms of metaphorical language and staging. Even if a critic wishes to deny the validity of this basic assumption and the cumulative consistency with which music can be shown to be employed in the dramatic design of this trilogy, the basic statements about the repetition of meters and the clarity with which different meters are contrasted remain true; repeated music would serve only to make these repetitions and contrasts more evident to the audience.

In addition, still more speculative statements are possible about the dramatic music that accompanies the choral songs within one play. Such statements depend on comparisons of songs in the same play or lines in the same ode to identify repeated musical measures, the rate of substitution, and the basic form of the music. For example, a repeated lecythion (–∪–∪–∪–), with its closely associated form the ithyphallic (–∪–∪––), is the basic meter in the choral passage at *Suppliants* 154–61 = 168–75:

–∪–∪––	ith
–∪–∪–∪–	lec
––∪–	ia
–∪–∪–∪–	lec
–∪–∪–∪–	lec
–∪–∪–∪–	lec
–∪–∪––	ith
–∪– –∪–∪–∪–	cr + lec

Clearly contrasting meters are found at the break between stanzas at *Agamemnon* 156–63:

da + sp

Although it may be impossible to discover the original melody and rhythm of an ode, it is at least clear from the bald schematization of the scansion patterns that the juxtaposition of a clearly dactylic stanza with a stanza of equally clear lecythion signifies a major difference in the music in this ode. Because such shifts occur frequently in the choral songs of the *Oresteia*, it is only reasonable for a critic to seek explanations within the context of the whole play.

Over years of attending the dramatic festivals the Greek audience developed an ear for the traditional forms of the most common meters. These basic metrical forms were the models that the poet varied when he introduced substitutions. The rate of such substitution and resolution can be determined from the scansion pattern of a choral ode. For example, lyric iambic meter can run along line after line in the same standard unresolved pattern. But when the poet begins to make a series of resolutions within the basic pattern, the shift should be perceptible to the hearer and would have been represented in the music and in the dance. Of course, there are always resolutions here and there in the basic meter—variations are necessary to avert sheer boredom. But there are also contrasting passages in dramatic meters where the poet seems to choose a highly resolved form of the meter as opposed to the basic iambic forms ($∪-∪-$, $∪--$, $-∪-$). Contrast the rate of resolution in two passages from the *Oresteia* (each resolved metron is underlined):

Agamemnon 367–76	*Choephoroi* 423–27
∪—— —∪— ∪——	∪—∪— <u>∪∪∪∪—</u> ∪—∪—
∪—— —∪— ∪——	∪—∪— ∪—∪—
∪—∪— ∪—∪— ∪——	∪—∪— <u>∪∪∪∪—</u> ∪—∪—
∪—∪— —∪— —∪—	<u>∪—∪∪∪</u> <u>∪—∪∪∪</u> ∪—∪—
∪—∪— —∪—	<u>∪—∪∪∪</u> ∪—∪— ∪—∪—

```
∪−∪−  −∪−
∪−−   −∪−
∪−−   −∪−
∪−−   −∪−  ∪−−
```

The barrage of resolutions in the second passage would have a strong effect on an audience because the departure from the customary iambic pattern occurs twice (in the strophe and antistrophe). The rapid pace of pronunciation, with an accompanying difference in the music, might also have been reinforced visually through the dancing. A poet who deviates this strongly is clearly using music to reinforce his meaning.[11]

Finally, there is the form of the choral lyric. The basic Aeschylean form is the stasimon formed by a sequence of two or more paired strophes and antistrophes, but there are striking variations from this scheme. Sometimes a refrain occurs at the end of each strophe and antistrophe, tending to unite a series of stanzas by common music. At other times a mesode or an ephymnion, either of which could be defined as a nonstrophic element, is introduced into the midst of a strophic system.[12] Because these stanzas lack a corresponding antistrophe, such units tend to break up the symmetry that is the basis of most choral odes; and such asymmetrical elements would be especially noticeable within a larger symmetrical pattern of music and dance. There are also freestanding lyric passages in the midst of spoken lines lacking an antistrophe and thus sung only once, though to a perfectly traditional meter; these stanzas are customarily called "astropha."

These two features of dramatic lyric—the repetition or variation of meters, and the symmetry or lack of balance in the basic forms—can be analyzed without any knowledge of the melodies or the rhythms of Greek tragedy. Such features are so highly conditioned by the drama in which they occur that no independent fragment of choral lyric can be confidently interpreted in this way; yet because the poet both wrote the words and music and choreographed the odes, such analyses can have great significance when incorporated within the unified conception of a specific play. Because an ancient dramatic premiere was in the fullest possible way the creation of the individual poet, he could directly manipulate the expectations of his audience in regard to meter, music, and form in order to convey and enhance his basic ideas.

It is immediately striking that the meters of Aeschylean drama, which accompany some of the most sublime religious thought and the most complex grammatical structures in Greek poetry, are themselves quite simple—that is, largely unresolved and, to a high degree, repetitive.[13] Although there will always be differences among scholars in determining the precise length of particular lines, and thus in applying an exact name to the metrical pattern of any one individual line, an overview of a section of lines in an Aeschylean chorus usually reveals a simple general pattern. For example, whether one places the mesode in the parodos of the *Persians* after line 114 or in its traditional position, whether one identifies it as an astrophic unit or splits it into two balanced strophes, and whatever readings one accepts at the difficult textual cruces, it remains clear that Aeschylus is trying to reinforce the ionic tone of the middle section of the parodos by giving a succession of virtually unresolved ionic dimeters:

$$\cup\cup-- \quad \cup\cup--$$
$$\cup\cup-- \quad \cup\cup--$$

Similarly, the theologically important Hymn to Zeus at *Agamemnon* 160–91 is composed of unresolved, repeated lecythia in 26 out of its 30 lines ($-\cup-\cup-\cup-$); in six of the lecythia there is a simple addition of a single spondee ($--$) or bacchiac ($\cup--$). The other four lines are either dactylic ($-\cup\cup$) or cretic ($-\cup-$). In the first set of stanzas the inclusion of a long dactylic line links the hymn to the preceding dactylic section describing the prophecy of Calchas; in the second section the presence of a line of cretics foreshadows the predominant meter in which the chorus next sings of Iphigenia's murder. The first strophic pair (160–67 = 168–75) is scanned as follows:

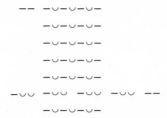

Meter is seldom clearer or simpler in Greek drama, and for this reason it is relatively easy to use the schematic pattern of Aeschylus' odes to determine the effect that the artist created through his music.

In addition, because the choral songs in Aeschylean drama are generally composed of several short individual stanzas, there is greater opportunity than in the plays of Sophocles or Euripides to construct a series of strongly contrasting metrical sections. For example, the parodos of the *Agamemnon*, the longest choral song in Aeschylean drama, is clearly divided into metrical sections: 40–103, anapaests (astrophic); 104–159, dactyls (strophe-antistrophe-epode); 160–191, lecythia (four strophic pairs); 192–257, iambics (six strophic pairs). The normal Sophoclean or Euripidean structure of one or two pairs of strophe-antistrophe allows variation within a metrical pattern as a kind of counterpoint meter but does not contain enough independent units to permit effective movement from one established metrical pattern to another.[14] Aeschylean drama, therefore, offers clear evidence through the analysis of the metrical structuring of choral odes in terms of strophes, antistrophes, epodes, mesodes, refrains, and other nonstrophic elements for an understanding of musical variation and development within a dramatic unity.

Of course, a study of musical form must finally base its argument on the audience. Any production is a collaboration of writer, director, actors, and designers with the audience. In the fifth century, writers could assume that their audience, through their previous years of theatergoing, knew the conventions of the Greek theater, including the broad outline of the repeated mythological plots, the forms of dialogue, choral dance steps, and basic song forms. It is often surprising to learn from parodies how much detailed knowledge of previous productions playwrights could assume. Euripides parodied the recognition scene from the *Oresteia* some forty years after its premiere performance, and Aristophanes even depended on the recall of a specific line from the *Hippolytus*.[15] Consequently, it also seems justifiable to assume that the playwright could expect from his audience an easy recognition of customary choral meters, a sense of the traditional and hence predictable form of an ode, and thus an awareness of innovation when the writer deviated from those norms.[16]

The remainder of this chapter analyzes the elements of Aeschylean choral song in the *Oresteia*. After presenting the overall metrical scheme of an ode,[17] I discuss the relation of the meters to the words and then show how the form of the ode reinforces the musical effect created by the joining of words and meters. However, because the odes are highly unified creations, it is not always possible to divide the discussion precisely along these lines.

AGAMEMNON

The Parodos (40–257)

40–103: anapaests

104–21: str. a	104	–⏒–∪∪–∪∪–∪∪–∪∪–∪∪	6 da
122–39: ant. a		–∪∪–∪∪–∪∪–∪∪––	5 da
	125*	–––––––∪∪––	5 da
		∪–∪– –∪∪–∪∪–∪∪––	ia 4 da
	110	–∪∪––	2 da
		–––∪∪–∪∪–⏒	4 da
	130	–∪∪–––∪∪–∪	4 da
		–––∪∪–∪∪–∪∪	8 da
	115	–∪∪–∪∪–∪∪––	
		∪–∪– –∪∪–∪∪–∪∪––	ia 4 da
	135	–––∪∪–⏓	3 da
		–∪∪–∪∪–∪∪–∪∪–∪∪––	6 da

	120	⏝–∪– ∪–∪–	2 ia
		–∪∪–∪∪–∪∪––– (refrain)	5 da
140–59: epode	140	∪–∪– ––∪–	2 ia
		∪–∪– –∪∪– ∪––	ia ch ba
		–––∪∪–∪∪––	4 da
		–––∪∪–∪––	2 da + clausula
		–––––∪∪––	4 da
	145	–∪∪–∪∪–∪∪–∪∪	4 da
		∪–∪– ∪∪∪– ∪––	ia cr ba
		–∪∪–∪∪–∪∪–∪∪ –∪∪–∪∪––	7 da
	150	–––∪∪–∪∪–∪∪–∪∪ –∪∪––	7 da
		–––∪∪–∪∪–– –∪∪––∪∪ –∪∪–∪	9 da
	155	–∪∪–∪∪–––––∪∪––	6 da
		–∪∪–––∪∪–∪∪–∪∪––	6 da
		–∪∪–––∪∪–––∪∪––	6 da
		–∪∪–∪	2 da
		–∪∪–∪∪–∪∪––– (refrain)	5 da
160–67: str. b	160	–– –∪–∪–∪–	sp lec
168–75: ant. b		–∪–∪–∪–	lec
	170	–∪–∪–∪–	lec
		–∪–∪–∪–	lec
		–∪–∪–∪–	lec
	165	–∪∪–∪∪–∪∪–∪∪––	5 da
	175	–∪–∪–∪–	lec
176–83: str. g		–∪–∪–∪–	lec
184–91: ant. g	185	–∪–∪–∪–	lec
		–∪–∪–∪–	lec
		–– –∪–∪–∪–	sp lec
	180	–∪– –∪– –∪–	3 cr
		–∪–∪–∪–	lec

Section	Line	Scansion	Meter
	190	—∪—∪—∪— ∪——	lec ba
		—∪—∪—∪—	lec
192–204: str. d	205	∪—∪— —∪— ∪——	ia cr ba
205–17: ant. d		∪—∪— —∪— ∪——	ia cr ba
		∪—∪—	ia
	195	——∪— —∪— ∪—⏝	ia cr ba
		∪—— —∪— ∪——	ba cr ba
	210	∪—∪— —∪— ∪——	ia cr ba
		—∪—∪—∪—	lec
		—∪∪— ∪——	ch ba
	200	—∪∪— ∪——	ch ba
		—∪∪— —∪∪—	2 ch
	215	—∪∪— —∪∪—	2 ch
		—∪∪— —∪∪—	2 ch
		—∪∪— ∪——	ch ba
218–27: str. e		∪—∪— —∪— ∪——	ia cr ba
228–37: ant. e		∪—∪— —∪— ∪——	ia cr ba
	220 230	∪—∪∪∪ ∪—∪—	2 ia
		∪—∪— —∪— ∪——	ia cr ba
		∪—∪— —∪— ∪——	ia cr ba
		∪—∪∪∪ ∪—— ∪——	ia 2 ba
		∪—— ∪—∪—	ba ia
	225 235	—∪∪— ∪—∪—	ch ia
		—∪∪— ∪——	ch ba
		—∪∪— ∪——	ch ba
238–47: str. z		∪—∪— —∪— —∪—	ia 2 cr
248–57: ant. z		∪—∪— —∪— ∪—⏝	ia cr ba
	240 250	∪—∪— —∪—	ia cr
		—∪—∪—∪— ∪——	lec ba
		∪—∪— —∪—∪—∪—	ia lec
		∪—∪— —∪—	ia cr
		∪—∪— —∪— ∪——	ia cr ba
	245 255	∪—∪— —∪— —∪— —∪—	ia 3 cr
		∪—∪— —∪— ∪——	ia cr ba
		—∪∪— ∪——	ch ba

Meter

At the end of his speech (line 36) the watchman seems jolted from his train of thought. He has been soliloquizing about his good fortune at this happy moment; but something causes him to check his words and to show caution.[18] Most probably there is a sign of the impending entrance of a character, either the chorus or Clytemnestra. If Clytemnestra is about to enter, a servant could appear carrying her sacrificial materials to a small altar near the palace door; her entrance at this point would be motivated by the cry of the watchman telling her to rise up from her bed and to raise a joyous shout to greet the torch (25–30).[19] If the chorus is entering, he could hear the introductory notes of the aulos player leading them into the orchestra. Either preliminary entrance signal would be enough to make the watchman cautious of being overheard—thus motivating his exit.[20] The action, then, is continuous; there is no pause with a new beginning when the chorus enters.[21] This overlapping of prologue by choral entrance enhances through stage action the suspicions and darker tones of his preceding speech and sets an ominous background for the following song. The watchman not only implies that it is dangerous to speak openly and that something remains hidden within the house, but he becomes so excessively cautious at the appearance of another party that he visually portrays the citizens' fear the moment before the chorus begins its ode. Yet his action provides only the first instance in this play where fear and suspicion are suppressed by the assertion of fair words; as the watchman leaves, the chorus and—sooner or later—Clytemnestra enter to celebrate the good news of victory.[22]

Anapaests   The meter to which the chorus enters is anapaestic dimeter ($\cup\cup-\cup\cup-\cup\cup-\cup\cup-$) with its usual accompaniments, the paroemiac ($\cup\cup-\cup\cup-\cup\cup--$) and the monometer ($\cup\cup-\cup\cup-$). This song is not marked by any noticeable pattern of substitution; indeed, the rate of substitution (52 percent) is normal for Aeschylean anapaests. If there is anything unusual about the song, it is its length. It appears that Aeschylus here sought to establish the marching meter customary for a chorus that enters or is about to begin a song. There are two reasons for this extended introduction: first, the chorus can be heard even before its arrival onstage singing an obvious entrance march;[23] second, the members of the chorus have a sufficiently long song to travel the whole distance into the center of the orchestra slowly in character with their description of themselves as old men (72–82). Each of these musical effects is significant to the audience. The traditional entrance music is a clear cue that possibly also provides motivation for the watchman's secretiveness and immediate exit. The initial verbal and visual characterization of the old men is necessary later, when the chorus becomes inactive and helpless upon hearing the cries of Agamemnon from within the palace and again when it attempts its pitiful resistance to Aegisthus and his soldiers at the end of the play. Aeschylus is consistent over the years in characterizing old men by their music; the elders of Persia require the same number of anapaestic lines to make their entrance as do the old men here; the young suppliant maidens in their rush to elude their suitors enter in about a third less time.[24]

Lyric Dactyls   As soon as the chorus has finished its marching entrance, it moves to lyric meters. This song falls into two sections: one triad of strophe-antistrophe-epode (104–59), each stanza of which is tied to the others by a refrain line, and a series of five paired strophic stanzas (160–257).

In the first section of three stanzas (104–59) the old men recall the beginning of the Trojan expedition: the departure of the commanders, the omen that met them as they left the palace, and Calchas' interpretation of the omen. The meter of this section is dactylic with a few interspersed iambs; although the epode does not correspond to the pattern of the strophe, it echoes it closely in basic meter, approximates it in length, completes the prophecy of Calchas begun in the antistrophe, and is joined formally to the strophic pair by the repeated refrain line. Because the same basic meter pervades these three sections, the music and the dancing would probably be similar in the strophe and antistrophe and would be varied only slightly in the epode. These three stanzas, then, form a unit in terms of content, formal structure, and meter.

Although dactylic lines occur sporadically throughout the play, such a clustering of dactyls recurs only in the final processional hymn, at the end of the *Eumenides*.[25] Thus the whole trilogy is framed by dactylic meter, and most likely the melody and dance figures accompanying the ending would be strongly reminiscent of the opening dactylic strophes. In a drama so filled with music and dance this musical binding of beginning and end by a meter that is not extensively used elsewhere provides a sense of closure and resolution to the trilogy. The effect is not overly subtle; the length of the three opening dactylic stanzas allows the chorus to establish right at the beginning of its lyric the music and dance pattern associated with this meter.

Dactylic rhythm is undoubtedly used here because it is appropriate for oracular pronouncement,[26] but there is a more basic stage effect. Because of the heavy use of dactylic meter the spectators would recall the mass of folklore and saga surrounding the whole Trojan expedition. They might even remember Odysseus' speech at *Iliad* 2.284, where he recalls the events at Aulis and Calchas' hopeful prophecy given there.[27] But far more important to the effectiveness of this passage than recollections of various elements in the Trojan story are the general weight and validation given to the prophetic powers of Calchas by the tradition, which is largely epic. He guided the fleet to Troy, predicted the victory in ten years, and is the obvious trustworthy prophet to whom all turn in their moment of need in *Iliad* 1. Aeschylus' audience, through long familiarity with epic, would realize while hearing this report of his words that his prophecy had always been true. The chorus, recalling the events at Aulis, reports that Calchas predicted the success of the expedition and spoke of the possibility that Artemis would block it by the winds; the latter has already happened, and the elders will soon learn that Troy has just fallen. But they also remember these words: "There remains a fearful, ever-arising, treacherous housekeeper—an unforgetting wrath that exacts vengeance for children slain" (153–55). Soon only this of Calchas' prophecies will remain unfulfilled. Thus the ode provides not only recollection of the past but also the beginning of a new action.[28] The anticipation of this last element in the prophecy will continue through the first three stasima to disrupt the chorus's attempts to sing only happy and harmonious music on this festal day. Dactylic meter is appropriate to motivate anxiety about the future because it lends to the prophecy the inherited authority of the epic tradition.[29] In the chorus's music and words alike it is clear that "the craft of Calchas never lacks fulfillment" (249).

Lyric Trochees and Iambs   The rest of this long choral song consists of five paired lyric strophes separated into two groups by their use of two opposed meters. The first four stanzas (160–91) are almost pure lecythia, a trochaic meter ($-\cup-\cup-\cup-$); the rest are built from a combination of iambic dimeter ($\cup-\cup-$) and two syncopated iambic feet, the cretic ($-\cup-$) and the bacchiac ($\cup--$).[30] In some Greek dramatic texts a syncopated iambic dimeter is so difficult to distinguish from the lecythion that there is no definable difference in the metrical structure; yet in this choral song and frequently throughout the *Oresteia* Aeschylus has made this difference apparent.[31] Six of the seven lines in the first strophic pair, and seven out of eight in the second, repeat identical lecythia with no resolved syllables (160–91).[32] Regardless of the closeness in form between the lecythion and a lyric iambic line, Aeschylus has presented the lecythion as a separate metrical pattern by repeating its simple form several times in a brief passage. He then provides immediate and strong contrast at line 192 by switching to the combined iambic meters and establishing them in the ears of his audience with equal insistence. Thus the surviving text offers a schematic indication of Aeschylus' desire to define the difference in two metrical sections; the music and dance figures designed to accompany the words would have heightened this contrast for the spectators. A director who fails to differentiate the character of these two sections of the parodos will have omitted one of the trilogy's most fundamental musical effects, for much of the later thematic development is presented through the music and dance that accompany these two meters.

The lecythion is the meter of the Hymn to Zeus (160–83), the prayer extolling the kingship of Zeus and expressing trust that suffering in this world will decrease and perhaps disappear as he leads men to understanding. This is a basic statement of Aeschylus' optimistic outlook, although it is also the belief that will be challenged throughout the trilogy. At the moment this hymn is not sufficient to distract the thoughts of the chorus from Calchas' prophecy, and they continue their recollections of Aulis, singing of the murder of Iphigenia demanded by Artemis. In this section the lecythion is forcefully and clearly established as the meter that accompanies the theme of the beneficial kingship of Zeus and mankind's hope for betterment through his favor.[33]

The remainder of the parodos is predominantly the story of the fatal infatuation of Agamemnon when given the choice of killing his daughter or disbanding the expedition. The final stanza (248–57) returns to the theme of worry about the immediate future, when their king will return to Argos bringing his dangerous guilt with him. In the Hymn to Zeus the elders have tried to turn their minds to more cheerful thoughts, but in these final stanzas they sing in persistent iambic meter of the infatuation that has led a man to sin and will eventually bring him to punishment.

The content of this major section of the parodos is not as neatly divided as the meters. The last stanza of lecythia (184–91) begins to tell the story of the events at Aulis, and the concluding antistrophe on the compelling force of justice is sung in iambics (248–57). Yet even though the whole parodos is sharply divided into sections by meter, it is the chorus's attempt to express a unified concept that draws upon the patterning of past events in order to predict the future. The chorus characterizes the expedition; tells of the omen at its beginning and the interpretation of this omen, which rouses troubled thoughts for additional bloodshed; expresses trust in the continual working of Zeus even when he operates through painful human experiences; tells of the bloody cost of good winds for sailing; and finally leaves the future to the beneficent justice of Zeus's universe. In moving from one subject to another the chorus is structuring events in an attempt to rationalize the ambiguities of the past and to view the future with optimism. The elders' hope depends on a full trust in the effectiveness of Zeus as he establishes a plan for humanity and in his concern for the betterment of mankind. As this ode is a unity in conception, so also the overlapping of thought between the two opposed metrical sections combines them into one unified choral statement. The two thematic meters of the trilogy have been clearly defined and established, each within a context: lecythion for humanity's progress under the just kingship of Zeus, and iambic for the infatuation that leads men to sin and requires punishment.

Musical Form

The parodos of the *Agamemnon* presents choral music-making at its most ordered and impressive: a long anapaestic entrance, the strophe-antistrophe-epode structure, a refrain line binding the elements in this triadic structure and setting an oracular tone,[34] a long series of precisely corresponding strophic pairs, and a variety of meters. At line 104 the chorus begins its lyrics by singing that it is *kyrios throein* ("endowed with the power to proclaim"). The old men possess the authority to sing about the omen at the beginning of the expedition because they were present at the event; yet the emphatic initial position of the words also betrays an element of pride in their skillful telling of past events. The phrase means not only "I have the authority because I was an eyewitness," but also: "I, the confident chorus of the *Agamemnon*, possess the full ability to sing past events well"[35]—an ability they then demonstrate orally and visually in singing this most elaborate and ambitious ode. Both the *Persians* and the *Suppliants* among the surviving earlier plays of Aeschylus have similar ornate entrance songs composed of anapaests and long chains of strophic stanzas with intercalated mesodes or ephymnia. But there is no ode longer, more comprehensive in subject, more carefully wrought poetically, or more revealing of the singers' characters and thoughts than the entrance song of the *Agamemnon*. Here Aeschylus wanted to present a chorus that was highly proficient and polished in its poetic ability, its thought, its meter, music, and dance. The obvious contrast is the opening chorus of the *Seven against Thebes*, when the distraught women of Thebes enter singing a highly resolved, unstrophic series of dochmiacs which are so heavily emotional that they virtually avoid the themes of the play. Such an entrance is effective and appropriate, for their disorder and terror conveys vividly the pressures that will induce Eteocles to pledge a strong, unbending defense of the city. As Aeschylus designed an initial picture of panic and despair through the choral entrance in the *Seven against Thebes*, so also in the *Agamemnon* he created his most organized, able, thoughtful, and purposeful group of singers by giving them an ode that allows them to parade their self-confidence.

The chorus, however, discovers problems in its structuring of past events, especially when using its interpretation of the past to understand the present. This ode dwells heavily on the permanent lessons about justice that can be learned by a careful consideration of events. Yet in their account of the past, the elders occasionally find themselves describing a situation or aspect of an action that makes it difficult to maintain a consistently hopeful pattern of justice. For example, even though the fleet sailed to Troy in defense of justice and Paris has been punished, it is also true that the innocent citizens of Troy were compelled to pay for a crime they did not commit and that the fleet could sail only after a father had killed his daughter. In the most general view justice has been preserved through the expedition, but the chorus finds implicit cause to worry about the quality of the act and the means humans employ to maintain a just world. At such moments the old men customarily surrender themselves to a faith in the goodness of Zeus and express their inability to understand the future. At 60–71, when their thoughts turn to the excessive nature of Troy's punishment, a whole army destroyed for the sake of one promiscuous woman, they immediately avert their minds from the past and express faith that they are helpless, being caught up in an irreversible pattern of action:

> It is as it now is, and it will be accomplished toward what is fated. Neither by burnt sacrifice nor by libations from unburnt offerings will one soothe the stubborn anger [of the gods].   (*Ag.* 67–71)

At 153–55 they sing of the vengeful housekeeper who remains, the personified Wrath who will exact payment for slain children. At this point the real meaning of their refrain line becomes clear: "Sing sorrow" for the bloody events of the past, but "may the good win out" if—as they believe—there is a pattern of justice that is being fulfilled under the guidance of Zeus.[36] They immediately abandon their thoughts about the implications of Calchas' prophecy for future action and turn to a pious expression of trust and faith in Zeus.[37] Finally, at line 243 the chorus describes the slaughtered Iphigenia as the most innocent of victims: "Often at the rich feasts of her father in the men's hall the chaste maiden sang, and lovingly honored her dear father's joyful prayer at the third libation with her blessed voice." The words that would logically follow would reveal ugly expectations for the returning Agamemnon. Once again the chorus turns away from them— "What happened then I neither saw nor do I tell"—and then expresses faith that justice will bring understanding of these painful events to those who are currently anxious or uncertain about the future. This pattern of covering over thoughts about an unhappy future by hopeful words of faith is characteristic of these old men who find themselves unable to unite the events of the past comfortably with their conception of justice.[38]

This masking pattern was first established when the watchman left the stage, hinting of troubles in the house just as the chorus appeared to sing happy words about the justice of the Trojan expedition. When the chorus first avoids the implications of its characterization of Helen as a promiscuous woman, the change in subject is not especially jolting because there is no change in the meter (60–68). The same is true in the final stanza, which continues the iambic meter from the previous two strophic pairs (248–57). The audience must be made to see that the old men, in their quest for a just world, customarily resort to a complete trust in Zeus because their interpretation of the past reinforces their faith in a consistently just god: Zeus saw that Paris sinned and therefore provided an effective agent of vengeance in Agamemnon. Just as their king trusted in Zeus enough to kill his own daughter, the same degree of faith will allow them to reconcile the world of pain and bloodshed around them with their belief in a just god who wants men to earn understanding and knowledge through suffering. Thus it is highly appropriate that there is no strong break in the music at such junctures.

Yet the establishment of consistency is not easy, and the elders are honest enough to admit it. The degree of pain in their world is so great that they find it difficult to glimpse the goal toward which Zeus is leading them: "In sleep there drips before the heart the remembered pain of our suffering. . . the favor of the gods comes with force" (179–82).[39] They even admit that their Zeus is a thought structure that they have created to render the senseless harshness of the world intelligible: "Pondering everything I can liken him to nothing except Zeus if I truly need to cast the vain weight of anxiety away" (163–66).[40] The doubt is reinforced in the form of the music. At line 159, when the true meaning of the refrain line "Sing sorrow . . ." becomes clear, the chorus abandons the dactylic meter with its associations of the truth of Calchas'

prophecy and turns to a different type of meter (and undoubtedly a different type of music and dance) as well as to a
simpler grammatical style. The oral and visual break with the
epode is quite complete as they struggle to maintain their optimism by asserting their faith in Zeus. But the shift in the
music shows how forcefully they must thrust away the nag-
ging concerns from the past in order to let their faith repose
easily in a king god who cares for mankind. It is important
for modern readers to try to "hear" this passage as the audience in the theater would have. The designation "epode"
seems to normalize the structure of the song, and in fact there
are many parallels to the triadic structure of a choral ode.
Most of these parallels, however, are from dramas that were
written several years after the *Oresteia* or from nondramatic
lyric genres. The norm for Aeschylean choruses is a continuous series of paired strophic stanzas. Once these old men begin their lyrics, they tell of the omen and the prophecy in a
corresponding dactylic strophe and antistrophe (104–39).
The metrical pattern of the dactylic lyric shifts—but only
slightly—as they sing of the second lawless sacrifice that will
be demanded. When they finish this section of their song,
which is as long as each stanza in the preceding strophic pair,
there is no reason for the audience not to expect a second,
metrically corresponding dactylic section as an antistrophe to
this "strophe." But this expectation is unfulfilled; something
new begins. The designation "epode" might normalize the
triadic structure for readers, but in the living theater the audience would perceive a break in the expected pattern, a shift
emphasizing that there is a significant and bothersome intel-
lectual leap necessary in moving from the telling of past
events to a belief in an ordered and harmonious world. Even
though the old men of the chorus will often have difficulty
bending their faith to fit events, they will continually try
to impose their own structure. In using the device of the
"aborted antistrophe," Aeschylus disappoints the expectation
of the audience to show musically that there is a dislocation in

thought when the chorus invokes faith to remove itself from a dilemma.[41]

Thus the form of the ode reinforces the words. The old men enter confident in their powers of song as they perform this beautifully articulated and complex ode; but as they encounter problems in defining a consistent pattern of justice, there is that one moment of disjunction in their music where the self-protective nature of their thinking becomes clear. In fact the elders will find it increasingly difficult as the play continues to make their conception of Zeus's justice explain the events occurring onstage, and it will become correspondingly harder for them to sing the type of ordered song that they so confidently present at their first appearance.

The First Stasimon (355–488)

355–66: anapaests			
367–84 str. a	385	∪ — — — ∪ — ∪ — —	ba cr ba
385–402 ant. a		∪ — — — ∪ — ∪ — —	ba cr ba
		∪ — ∪ — ∪ — ∪ — ∪ — —	2 ia ba
370		∪ — ∪ — — ∪ — — ∪ —	ia 2 cr
	390	∪ — ∪ — — ∪ —	ia cr
		∪ — ∪ — — ∪ —	ia cr
		∪ — — — ∪ —	ba cr
375		*∪ — — — ∪ —	ba cr
		∪ — — — ∪ — ∪ — —	ba cr ba
	395	∪ — — — ∪ — ∪ — —	ba cr ba
		∪ — ∪ — — ∪ — — ∪ —	ia 2 cr
		— ∪ — ∪ — —	cr ba
380		— ∪∪ — ∪ — ⌣	ch ba
	(ephymnium rhythmicum)		
		— ⌣ — ∪∪ — —	pher
	400	— ⌣ — ∪∪ — ⌣	pher
		— ⌣ — ∪∪ — ∪ —	glyc
		— ∪ — ∪∪ — —	pher

403–19: str. b	420	⏑–⏑– –⏑– –⏑–	ia 2 cr
420–36: ant. b		⏑–⏑– –⏑–	ia cr
	405	–⏑– ⏑––	cr ba
		⏑–⏑– ⏑–⏑– ⏑–⏑–	3 ia
		⏑–– –⏑⏑⏑	ba cr
	425	⏑–⏑– ⏑–⏑⏑̲̆ ⏑–⏑–	3 ia
		⏑–⏑– –⏑– ⏑––	ia cr ba
	410	⏑–⏑– –⏑–⏑–⏑–	ia lec
		⏑–⏑– –⏑–⏑–⏑⏑̄	ia lec
		*⏑–⏑– –⏑– –⏑–⏑–⏑–	ia cr lec
	430	*–⏑–⏑–⏑–	lec
		⏑–⏑– –⏑–	ia cr
	415	–⏑– –⏑– ⏑––	2 cr ba
		(ephymnium rhythmicum)	
		–––⏑⏑–⏑̄	pher
		–⏑–⏑⏑–⏑̆	pher
	435	–⏑̆–⏑⏑–⏑–	glyc
		–⏑̄–⏑⏑––	pher
437–55: str. g		⏑–⏑– –⏑– –⏑–	ia 2 cr
456–74: ant. g		–⏑– –⏑–⏑–⏑–	cr lec
	440	⏑–⏑– –⏑–	ia cr
	460	⏑–⏑– –⏑–	ia cr
		–⏑–⏑–⏑–	lec
		–⏑–⏑–⏑–	lec
		–⏑–⏑–⏑–	lec
	445	⏑–⏑– ⏑–⏑–	2 ia
	465	⏑–⏑– ⏑–⏑–	2 ia
		⏑–⏑– ⏑–⏑–	2 ia
		–⏑⏑– ⏑–⏑–	ch ia
		–⏑⏑– ⏑–⏑–	ch ia
	450	–⏑⏑– ⏑–⏑–	ch ia
	470	–⏑⏑– ⏑––	ch ba
		(ephymnium rhythmicum)	
		–––⏑⏑––	pher
		–––⏑⏑––	pher
		–––⏑⏑–⏑–	glyc
	455	–⏑–⏑⏑––	pher

475–88: epode	475	∪–∪– –∪–	ia cr
		∪–∪– –∪–	ia cr
		–∪–∪–∪–	lec
		∪–∪– ∪–∪– ∪–∪–	3 ia
		∪–∪– ∪–∪– ∪–∪–	3 ia
	480	∪–∪– –∪–	ia cr
		∪–∪– –∪–∪–∪–	ia lec
		–∪–∪–∪–	lec
		∪–∪– –∪–	ia cr
		∪–∪– –∪–∪–∪–	ia lec
	485	∪∪∪∪– ∪–∪∪∪ ∪∪∪∪–	3 ia
		∪∪∪∪– ∪∪∪∪–	2 ia
		∪–∪– –∪–∪–∪–	ia lec

Meter

Following a short anapaestic introduction are six long strophic stanzas highly unified in meter, form, and thought. The most obvious unifying element is the metrically identical, four-line coda that concludes each stanza. The subject matter of these coda sections is not similar nor do they recall a recurring theme at the end of each of the strophes; in fact each is very close in content to the stanza that precedes it. Given the assumption that the music in corresponding stanzas is the same, this ode is filled with constant musical reminders that the thoughts of the chorus about the victory at Troy do have at root a unified conception.[42]

In addition, the basic metrical pattern is similar in each stanza. The meter is mostly iambic with its accompanying syncopated forms familiar from the parodos, the cretic and the bacchiac. Of the fifty-three lines in the strophes and the epode (excluding the pherecratean/glyconic coda sections), thirty-five are composed exclusively of these three metrical feet; in other words, 66 percent of the stasimon consists of simple iambic lines. The only real departures from the basic iambic rhythm are the lecythia in the second and third strophic pairs and in the epode, which are grouped together so that the rhythm is not lost (especially after it has been so strongly

and clearly established in the parodos); and the four choriambic lines at the end of the third strophic pair. The use of
lecythia sustains the audience's awareness of this meter, and
the choriambs will appear in the next stasimon; thus they
provide the kind of musical connection to previous and later
odes that was seen in the Hymn to Zeus. With these exceptions this long choral song presents a largely unvaried and
uniform iambic meter. Even the precise form of several individual iambic lines is repeated an extraordinary number of
times; especially notable are:

$$\cup-- \quad -\cup- \quad \cup-- \qquad \text{4 repeats}$$
$$\cup-\cup- \quad -\cup- \quad (-\cup-) \qquad \text{10} (+\, 4)$$
$$\cup-\cup- \quad \cup-\cup-$$
$$\text{or} \qquad\qquad\qquad 9$$
$$\cup-\cup- \quad \cup-\cup- \quad \cup-\cup-$$

All these metrical ingredients—the six corresponding codas,
the lack of significant metrical variation throughout the song,
and the repetition of line patterns—make this one of Aeschylus' most organized and unified odes in terms of metrics, and
thereby, of music and dance.[43]

The words of this chorus follow a logical progression. The
old men begin by announcing as the new theme of their song
the justice wrought by Zeus in the devastation of Troy; their
lyric begins: "They [the Trojans] can tell of the stroke of
Zeus" (367). The chorus then interprets the fall of Troy as
corroboration of its optimistic view of the world: the evil
man will pay because the world is just and ordered. But the
old men do not deny that justice was achieved only with a
great deal of suffering for the Greeks. Helen sailed away and
left nothing but unsatisfied craving in the palace of Menelaus.
Even greater grief remained for those who stayed at home
from Troy as they saw their dead sons and brothers shipped
home in urns. There is traitorous talk among the citizens and
a suspicion that the commander of the expedition has yet to
pay the price for the suffering he has caused. Finally, when
they admit that they themselves would not want the title

"sacker of cities," their logic has brought them only a step away from directly saying something hostile or unfavorable about Agamemnon. But, of course, it is the common pattern for this chorus to avoid the implications of its thinking at such a moment, a retreat accomplished here by throwing doubt on the truth of the torch's message. In effect, the old men's thoughts have led to conclusions that are so disturbing that they do not want the message from Troy to be true. Every step in the development of this lyric flows quite reasonably and consistently from the previous ideas. The justice of Zeus is seen to have such horrible immediate consequences that the chorus must seek refuge in the hope that the cause of its thoughts is untrue—that the torch is unreliable and can be dismissed as the kind of thing a woman would believe in.

This ode is presented as a hymn of honor to Zeus and as such is a statement of faith in the world ordered under his sovereignty. The first stanza contains several general principles about the working of justice: Zeus has worked as he has decreed; men say that gods show no care for those who commit a crime, but they are wrong. The wrongdoer has no protection in wealth once he has kicked the great altar of Justice out of sight. Such statements present the constant hope of the old men, but when they apply their idea of justice to an actual event, they must admit that Zeus's justice is a stroke or blow, an act of violence, and that rather than appearing openly to any observer it must be "tracked down" (367–8). Thus the theme of the song is the optimistic "learning through suffering" theme familiar from the parodos. However, whereas the old men sang their theme there to a clear lecythion meter, here they sing it to a different rhythm; if the lecythion is to be associated throughout the drama with the just working of Zeus, they are singing the wrong song. This is only the first time in the *Oresteia* that someone will find himself singing his words to the wrong thematic music; eventually he discovers that the music has been right as his words slip gradually but ineluctably into the thought proper to that music. The insistently repeated uniformity of the meter in this ode reveals the logically interconnected direction of their thoughts as the old men try to sing of their concept of Zeus's justice but find that the defeat of Troy does not fit their theory closely enough. By the end of the ode the elders quite naturally come to dwell on the excessive behavior of Agamemnon and the punishment that their faith requires of such men. As if to remind the audience that there is another meter that might be more appropriate in this context, the sections of lecythia stand alone and are never developed.

The dislocation implicit in singing the wrong song opens the possibility for irony: in their words the old men show that they intend to look on the bright side—and yet they begin by singing the wrong song. Even more ironically, their music is correct; the justice administered by Agamemnon did involve crime, and he will receive punishment before the play is over.[44]

There is even evidence in metrical patterning that the elders are beginning to realize how inconsistent their belief is. Up to this point in the *Oresteia*, lyric meters have been largely unresolved; the metrical feet take their simplest, most basic form. At the end of the epode are two lines of highly resolved iambic meter (485–86). In keeping with the lack of metrical variety characteristic of this stasimon, there are almost no resolved iambic feet in the whole ode.[45] Resolution shows that anxiety has begun to work its way into the previously uniform and simple meter as the chorus reveals its concern that the message from Troy may be true.

The music of this stasimon is probably religious in tone, in keeping with the chorus's intention to sing a hymn to Zeus. In addition, the uniformity of the meter suggests that the music would have been homogenous and the dancing similar from beginning to end, with a repetition of a figure at the coda sections to stress the unity of the whole piece. Music and dance would probably have strongly echoed the visual and oral effects accompanying the iambic meter in the last part of the parodos, underlining the irony that the chorus is singing the wrong song for its subject.[46] Finally, there would be some noticeable musical variation in the chorus's ordered song at the end of the epode, where the meter is resolved for the first time.

Form

The first stasimon falls into three sections clearly marked by meter: a brief introduction by the chorus in anapaests; the three pairs of lyric strophes closely connected by meter, repetition of lines, and the coda sections; and an epode continuing the meter from the strophes but probably not sung in unison by the whole chorus.

The anapaestic introduction is by no means unusual in this position; it marks the beginning of a formal ode and is much in character for a chorus that has demonstrated its musical virtuosity in its performance of the parodos. By such a formal introduction Aeschylus allows the members of the chorus to position themselves and to signal that the song to come will be an organized and artistic example of choral lyric. In keeping with this announcement through form, the chorus in an orderly way explains the subject of its song, the general principles underlying the immediate action, and finally applies these general principles to the case of Helen and Paris. The ideas proceed logically; the meter is simple and repetitious. The succession of balanced and metrically interrelated strophic stanzas portrays the effect that Aeschylus also sought in his words: a formal choral statement synthesizing the event at Troy with the religious principles of the chorus.

Yet there is a problem. What began as a methodical statement of phenomenon–general principle–particular cause gradually attracts related ideas that must also be included in a unified statement. At line 409, in the second strophe, the subject shifts from the suffering at Troy to the suffering in Greece; in the second antistrophe the subject turns from the suffering of the past to that of the present. The last strophe is filled with threats against Agamemnon: "The gods do not ignore those who have killed many men" and "May I never be a sacker of cities" (461–68 and 472). The laws of the universe, which the chorus attempts to define, are transmitted to men only by their recurrence in human events. Because there is no Bible nor sacred book, mortals must make these principles live by applying them to each event consistently. Paris sinned—he and his people have suffered terribly; but Agamemnon has also sinned—and the same laws that the chorus praises in this hymn demand that there be further retribution.[47] The tightly unified choral form reflects its rigorously unified content: the punishment of Troy, the sacredness of certain relationships, the violation of justice and its consequences, the fate of a man who is easily led into ruin, the human cost of the expedition to Troy, disapproval of the generalship of Agamemnon, and the certainty that a Fury will track down men who are responsible for many deaths.[48]

To confirm this interpretation there is the epode.[49] At the beginning of this stasimon the chorus has assured Clytemnestra that it is confident that Troy has fallen just as she reported, even though no messenger has come to verify her news. But as the old men reflect on the implications of Troy's defeat, they realize that they do not like the conclusions they must draw. At the point where they would have to predict something dire for Agamemnon, they turn away from their train of thought and express the hope that her report is pure rumor. From its form the audience would not necessarily realize that this is an epode but would expect a corresponding stanza to serve as an antistrophe. Once again this disappointed expectation reflects the inadequacy of such avoidance as a conclusion to an ode that has promised much in its poetry, its logic, its religion, and its music. For an audience that has heard a pattern three times, it would be jarring to find that there is no antistrophe and that the repeated coda has been replaced by highly resolved iambics expressing a snorted exasperation. At the end of an ode that is even more highly unified than usual, Aeschylus' choice of a non-strophic form has special significance.

In addition, Aeschylus seems for the first time in the play to have split the chorus into at least two groups of singers.[50]

For a chorus that has prided itself on its ability to sing and
dance to highly organized and complex music, this ending
betrays a temporary paralysis. The old men are lost and have
nothing purposeful to say. In their uncertainty and apprehen-
siveness their competence at musical organization breaks
down. The very structure of the chorus is split as they catch a
glimpse of a future they do not want. The breakdown in their
thought is conveyed by a disruption of the orderly continuance of strophic stanzas in simple meter, in formal balance,
and in the unity of the chorus as a group.[51]

The Second Stasimon (681–782)

681–98: str. a		— ᴗ — ᴗ — ᴗ —	lec
699–716: ant. a	700	— ᴗ — ᴗ — ᴗ —	lec
		— ᴗ — ᴗ — ᴗ — — ᴗ —	lec cr
		— ᴗ — ᴗ — ᴗ —	lec
685		— ᴗ — ᴗ — ᴗ —	lec
	705	— ᴗ ᴗ — ᴗ — ᴗ —	ch ia
		— ᴗ ᴗ — ᴗ — ᴗ — ⏒	?
		ᴗ ᴗ — ᴗ — ᴗ ᴗ —	?
690		ᴗ ᴗ — — ᴗ ᴗ — —	2 ion
		ᴗ ᴗ — ᴗ — ᴗ — —	anac
	710	ᴗ ᴗ — ᴗ — ᴗ — —	anac
		ᴗ ᴗ — — ᴗ ᴗ — ᴗ — ᴗ — —	ion anac
695		ᴗ ᴗ — ᴗ — ᴗ — —	anac
		*— — — ᴗ ᴗ — ᴗ —	glyc
	715	*— ᴗ ᴗ — ᴗ — —	ch ba
		ᴗ ᴗ ᴗ — ᴗ ᴗ — ⏒	pher
717–26: str. b		ᴗ — — ᴗ ᴗ — ᴗ —	glyc
727–36: ant. b		— ᴗ — ᴗ ᴗ — ᴗ —	glyc
		— ᴗ — ᴗ ᴗ — ⏒	pher
720	730	— ᴗ ᴗ — ᴗ ᴗ — —	(pher)[52]
		— ᴗ ᴗ — ᴗ ᴗ — ᴗ	(pher)
		— ᴗ ᴗ — ᴗ ᴗ — —	(pher)
		ᴗ ᴗ ᴗ — ᴗ — ᴗ —	lec
		ᴗ ᴗ ᴗ — ᴗ — ᴗ ⏒	lec

725	735	−⏒−∪∪−∪−	glyc
		−∪−∪∪−−	pher
737−49: str. g	750	∪−∪− −∪−∪−∪−	ia lec
750−62: ant. g		∪−− ∪−∪−	ba ia
740		−∪− ∪−−	cr ba
		∪−− −∪− ∪−−	ba cr ba
	755	−∪∪− ∪−∪−	ch ia
		−∪−∪∪−∪−−	hipp
		∪∪−− ∪∪−−	ion
745		∪∪−∪ −∪−−	anac
		∪∪−− ∪∪−−	ion
	760	∪∪−− ∪∪−−	ion
		−−∪ −∪∪−	ch. dimeter
		−∪−∪∪−−	pher
763−72: str. d		∪−∪− −∪−	ia cr
773−82: ant. d		−∪− −∪−	2 cr
765	775	−∪−∪−∪−	lec
		∪−∪− ∪∪∪∪−	2 ia
		∪−∪− ∪−∪−	2 ia
		*−∪∪∪− ∪∪∪∪∪∪	2 ia
		*∪∪∪∪− ∪−∪−	2 ia
770	780	−∪∪− ∪−−	ch ba
		−∪∪− ∪−−	ch ba

Meter

Four basic meters appear in this stasimon: the lecythion; the iambic and its familiar substitutions; the ionic with its related form, the anaclast; and the glyconic with its companion, the pherecratean. As a whole, however, the ode is predominantly ionic and the glyconic; forty-four of ninety-four lyric lines (47 percent) are given to these two meters. Because these are used rarely in the *Oresteia* and seem to have no connection to a dramatic theme, the high frequency of their occurrence in this ode immediately suggests that the chorus is trying to escape the two themes with which it has been preoccupied in the previous odes, a suggestion further corroborated by the arrangement of meters within this lyric.

The chorus begins its song with five lines of unresolved lecythion interrupted by only a single cretic; then the meter modulates to ionic, with two lines of glyconic at the close of the strophe.[53] To the lecythion meter the elders marvel at the appropriateness of Helen's name: there must have been a name-giver who remains invisible but who knew from the beginning that she would be a source of destruction. They sing of this ordering force, which knows future patterns of development and can thus assign proper names to people, in the meter of the Hymn to Zeus; the musical reminiscence is appropriate because both passages express a trust in an orderer who defines a pattern in human events. In the corresponding section of the antistrophe they sing of the Wrath that sent destruction against Troy because the code of Zeus, the god of guest-friendship, was violated; again their belief in the pattern of Zeus's justice is sung to the lecythion. At this point the chorus is singing clearly and repeatedly to the meter appropriate to its words, and the music and dance would probably be similar to those performed to the basic lecythion theme in the parodos.

But at the point in the strophe and antistrophe where the meter shifts to ionic the words turn from theories to acts: the escape and marriage of Helen. The lecythion is used to sing of the large forces shaping and controlling events; the ionic to tell of those events. The old men contentedly sing of the crime of Helen and Paris, lavishing careful attention on it while drawing no conclusions that will cause them consternation. They take their time in this comfortable and safe reminiscence of the past; they sing of the delicate draperies at Sparta and the speedy voyage to Troy, and they revel in their moralizing as they see a bloody Eris driving Helen on to Troy and virtually hear the Trojans modulating their wedding hymn to a lament. Such enjoyment of the past is an indulgence for this serious chorus; they are escaping from their worrisome thoughts about the return of their threatened king, and the meter framing this escapism appropriately has no thematic import.[54]

The next two strophes tell the equally harmless animal fable of the lion cub who fulfilled the predictable pattern of nature by growing into a wild beast. The parallel to Helen, who reveals the true nature known by the name-giver, is all too clear. Once again the chorus ruminates in a leisurely way on a story that has interesting applications to the life of Helen, telling how the small lion was loving of the children and a joy to the older members of the family, how it was kept like a child, and how its eyes shone. Again they exult in the moral message: the unsuspecting cub was reared as a priest of Ate by the will of the god.[55] The meter repeats the glyconic/ pherecratean from the end of the previous strophic pair. Because this meter has no thematic connotation, the music continues to reinforce the chorus's desire to avoid considerations that the action of the play will eventually force upon it.[56]

The third strophic pair begins with another meter familiar from the parodos, the iambic and its substitutions, but this meter is soon lost in an extension of the ionic. In the first of these stanzas the chorus continues to delight in describing what people thought Helen was when she came to Troy and what she actually turned out to be; she came as a windless calm and a gentle glory of wealth but soon revealed hints of peril—a gentle arrow from the eyes, a flower of love that strung the heart. Finally her destructive nature became apparent: a bitter marriage rite, a woman dangerous to be with, and (as the chorus self-righteously asserts) an Erinys sent by Zeus, the god of guest-friendship, to bring weeping to brides. As expected, while the chorus exults in its moralizing from the past, it reverts to the ionic meter. But at the beginning of the third antistrophe the chorus begins to return to general statements about the pattern of justice that it sees in the punishment of Helen and Paris.[57] The old men find themselves (perhaps almost as a surprise) singing in iambic meter but soon lose themselves in the ionic as they assert their strong personal belief that evil begets evil while justice will always produce beautiful children.

As they continue their statement of principles into the fourth strophe they also continue their metaphor of birth and growth under order.[58] Helen grew in accord with her name, and the lion cub in accord with its nature; acts of pride and insolence also generate a patterned growth controlled by justice, who "guides everything to its proper end" (781). In terms of their own logic the old men have finally sung a successful lyric ode that does not compel them to turn aside from the inescapable direction of their thoughts. They have begun by singing of permanent patterns that are apparent in the world; they have triumphantly applied this ordered structure to the case of Helen, Paris, and the citizens of Troy; and they have drawn some deeply religious and quite consistent ethical conclusions while bringing their ode to an orderly, methodical, and systematic end.[59]

Yet there are troublesome verbal hints in the final three stanzas. The chorus begins to talk in architectural terms: "a black Ate for the house," "Justice shines in smoky houses," and "Justice deserts guilded halls" (769–79). Because the scenic background represents the actual house of Atreus, which will take on a living force in Cassandra's words, the audience is aware that the palace of the king is by no stretch of the imagination a "smoky house." The old men also say that Justice does not honor the power of wealth misstamped with praise (779–80). Although they again draw no conclusions nor look to the present situation, the iambic meter of sin and infatuation recurs as the clearly dominant meter of the fourth strophic pair. There was a trace of this meter at the beginning of the third strophic pair, but it was inapplicable in a strophe in which the chorus was relishing its condemnation of Helen. In the corresponding antistrophe the chorus began to draw a moral, and the intrusion of the iambic may have been a surprise to them but it was soon forgotten in the continued ionics. In the fourth strophe the ionic and glyconic disappear, and the iambic reasserts itself strongly where the elders sing of the *daimon* that cannot be fought against and the unholy boldness that brings destruction. The high resolution of the iambic toward the end of the stanza stands in marked contrast to the preceding three sets of strophes, in which there are few resolutions of any kind. The chorus thus offers a musical clue that it realizes that it has reached another point at which it will have to repress anxiety about the future, but it is able to finish its song successfully without retreating to an expedient diversion.

When the chorus begins to sing of order and direction in the world, it sings the lecythion. Then it turns to subjects that are indulgent to its confusion and sings in meters that have no thematic association, and thus suggest no problematic issues. But at the end, even though the old men do not overtly acknowledge present danger in their view of justice, there is an obvious application to Agamemnon, and the meter shows that in their hearts they have not forgotten the dilemma which their faith poses for them. Once again meter is a truer guide to the feelings of the chorus and to the intent of the poet than words; the music reflects the true situation: the destruction of Troy—scarcely a type case for perfect justice—is an act of blood which will be avenged. Against a clear statement of a thematic meter their words sound hollow.

To shatter their pleasant excursion into abstract theorizing about the past, Agamemnon appears as they complete the ode with these words: "[Justice] guides all things to their fulfillment."[60]

Form

As Agamemnon and his group of survivors appear, the chorus changes its tune and begins to sing anapaests.[61] This break between the strophic music of the chorus and the anapaestic entrance is complete in terms of form, meter, and music. Yet in content the break is not complete; the general statements of the chorus in its final two stanzas can be understood to apply to the present master of the House of Atreus, and their

expression in iambics suggests that the chorus actually realizes the possibility of such an application. When the old men
begin the anapaests for the formal entrance of the king, they
immediately address him in three separate ways: "Tell me,
my king, destroyer of the city of Troy, offspring of Atreus,
how shall I address you?" (782–85). First they call him
"king"; but they have just spoken about the fate that awaits
those who are wealthy and who live in palaces—and Agamemnon enters in state as king. Then they call him "sacker of
Troy," which surely would recall to the audience the use of
ptoliporthes in the previous stasimon at 472, when the chorus
spoke of the dangerous talk of the citizens and the threat of
a stalking Fury. Finally they address him as "offspring of
Atreus"; following a lyric that has been constructed around
the predictable pattern of growth from young to old and
from generation to generation, the epithet must raise thoughts
of crime deeply rooted and growing in the house of which this
man is now master. Thus, although the form and meter of
the anapaestic entrance song provide a sharp break from
strophic song, the themes of the previous ode continue. For
the audience the warning signals are clear; but the old men on
the stage, in their joy at the end of the war and at the sight of
their returning king, have momentarily forgotten the ominous import of their reflections on the past. They can openly
acknowledge their negative feelings of ten years ago without
reverting to their gloomy thoughts for Agamemnon's future,
but Aeschylus will not let his audience forget those thoughts.
The chorus has sung an ode that avoids present problems despite specific hints toward the end of the song. In fact the previous reasoning of the chorus shows that it too continually
insists on the necessity of connecting past and present, but at
the moment it chooses to ignore this need. The poet makes
musical form demonstrate this avoidance by splitting the past
from the present—the past in the lyrics and the present in the
anapaests. But he bridges this separation of events by having
the themes from the first section continue into the second.

The unity in conception is there but it is a deeper and more painful unity than the chorus wants to admit. This stasimon with its following anapaests is the reverse of the previous ode. There the pattern that the chorus derived from the past and applied to the future caused grave doubts and discomfort. The development of logical thought was appropriately unified in meter and highly symmetrical in structure. In the second stasimon the chorus continues to develop and examine the same pattern more closely but it never moves to conclusions about the future. Rather, the old men pamper their faith by mulling over past events and seeming to ignore the implications of the pattern that they themselves want to assert for past, present, and future. In place of the final strophes in the first stasimon, where the chorus drew conclusions that were dangerous for Agamemnon, Aeschylus provides a separate entrance song for the king, thus sharply separating the emotions of the present from moralizing about the past. As long as these subjects can be segregated, the chorus can continue to sing happily, if inconsistently, about each. Form expresses this artificial separation, but the continuing action of the play will bring the unity of past and present so clearly onstage that the chorus will not long be able to avoid constructing a pattern of justice that explains both.

The Third Stasimon, The Cassandra Scene, and the "Fourth Stasimon" (975–1034, 1072–1177, 1331–42)

Third stasimon

975–87: str. a	975	—∪—∪—∪—	lec
988–1000: ant. a		—∪—∪—∪—	lec
	990	—∪—∪—∪— ⌣——	lec ba
		—∪∪—∪∪—∪∪—∪∪——	5 da
		—∪—∪—∪—	lec
	980	—∪—∪—∪—	lec
	995	—∪— —∪—	2 cr
		—∪—∪—∪—	lec
		*—∪—∪— ——∪— ∪—∪⌣	3 ia

985		*⏑— —⏑—	2 cr
		—⏑—⏑—⏑—	lec
	1000	—⏑—⏑—⏑—	lec

1001–17: str. b

1018–34: ant. b

		⏑⏑⏑— ⏑⏑⏑— ⏑⏑⏑—	3 cr
	1020	⏑⏑—— ⏔⏕ ⏔⏑—	ion anap?
		⏔⏑— ⏑⏑— ⏑⏑— —	paroemiac
1005		—⏑⏑—⏑⏑—	hemiepes
		—⏑⏑—⏑⏑—	hemiepes
		—⏑⏑—⏑⏑—⏑—⏒	alcaic deca-syllable
	1025	—⏑—⏑—⏑—	lec
		—⏑—⏑—⏑—	lec
1010		—⏑—⏑—⏑—	lec
		—⏑—⏑—⏑—	lec
		—⏑—⏑—⏑—	lec
	1030	—⏑—⏑—⏑—	lec
1015		———⏑⏑—⏑⏑—⏑⏑	8 da
		—⏑⏑—⏑⏑—⏑⏑——	
		—⏑—⏑—⏑—	lec

Cassandra scene [kommos] (1072–1177)

1072–75: str. a	Cass:	⏑⏑⏑⏑— ⏑——	ia ba
1076–79: ant. a		——⏑— ——	ia sp
	Chor:	2 trimeters	
1080–84: str. b	Cass:	——⏑— ——	ia sp
1085–89: ant. b		⏑—— ⏑——⏑—	ba doch
		⏒—⏑— ⏑—⏑— ⏒—⏑—	3 ia
	Chor:	2 trimeters	
1090–94: str. g	Cass:	—⏑⏑—⏑— —⏑⏑—⏑⏒	2 doch
1095–99: ant. g		—⏑⏑⏑⏑⏑ *⏑—⏑—	2 ia
		——⏑— ——⏑— ——⏑—	3 ia
	Chor:	2 trimeters	
1100–6: str. d	Cass:	⏑—⏑— ⏑⏑⏑—⏑—	ia doch
1107–13: ant. d		⏑⏑⏑⏑⏑⏑⏑—⏑⏒	lec
		⏒—⏑— ⏒—⏑— ⏑—⏑—	3 ia

	⏑ — — ⏑ — — ⏑ — — ⏑ — —	4 ba
	⏑ ⏑ ⏑ ⏖ ⏑ —	doch
Chor:	2 trimeters	

1114–24: str. e	Cass:	⏑ — ⏑ — ⏑ ⏑ ⏑ — ⏑ —	ia doch
1125–35: ant. e		— — ⏑ — ⏑ — —	ia ba
		⏒ — ⏑ — ⏑ — ⏑ — ⏑ — ⏑ ⏒	3 ia
		⏕ — ⏑ — ⏑ ⏑ ⏑ — ⏕ —	ia doch
		⏑ ⏑ ⏑ — ⏑ — — ⏑ — — ⏑ —	doch 2 cr
	Chor:	2 trimeters	
		⏑ ⏑ ⏑ — ⏑ — ⏑ ⏑ ⏑ ⏖ ⏑ —	2 doch
		⏑ — — ⏑ — ⏑ — — ⏑ —	2 doch
		⏑ ⏑ ⏑ — ⏑ — — ⏑ — —	cr 2 ba
		⏑ — ⏑ — — ⏑ —	ia cr

1136–45: str. z	Cass:	⏑ ⏑ ⏑ — ⏑ — — ⏑ ⏑ ⏑ — ⏑ —	cr ba doch
1146–55: ant. z		⏑ ⏑ ⏑ — ⏑ — ⏑ ⏑ ⏑ — ⏑ —	2 doch
		2 trimeters	
	Chor:	⏑ ⏑ ⏑ — ⏑ — ⏑ ⏑ ⏑ — ⏑ —	2 doch
		⏑ — — ⏑ —	doch
		⏑ ⏑ ⏑ ⏑ ⏑ — ⏑ — — —	2 cr sp
		⏑ ⏑ ⏑ — ⏑ — — ⏑ — — ⏑ —	doch 2 cr
		⏑ ⏑ ⏑ — ⏑ — — ⏑ ⏑ — ⏑ —	2 doch
		⏑ — — ⏑ —	doch

1156–66: str. ē	Cass:	⏑ — ⏑ — ⏑ — ⏑ ⏑ ⏑	2 ia doch
1167–77: ant ē		⏑ ⏑ ⏑ — ⏑ —	
		⏑ — ⏑ — — ⏑ ⏑ — ⏑ —	ia doch
		⏑ ⏑ ⏑ — ⏑ — — ⏑ ⏑ — ⏑ —	2 doch
		— ⏑ ⏑ — ⏑ —	doch
		2 trimeters	
	Chor:	⏑ ⏑ ⏑ ⏑ ⏑ — ⏑ ⏑ ⏑ — ⏑ —	2 doch
		⏕ — ⏑ ⏑ ⏑ ⏑ — ⏑ —	2 ia
		⏑ — — ⏑ — ⏒ ⏖ — ⏑ —	2 doch
		⏑ — — ⏑ — ⏑ ⏑ ⏑ ⏑ ⏑ ⏑ ⏖	2 doch
		— ⏑ ⏑ — ⏑ —	doch

"Fourth stasimon"
1331–42: anapaests

The third stasimon is a short and highly ordered song consisting of two strophic pairs. The basic meter is the lecythion: thirty of fifty-four lines contain unresolved lecythia (55 percent). The remaining meters are diverse and so scattered throughout the lecythia that the poet seems to have made little attempt to establish any meter. Immediately before this ode Clytemnestra calls upon Zeus as the enforcer of patterns as she prays while her husband enters the palace: "Zeus, Zeus, you who direct matters to their proper end, make my prayers complete; may you take charge of those things that you intend to bring to pass" (973–4). The lecythion, as the meter of the Hymn to Zeus and also of the opening of the second stasimon, where the chorus theorized about the name-giver, is appropriate in the response to her prayer.

The chorus can no longer luxuriate in moralizing about the past nor can it merely express happiness that the king is home and the war over. Clytemnestra compels them to consider the present, and a critical moment appears to be at hand.[62] Her prayer has brought the perplexity of the old men to a head. Despite their forebodings about Agamemnon they have seen with their own eyes that he is safely home (989). Present good fortune should overcome their fear of impending vengeance, and yet there is the continuing feeling that Agamemnon must suffer some sort of punishment for the bloodshed which he has caused. Consequently, the thoughts of the chorus run in two directions. The discomfort they feel is similar to the discomfort caused by dreams that are hard to interpret and bring only doubt (981). They yearn for a sense of settled, persuasive confidence because they lack firm belief in their optimistic expectations (982 and 993).

The old men, distressed by having to think of irreconcilable possibilities, express their torment in two ways: in anatomical words—dread flutters before the heart, they feel something inside that they want to spit out, and their hearts spin around against their minds (975–83 and 995–97) and in terms of sound—from inside there is a song that is unwanted and unrewarded as their spirits sing the dirge of the Erinyes without the accompaniment of the lyre (979 and 990–94). The thoughts that upset them are evident from the adjectives that accompany the two types of description. Their hearts are prophetic, and the music from within forebodes (997–79); the heart spins in circles that bring the fulfillment of previous actions, and it brushes against the mind that knows justice (995–97); the music from inside is the dirge of the avenging Furies (990–92). At this point Aeschylus' mixture of metaphors may become difficult to grasp, but the intent is clear. The old men's anxiety arises from their thoughts of the immediate future and the irreversible pattern of vengeance that seems to apply to Agamemnon.

In the second strophe (1001–17) the chorus continues the idea of the voyage from the first strophe (984). The trip to Troy was blessed with victory, and the return home seems to have been favored by one of the gods. Combining the motifs of the ship and the house, they express hope that the success of the voyage bodes well for the king. Zeus might be protecting Agamemnon because there has been no excess of pride in his life—or, if there has been, he may have already discarded it. But the old men are by no means convinced that the ethical model of the ship's captain casting his excess cargo overboard has much relevance to the crime involved; they admit that it is hard to think of any way in which Agamemnon could have atoned for the murder of Iphigenia except by bringing her back to life. From the story of Asclepius it is clear that death is one barrier that Zeus strictly enforces (1018–24).

The elements that unify the stasimon through line 1024 are: (a) a belief in Zeus as the powerful ruler of the universe, (b) an unwanted conviction that the old men know the next event required by their own conception of justice; (c) the established fact of the safe sea voyage of their king and his glorious entrance into his palace (the one firm fact available to the chorus); (d) the existence of disquieting feelings that all is not well, feelings expressed in terms of physical discomfort and unpleasant music coming from within; and (e) the continued presence of these uncomfortable feelings ever since the fleet left Aulis and their persistence in the face of clear, visible evidence of the king's safety.

Hence their perplexity: to have their innate sense of justice fully edified, their king must die; but to satisfy their belief in the justice of Zeus, their king must live. If he dies, they will lose their faith in Zeus as the enforcer of justice; if he lives, they will see that there are bloody exceptions to the most basic laws of the ordered universe: fathers who murder their children must find a place in the system of justice. These are the two fates that the old men have been juggling since the parodos where they recalled the slaughter of Iphigenia and the general principle of justice that demanded revenge for the crime of Paris. The prayer of Clytemnestra to Zeus asking for the final act has driven the chorus to focus its thoughts on these two *moirai* (fates). In the deliberations of the chorus, however, neither *moira* is totally convincing; the established fate of all mortals prevents the idea of the special fate from the gods from winning total victory and prohibits a persuasive confidence from taking over the throne of the old men's minds (1025–27 and 982–3).[63]

Finally the members of the chorus return to physical descriptions of their dilemma. If one of the two *moirai* were established in their minds, they would speak out their happy resolution even faster than their tongues could form the words. But because neither *moira* achieves dominance, their inner discomfort remains something that they would like to spit out but cannot (980). As a result the noise from within continues; the heart mutters and keeps paining the soul while the mind is burning (1030–34).

The present situation seems too complex for their religion, or—what is more worrisome—their religion all along has been too simple to explain the events of their world. Either way, they cannot answer questions convincingly or obtain that desired confidence as long as they think in terms of two possibilities, both of which are unsatisfactory. The last part of the final antistrophe is phrased in terms of the first part of the ode: the symptoms of discomfort are physical, and the inner sound, which is disturbing, continues as they contrast alternative fates that Agamemnon may experience. In this ode there is a unity of ideas, mood, and images.

Underlying these unities is a similar consistency in the predominant lecythion meter. It would be appropriate for the old men to sing to the meter of sin and infatuation that accompanied their description of the murder of Iphigenia and to which they were led to condemn their king as the "sacker of cities"; in their hearts they feel that there is a strong case against the prideful, arrogant, and bloody king who has acted in a way that openly begs for the justice which overtook Paris and Helen. Instead they assert the meter associated with a complete trust in Zeus as a god guiding men through a world of suffering to greater understanding. They also admit, however, that there is another type of music in this ode, a music that rises up from inside them unbidden and that they do not want to hear. Over this music they sing out strongly to the lecythion meter hoping that their suspicions about their king's danger will prove unfounded.

The regular form of the third stasimon contrasts with the confusion and anguish of its content. For its role to be understood, this contradiction must be viewed within the larger framework of the entire musical movement spanning the opening of the third stasimon through the conflicting utterances of the chorus after the death of Agamemnon. The third stasimon, unlike the previous three long lyrics, does not precede a long iambic episode. Rather, Clytemnestra coming from the palace directs attention to the silence of Cassandra. After this brief scene Cassandra and the chorus share a musical kommos followed by a spoken exchange. The chorus closes this scene with the anapaests that immediately precede the death cries of Agamemnon.

In the third stasimon the members of the chorus are conscious of the noise and the music from within, which they do not want to hear because it is associated with their forebodings of Agamemnon's death. The behavior of Cassandra aggravates their confusion. She shrieks out in unhappiness to the god Apollo (1072). The old men answer in iambics that Apollo has no need to hear such songs. Cassandra repeats her cry of sorrow, and they once again tell her that she is singing the wrong kind of music for the occasion. The hidden music of anxiety, which was internal and suppressed in the stasimon, becomes external and public in the scene with Cassandra. It begins when they sing:

> What Erinys is this that you summon to rise up above this house? Your words bring me no joy. A red drop ran to my heart—the very drop that arrives together with the rays of dying life for a soldier slain by the spear. Doom comes on swiftly.   (*Ag.* 1119–24)

The words *Erinys* and *house* indicate that they are thinking in much the same terms as in the stasimon, when they sang: "My spirit—self-taught—sings the lyreless song of the Erinys" (990–92), and when they spoke of the shrewd captain who would not let his whole house sink (1008–14). The anatomical description of their feelings, the drop that rushed to the heart, is reminiscent of the physical symptoms of discomfort in the ode.[64] At the very moment when Cassandra has made them think of their previous confusion, they begin to sing a combination of dochmiac and iambic meter, and the music that was previously a dimly heard tune from within is now sung openly onstage. It is still the unwanted and unrewarded song; they call her music a tuneless tune (1142); inarticulate shrieks and loud notes (1152–3); whining notes, shattering to the ear (1165–6); and songs that are laden with death (1176)—but they imitate her meter and probably also her music.[65]

The music of foreboding that the old men felt so strongly in the stasimon was only a hint of the musical exchange that is a vital part of the staging in the Cassandra scene. Even as they seek to quiet the Trojan princess and profess ignorance of the meaning of her words, the music betrays the inner fear that their king may die. Perplexity still reigns in their minds.

The lyric meter during the Cassandra scene is largely dochmiac in highly resolved and varied forms with interspersed iambics, bacchiacs, and trochaics, including one lecythion (rendered virtually unidentifiable because it is so highly resolved). The dochmiac meter is traditionally associated in Greek tragedy with a high level of excitement or vexation;[66] it seems appropriate to this musical passage, where the members of the chorus want to remain calm but their knowledge of what may happen raises their anxiety and preys on their minds. The music from within is a music of fear; they are anxious for their king, but they are also pious men clutching to a faith and hope in a simple religion that they anticipate will be taken from them by impending events.[67]

In terms of musical effect the chorus first sings a carefully crafted ode dominated by the meter associated with the order of the world under the reign of Zeus; but its words indicate that it is suppressing another kind of music, and from the previous usage of the two meters—the lecythion and the iambic—it is clear what music they do not want to hear. Then Cassandra enters and leads the old men from a very prosaic level of conversation (for example, at 1087–89 and 1112–3) to an awareness of the full danger to Agamemnon at that moment.[68] She, who sees clearly the treachery within the palace, by her singing leads the music of distress from within the chorus onto the stage at 1121–24. Yet when Cassandra leaves the stage, the chorus reiterates in an orderly sequence of anapaests its belief that Agamemnon should be protected by Zeus:

> Now if he should pay for the blood of earlier people and by dying pay the penalty of death to the dead, then who of men hearing these things would boast that he has been born with a fortune which will do him no harm?
>
> (1338–42)

Even though Cassandra has suggested that Agamemnon is going to be killed, the old men immediately take the opposite stand because they fervently want to believe in a Zeus who will honor the men who carry out his work on earth.[69]

Scarcely does the chorus finish these anapaests when the cries of Agamemnon are heard from inside the house and his death is an accomplished fact. At the beginning of both the parodos and the first stasimon, the audience has heard an anapaestic introduction to a formal ode. Hearing the twelve anapaestic lines sung by the chorus and seeing no actor present, it would now expect to hear a formal choral ode—the "fourth stasimon"—enlarging on the theme elaborated so often before by the chorus and just mentioned in the introductory anapaests: the actions of Agamemnon against Troy and the justice of Zeus that exonerates him because of his special mission.[70] The chorus's words and music, however, are interrupted by a highly unmusical sound—the death screams of Agamemnon. Not only would a fully formal, meditative choral song be inappropriate at such a moment, but the old men's confidence is so shattered that it is impossible for them to organize the elements of such a song. To make the breakdown even more pronounced, the poet now gives each member of the chorus two spoken iambic trimeter lines showing the group's complete bewilderment.[71] One citizen wants to call all the citizens to a meeting. One wants to burst into the palace and see what is really going on. Some of the comments contain no plan at all, being merely the ineffectual expressions of numbness following such an event. Some lament their inactivity; some fear a tyranny; some urge immediate resistance to any show of force by the assassins. And finally, as several members encourage each other to ascertain the facts before making any decision, they are thwarted by the appearance of Clytemnestra standing over the two bodies.

The murder of Agamemnon is the pivotal moment in this play. It is an act that embodies major inversions and reversals for many of the characters. A man is killed by a woman, a husband by his wife, a king by his queen, a tyrant usurps the throne and uses arms against the citizens, a welcome is turned into a funeral, and the hope of all for a return to normal living is ended. This event makes the promise of Zeus in punishing the Trojans seem a thing forgotten, for the universe appears godless or cruelly tyrannical. And as this truth has become clearer in the progression of events toward Agamemnon's death, the chorus has increasing difficulty in making music. During the parodos the chorus confidently expressed its be-lief in Zeus and in its own ability to make music. When this belief in Zeus is shattered, it is fitting that, in a play in which music-making is used as a visual and aural metaphor, the abil-ity to sing and dance also vanishes. This long scene, which depends largely for its organization on music, began with the strict and simple formalism of the third stasimon. Then the elders, though unwilling, were compelled by Cassandra to sing, and finally, when they made their hopeful assessment about Agamemnon, they were not even permitted the op-portunity to finish their thoughts—indeed, they now do not even look like a chorus. They do not dance or sing lyrics; they stand still and talk like the other characters. They do not even sing together; they utter their conflicting pieces of ad-vice individually.

What has happened in this scene is typical of Aeschylus the dramatist. Just as other metaphors are brought onto the stage and not left solely in the realm of verbal ornamentation, the verbal motif of music and sound is now developed physically onstage as the audience watches tragedy's basic formal com-ponent, the chorus, break apart under the impact of Aga-memnon's death.[72]

The End of the Agamemnon (1407–1673)

Last Song (1407–1576)

1407–11: str. a	⏑⏑⏑–⏑–	doch
1426–30: ant. a	⏑⏑⏑⏑⏑ ⏑–⏑–	2 ia
	⏑⏑⏑–⏑–	2 doch
	–⏑⏑⏒⏑⏑–	
	⏑⏑⏑–⏑– –⏑⏑–⏑–	2 doch

	1410	⏒⏑⏑⏑⏑⏑⏒	2 doch
		⏑⏑⏑−⏑−	
	1430	−⏑−⏑⏑−−	pher
1448−54: str. b		−⏑⏑−⏑− −⏑⏑−⏑−	2 doch
1468−74: ant. b		−⏑−⏑⏑−−	pher
1450	1470	⏑−⏑− −⏑− ⏑−−	ia cr ba
		−⏑⏑−⏑⏑−⏑−−	alcaic decasyllable
		⏑⏑⏑−⏑−⏑−	lec
		⏒⏑⏑− −⏑− −⏑−	3 cr
		−⏑− −⏑−⏑−⏑−	cr lec
1455−61:		⏑−	
ephymnion a		⏑⏑− ⏑⏑−	anap
(NOT REPEATED)		⏑⏑− −− −⏑⏑ −−	anap
		−− ⏑⏑− ⏑⏑− −	paroemiac
		*−⏑⏑−−⏑− −⏑⏑−⏑−	? (doch)
	1460	⏑−⏑− ⏑−⏑− ⏑−⏑−	3 ia
		⏑⏑⏑− −⏑− ⏑−−	2 cr ba
1481−88: str. g	1505	*−⏑⏑−⏑⏑−	hemiepes
1505−12: ant. g		−⏑⏑−⏑⏑−⏑−−	alcaic decasyllable
		−−⏑⏑−⏑−	?
		−⏑−⏑⏑−−	pher
1485		⏑−⏑− ⏑−⏑−	2 ia
	1510	⏑−⏑− ⏑−⏑−	2 ia
		⏑−⏑− ⏑−⏑− ⏑−−	2 ia ba
		⏑−−⏑⏑−⏑−−	hipponacteum
1489−96:		−− −− ⏑⏑− ⏑⏑−	anap
ephymnion b 1490		−⏑⏑ −−	anap
(Repeated 1513−20)	1515	⏑⏑− ⏑⏑− ⏑⏑− −	paroemiac
		−− ⏑⏑− ⏑⏑− ⏑⏑−	anap
		⏑⏑− ⏑⏑− ⏑⏑− −	paroemiac
		−−−−− −⏑⏑−⏑−	2 doch
1495		⏑⏑− ⏑−⏑−	?
	1520	−⏑⏑−⏑⏑−⏑−−	alcaic decasyllable

1530–36: str. d		∪–∪– –∪– ∪––	ia cr ba
1560–66: ant. d 1531	1561	–∪∪– ∪–⌣	ch ba
		∪–∪– –∪– ∪––	ia cr ba
		⌣–∪– –∪– ∪–∪–	ia cr ia
		∪–∪– –∪– ∪––	ia cr ba
1535	1565	∪–∪– ∪–∪– ∪–∪–	3 ia
		∪–– –∪– ∪––	ba cr ba

1537–50:		–– –– –∪∪ ––	anap
ephymnion g		–– ∪∪– –∪∪ ––	anap
(NOT REPEATED)	1540	–– ∪∪– ∪∪– –	paroemiac
		∪∪– –– ∪∪– ––	anap
		–∪∪ –– –– ––	anap
		–∪∪ –– ∪∪– ––	anap
	1545	–– ∪∪– ∪∪– ––	anap
		∪∪– ∪∪– ∪∪– –	paroemiac
		–∪∪–∪∪–∪∪–∪––	praxillean
		–∪∪– ∪––	ch ba
	1550	∪–– –∪– ∪––	ba cr ba

Meter

The final scene between Clytemnestra and the chorus provides a musical contrast to the Cassandra scene. At first the
chorus sings while the main character speaks, but its agitated
responses soon lead her to song.

Clytemnestra, throwing open the doors and proudly revealing her work, interrupts the confused movements of the
chorus. Her tone is confident as she speaks with characteristic
strength, articulation, and poetic subtlety, but her sense of se-
curity wavers as she tries to strike a bargain with the *daimon*
of the family, hoping that he will desert the house and allow
her to live on with her small share of the possessions (1567–
76). At the end of the play she is impelled to tell Aegisthus
that they have done enough evil and have been struck down
by the heavy hoof of the *daimon* (1654–60).[73] This extreme
change in tone is accompanied by a shift from speaking to
music as Clytemnestra realizes that she is not succeeding in

her attempts to persuade the chorus of her righteousness. Her speeches grow shorter and then she begins to chant to the anapaestic meter. In her first two anapaestic stanzas it almost seems as though she is trying to sing in corresponsion (1462–67 and 1475–80); fittingly, as she tries to order her music, her words reprove the chorus and seek to impose her interpretation of the event upon them.[74] At 1497 she is still assertive, but by 1521 it is clear that she has failed to convince the old men and concomitantly has failed to make her anapaests correspond as a type of ordered strophe-antistrophe. Now she merely finishes out this scene (up to the entrance of Aegisthus) with unmatched anapaestic stanzas which portray increasing discouragement.[75]

The responses of the chorus become more cogent and complex as, in a series of musical stanzas, it refuses to answer her rational appeals. At first the old men are shocked that the deed has been done and is so arrogantly displayed; by the end of the scene they have come to understand that only one response is called for, and they predict with gloomy certainty the continuation of killings within the house, a threat that Clytemnestra must realize is aimed directly at her. In their first two strophic pairs the dochmiac is the predominant meter as the chorus expresses its instinctive abhorrence of this deed of blood; the elders ask what root or drug could have produced a woman so crazed, for they see evidence of a mind that is deranged (1407–11 and 1426–30). At 1448 they pray for death to remove them from such a world, and in the first ephymnion they identify the Eris that has existed in the house since the days of Helen; in the corresponding antistrophe they sing of the *daimon* in the house who sings a tuneless hymn over the body. The meter in these two pairs of strophic stanzas is varied—dochmiac, pherecratean, iambic, Alcaic decasyllable, and lecythion. As the chorus recovers from its initial shock—expressed in dochmiacs—it gradually assimilates all the elements of the complex crime, seeks a pattern, and makes firmer statements about the future. Accompanying this growing certainty there is the reappearance of a clearly-stated thematic meter in the ephymnion about Helen (1455–61); it begins with anapaests, then moves to iambics in a short six lines.

In the third strophic pair the meter is varied at the beginning, but there are three repeated lines of unresolved iambic toward the end, and the repeated ephymnion to these stanzas is more settled on an anapaestic meter. To these more organized and uniform meters the chorus begins to confront the problem inherent in its view of the universe since the opening of the play: how the role of Zeus relates to human responsibility. The old men see that both Zeus and Clytemnestra must be involved, and they therefore pronounce Agamemnon's murder to be impious and guileful.

Finally, to a very steady iambic meter they claim that they are at a loss, bankrupt of any further means of thought. The universe has not worked in accord with their pious hopes but seems to be run by a god of whim and caprice who shows very little concern for mortals. The old men must now discard their belief in progress through suffering under the guidance of Zeus and confess that there is only more bloodshed in the future. As they renounce all hope in the ordering force of Zeus, they drop all pretense of singing the lecythion and assert firmly the iambic meter that was first used to describe the slaying of Iphigenia.[76] The final ephymnion is sung to a clear anapaestic meter—eight lines of anapaests with a final three lines of praxillean and iambic.

Both parties are singing at the end of this scene but not to the same music, for there is little harmony of thought between them. Clytemnestra has tried to convince the old men to see her as the agent of justice in Zeus's world, but they cannot find any way in which she can justify herself in that role. She hopes to be regarded as a cleanser and sanctifier of the house, but the elders can see only that she has renewed the pattern of sin and infatuation that they hoped had ended, and now they sing to the iambic meter: "Who would cast the cursed seed from the house? The family has been glued to ruin" (1565–66). During this scene Clytemnestra realizes that

her role is not as clear to the chorus as it was to her and therefore, insists on the rightness of her cause all the more vehe-
mently. But the chorus maintains that the only result of this
murder can be another murder and becomes increasingly
more apprehensive about the future. Neither singer can accept the reasoning of the other—and so they both continue to
sing their own songs, but there is a slight move toward agreement at the end of the scene. Their mutual understanding is
both verbal and musical: Clytemnestra declares that they
have spoken truthfully of Zeus's law and hopes that her act,
though not glorious, may be sufficient to create peace in the
house; they concur in her judgment of the act but can see another killing that is not far off. Each party shows a move toward agreement on the anapaestic meter, the chorus in its last
ephymnion and Clytemnestra in her last anapaestic stanza.
Although these stanzas are not juxtaposed to show full harmony, there is a modicum of agreement in their words along
with a musical hint of common element in their attitudes.[77]

The quality of Clytemnestra's music throughout the scene
is indicated in lines 1472–74, where the chorus says that she
stands like a hateful raven over the body and sings a tuneless
hymn. As she becomes more distressed at her situation, her
music becomes discordant and may be echoed in the chorus's
ephymnia, which become increasingly insistent on the anapaestic meter.

Form

The final scenes of *Agamemnon* show the shattering of belief
in a cosmic order and the imposition of a new type of order
through military force and tyranny. This disillusionment is
represented visually by the breakup of the chorus and aurally
by the disappearance of its music; the new regime is represented by Aegisthus and his soldiers, the brave but helpless
resistance of the chorus, and its silent exit as it realizes nothing
in the future is worth singing about.

When Clytemnestra displays the two bodies and tries to
justify her actions, the chorus replies once in iambics and

then turns to lyrics to answer her. Musical form underlines the complete divergence of Clytemnestra's thinking from that of the chorus. As mentioned above, only at the end of this scene do they attain some small agreement in terms of the situation and their music; otherwise the chorus never sings in the musical form that Clytemnestra uses. She sings nonstrophic anapaests while the old men sing a more elaborate lyric response that works its way into a final iambic statement. In the end, only the superior force of Aegisthus restores order. Music, then, serves two functions in this scene: first, it indicates the rising emotional level of Clytemnestra—from speech to song, from iambics to anapaests; and second, it presents aurally and probably also visually the basic disagreement in the interpretation of the deed and its implications as Clytemnestra and the chorus both sing and move to different rhythms and music.

The form of the music is crucial in reinforcing the conflict portrayed in this scene. When Clytemnestra asserts her righteousness in killing her husband, the chorus replies in an agitated meter but in a strophic form. She then turns to personal justification in an iambic speech, reminding them of the protection Aegisthus offered her and talking of her joy at the two murders; the chorus answers with a lyric strophe implicitly rejecting her explanation and continues in an ephymnion whose language is reminiscent of that previously used to describe the crime of Helen and Paris.[78] Clytemnestra immediately repulses any attempt to identify Helen as a cause, because she knows that this type of punishment cycle directly threatens her. The old men respond by addressing the *daimon* in the house, which seems to them incorporated in Clytemnestra. At line 1474 the audience, which has heard one balanced pair of strophe-antistrophe, another lyric strophe of thirteen lines, and now a repetition of the first seven lines of that lyric, would expect the song to continue in corresponding meter for another six lines; but this expectation is not fulfilled.[79] When Clytemnestra assures them that she likes the idea of serving the *daimon* far better than any talk of Troy

(1475–77), the song of the chorus appears to be cut short by the omission of the ephymnion corresponding to 1454–61. Thus Aeschylus has again composed a musical form for a choral song that disappoints the expectations of his audience. Making the effect all the more unsettling, an ephymnion after the third strophe is repeated after the third antistrophe; but the ephymnion after the fourth strophe is not repeated. In any scene with two speakers, one offering arguments and the other responding, there is a built-in expectation of symmetry;[80] but orderliness does not suit the prospect of continued violence that the chorus now sees. Aeschylus has therefore broken up any impression of orderly exchange by attaching musical units in an unsymmetrical fashion so that the audience will not be able to predict what form the music will take in the next stanza.[81]

It is also possible that the lack of repetition of the two ephymnia results from interruption by Clytemnestra rather than from a deliberate omission by the chorus. At 1475 Clytemnestra's words show that she is eager to have the chorus confirm her own structuring of the event, and she could well break in on their words to say: "Now you have corrected your thought . . ."—especially after their previous stanza, where they wanted to relate this event to the sin of Helen. Following 1520, as she corrects the chorus's lament concerning the manner in which Agamemnon died, her tone is more that of a persuader; she lacks the desperate quality that motivated her to interrupt the previous song. At 1541–50 the chorus asks who will preside at the funeral and Clytemnestra again has a motive to respond sharply. She surely does not want this hated man to receive a hero's burial; that would undermine her whole role as the cleanser and healer. Once again, therefore, she may actually interrupt the chorus's song and cause the dancing to stop in the midst of a pattern, thus creating a visual disjointedness to the scene. At 1567 she interrupts their general summary statement by responding in a direct and abject tone. After so many impassioned interruptions the chorus accepts her considered final statement as direct response. They willingly let her reply, because their hope to create a symmetrical song is now gone and they expect an interruption to their prediction of coming dangers. Here Clytemnestra delivers a correct and reasoned summation in a lowered tone in keeping with her expectations.

Consideration of the staging of the ephymnion demonstrates the importance of visualizing the plays instead of merely reading the text. Although editors have attempted to make these stanzas seem a usual part of a lyric ode by identifying them on the page with the notation "ephymnion," the evidence that Aeschylus is playing upon musical form in the play casts doubt on such normalization. Probably these notations should be removed so that a reader can see clearly that "normalizing" is neither necessary nor appropriate, rather this portion of the text should look as choppy as it acts.

The musical dislocations of this scene continue to the end of *Agamemnon*. The most striking feature of the play is that there is no exodos. In every other surviving Aeschylean play except *Prometheus Bound* there is music to which the chorus can exit; and it goes almost without saying that in a theater with no curtain, there must be some way of clearing the stage and indicating the end of the drama. With no exit song, the ending of the play conveys a sense of incompleteness, the expectation of yet another action before the full drama can be concluded; and this is exactly the feeling that the chorus has expressed in its words (1560–66). In addition, the chorus leaves the stage silently, not singing as a normal chorus would. Thus the departure of each member would not be organized to a rhythm or a grouped formation, but would be scattered and random.

Such an ending is suited to the words and staging of the last scene. The queen urges her husband to ignore the threats of these men and stresses the power the two of them share. There is not a doubt who holds the upper hand in Argos. The new king and the queen turn and enter the palace; the doors shut, and the chorus is left confronting the soldiers who now guard the palace entrance. One by one or two by two, they silently leave the stage until it is empty. Only then does the audience realize that the play is over.

This formless conclusion is the fullest extension of music-making as metaphor in the *Agamemnon*. The chorus in its helplessness simply has no more to say. The elders are a symbol of great despair as they find no words to express their feelings and walk offstage. From the moment of the death cries of Agamemnon, the chorus has had difficulty in maintaining the pattern of singing that it achieved so effectively in the parodos and the early stasima. Its weak and irregular exit is a fitting culmination of this progressive disability.[82]

Although each of the stasima and songs of the *Agamemnon* can be discussed individually, the total musical effect of the play—both in meter and in form—is clear only when one imagines oneself as a spectator. From the first lyric words of the chorus there is an intensive effort by Aeschylus to identify two themes implicit in the story of Agamemnon: the justice of Zeus and the necessity of punishment for sin. History enforces a belief in the latter, but the old men's faith inclines them to incorporate it with the former. These two formulations are by no means necessarily exclusive. It is the manner in which past actions have been performed that renders it impossible to hold both in one consistent belief; Zeus's justice has been accomplished by men of excess. Accompanying the words that describe and define this dilemma are two thematic meters that are stated simply and insistently. The lecythion is established as the meter associated with the theme of the justice of Zeus, the iambic as the meter accompanying that of sin and retribution. For the first half of the play the chorus tries to combine its interpretation of the fall of Troy with hopeful expectations for the future, and in doing so it encounters problems. Often the thematic meters established in the parodos show the difficulty the old men are having or the feature they are ignoring. Finally, in the third stasimon they are forced to admit that there are two types of music; one of these they want to suppress but it keeps asserting itself. Cassandra leads them to sing about the threat to Agamemnon. They begin to organize themselves into a formal chorus, but immediately after their strong statement that Agamemnon cannot die, they hear the screams of the dying Agamemnon; their organization falls apart and their music fails. Clytemnestra by her attempts at justification goads them into organizing, but they can form no clear statement until they reluctantly settle on the iambic rhythm of sin and retribution, prophesying another murder in the family. Then with the appearance of Aegisthus and his soldiers the chorus sees clearly the violence and caprice rampant in its universe and realizes how irrelevant its theoretical structuring of its world was. In this play, group singing and dancing to complex, lengthy strophic songs are usually intended to celebrate the order of Zeus's universe; murder, which opens a chilling view of the real nature of a harsh world, provides no cause for happiness and is probably better pondered quietly by each individual man. Fittingly, the chorus disintegrates into a group of individuals who leave the stage in silence. The music at the end of the *Agamemnon* has itself been murdered. And like the spirit of the dead king Agamemnon the same musical themes will return to haunt the characters in the *Choephoroi*.

CHOEPHOROI

The Parodos (22–83)

22–31: str. a		∪−∪− ∪−∪−	2 ia
32–41: ant. a		∪−∪− ⏒−∪− ∪−∪−	3 ia
		∪−∪− ⏒−∪−	2 ia
25	35	⏒∪∪∪∪∪ ∪∪∪∪−	2 ia
		∪−− −∪−	ba cr
		−∪−∪−∪−	lec
		∪−∪− ∪−∪−	2 ia
		∪∪∪∪∪∪ ∪−∪−	2 ia
30	40	−−−−−−−−∪∪−−	5 da
		−∪−∪−∪−	lec

42–53: str. b		⌣–∪∪∪ ∪∪∪∪∪ ∪–∪–	3 ia
54–65: ant. b	45	∪––∪–∪–∪–∪––	?
		–∪–∪–∪–	lec
		–∪–∪–∪–	lec
	60	∪–∪– ∪–∪– ∪–∪–	3 ia
		∪–∪– ∪–∪–	2 ia
	50	∪–∪– ∪–∪–	2 ia
		∪–∪– ∪–∪–	2 ia
		∪–∪– –∪∪–	ia ch
	65	–∪–∪∪–⌣	pher
66–69: str. g	70	∪–∪– ∪–∪– ∪–∪–	3 ia
70–74: ant. g		∪–∪– ∪–∪– ∪–∪–	3 ia
		*∪–– –– ∪∪∪– ∪–∪–	ba sp cr ia
		*∪–∪– ∪–∪–	? + ia
		–∪– ––∪–	
75–83: epode	75	∪–∪– –∪– –∪–	ia 2 cr
		∪–∪– –∪– ∪––	ia cr ba
		∪–– –∪– ∪–∪––	ba cr + ?
		*∪–∪––∪–∪	?
		∪–∪– –∪–	ia cr
	80	∪–∪– –∪– ∪–∪–	ia cr ia
		∪–– ∪–– ∪–∪–	2 ba ia
		∪–– ∪–∪–	ba ia
		∪–∪– ––∪– ∪–∪–	3 ia

Meter

The *Choephoroi* is a play of compulsory revenge staged in an atmosphere that is gloomy and dark from the entrance of the black-draped chorus to Orestes' frenzied flight from the gray, snake-haired Furies at the end. The plot centers on a murder that the conspirators believe will be the last of the killings in the house, yet because each of them confuses revenge with justice, it is only to be expected that there will be a further demand for blood.

The chorus of slave women brings to the stage a less rigorous quality of theological thinking than the chorus in the *Agamemnon*. There the old men built an optimistic structure of the world by searching history for examples to show the workings of their god; here the chorus enters stating that the reverence and awe that men used to feel is gone and has been replaced by fear (55–65). Instead of looking back into history for evidence of the gods' actions, this chorus dwells on the distress of the present moment: the horrifying scream in the night, the sleeplessness, the blood clotted on the ground, and the frightening reminders of Agamemnon's murder. In the previous play the old men were citizens who could discuss and develop their thoughts forthrightly; here the chorus enters as slaves, not gathering eagerly to hear news of their king, but rather commanded by their mistress. There the chorus sang a complex, highly imagistic entrance song of varied meters displaying its pride and ability in song; here the chorus sings a repetitious song of woe. The atmosphere from the start is one of unrelieved, brooding oppression.[83]

Appropriately, the meter of this ode is unresolved iambic that almost completely excludes even the standard variations, the cretic and the bacchiac, until the epode. The first three lines of the opening strophe are basic iambic, with two minor resolutions of a long for an initial short that are not echoed in the antistrophe. From this point on there is an attempt at some variety through the use of a highly resolved iambic, one bacchiac and cretic, a lecythion, and a dactyl. In contrast to the previous simplicity and clarity of meters in the *Aga-memnon*, the chorus appears to be groping for an organizing meter. It is undoubtedly significant that the iambic meter is highly resolved when the chorus speaks of manifest signs of horror: their gashed cheeks, their ripped clothes, the screams and gloomy prophecies from the house (25, 29, 35, and 39). Yet there is also a broader musical effect; the metrical direction of the parodos is from some variation to none. This chorus will come to settle firmly on the iambic meter for the rest of the parodos, and this insistence on the iambic rhythm is communicated all the more forcefully because the meter wanders in the initial pair of stanzas.

The first line of the second strophe is also highly resolved, but variation disappears by the end of the stanza, where there are four lines of repeated iambics with no substitutions. In the third strophic set the meter is so solidly iambic that it almost approximates the spoken trimeters. Finally, in the epode the iambic meter associated with sin and retribution in the previous play sounds strongly in the persistent combination of iambic, bacchiac, and cretic.

There are scattered lines of lecythia in the first two strophic pairs to remind the audience that another type of thematic music could be sung, but this meter remains undeveloped by the chorus, which openly yearns for another act of bloodshed. The slave women easily accept the universe of force that appeared so clearly through the actions of the *Agamemnon*. They define justice as a violent single deed, an act that need not be validated by comparison with previous actions. Therefore, when they sing, music is a true guide to their type of justice. In this case they are not singing the wrong song unconsciously, but their view of the world makes the music of sin and retribution appropriate for the kind of bloody and painful justice that is the only alternative available to men.[84]

Form

Of the previous plays of Aeschylus both the *Persians* and the *Suppliants* (and, of course, the *Agamemnon*) contain anapaestic "marching" introductions to the chorus's entrance. The *Seven against Thebes* does not contain such an introduction because a free-form dochmiac song is more truly representative of the hysterical ladies of Thebes, whereas in the first two plays the situation allows each chorus the leisure to come onstage to a set meter and in an ordered formation. Even though the chorus of the *Choephoroi* is no more pressed for time or agitated than the suppliant maidens at their arrival in Argos, there is no anapaestic entrance song for the slave women. They begin to enter with no words or music at line 10, when Orestes notices them coming from the palace preceding Electra, who does not come out of the palace until just before Orestes' comment on her at line 16.[85] Their silence and lack of formation recall the exit of the chorus in the *Agamemnon* and should thereby suggest to the audience that matters have become no better in Argos and that this chorus, though composed of different characters, will also have trouble singing. The slave women quickly dispel that suspicion by singing a long, organized ode.

In the first strophe they describe their costume, their masks, and the breast-beating and cheek-clawing kind of activity that they would probably pantomime during their entrance. Because they are a dour, gloomy chorus, the lack of any variation in their meter is quite consistent with their characterization. Yet it is significant that they have little difficulty in organizing their song. Far from the confusion of their predecessors, the slave women are fixated on the idea of getting the murder done. Others in this play may have to be persuaded to do the deed, but the chorus is unvarying in its conviction that Clytemnestra must be killed. Consequently the slave women are confident in their statements and readily find music for their words. Their song touches on a number of themes, all of which fit easily into their conception of the deteriorating situation in the House of Atreus: terror, sleeplessness, torn cheeks, and ripped clothes. Guilt and misery thrive. They recall the murder of Agamemnon, comment on its religious implications for the house, describe the troubled minds of the rulers who sit on an uneasy throne, and report the voice of the dead calling for vengeance. As resentful slaves they symbolize an abiding threat to their rulers. In this ode guilt, fear, and tyranny are woven together into a consistent whole, and the organized form of the three strophic stanzas embodies this order.[86]

The epode strongly recalls the meter of the iambic strophes in the *Agamemnon*; but when the slave women sing for ten lines and then stop without a corresponding antistrophe, they disappoint the audience's expectations once again. Indeed, throughout the play there will be recurrent signs that Aeschylus wants to discomfit his audience. Not only are the slave women bloody and vindictive, but also their counsel will prove wrong at the end of the play. Although they make music easily, the poet will also show through their music that there is more to establishing a new ordering of the world than pursuing the brutal vengeance that they call justice. The epode in the entrance song thus provides a musical foreshadowing of the dislocation that the audience will later feel while watching the conspirators develop their plot.[87]

The First Interlude (152–63)

	∪∪∪∪∪ ∪∪∪∪∪	2 ia
	∪∪∪– –∪–	2 cr
	––∪∪ ––∪–	2 ia
155	∪∪∪∪∪ ∪–∪–	2 ia
	∪∪∪–∪–	doch
	∪∪∪–∪– ∪––∪–	2 doch
	∪––∪–	doch
	∪∪∪∪∪∪–	doch
160	∪––∪– ∪–∪–	doch ia
	∪∪∪–∪–*∪∪∪–∪–	2 doch
	*∪–∪∪––∪– ∪––∪–	? + doch
	∪∪∪–∪– ∪––∪–	2 doch

The chorus takes the initiative in the first scene of the play as Electra wavers, unable to decide what to do. Because the slave women want blood, they happily accept the role of teacher to Electra's doubt. In fact, until Electra recognizes Orestes there is no visible force onstage organizing revenge except the chorus, which characteristically gives heightened aural and visual corroboration to the timid prayer of Electra in this short song.

Beyond the weak actions of mortals a power is at work,

even though mysteriously, at the opening of the play. The murdered king insists on vengeance through the dream sent to Clytemnestra, and Apollo has sent Orestes back to Argos. This choral prayer shows by its intensity and excitement the active presence of the dead in the heightened emotions of the living. Such emotion is appropriate to the moment; the audience has already seen that Orestes is present as the avenging agent of his father, and he is just about to appear to begin plotting. This small choral song is sung to a highly varied dochmiac meter at the very moment when Electra, having finished her prayer, pours her offerings on the tomb and asks the chorus to sing a fitting lament. As the women pray for vengeance, their excited movement and song reveal the presence of an unseen power that will drive the unwilling conspirators, especially in the kommos.[88]

The motivation for this song arises from Aeschylus' structuring of the first half of the play, which is largely concerned with the actual and psychological uniting of the conspirators. In an intrigue story it would be possible to focus the plot entirely on the mundane details of formulating the plan and carrying it out. But in the *Choephoroi* the constant relation of human actions to the desires of the larger powers in the universe as expressed through Apollo and Agamemnon is never lost in the minute details of plotting. The first part of the long opening scene, devoted to the demands of those outside mortal life, is separated from the second part, in which Electra and Orestes are reunited, by this song marking the culmination of the libation scene through its intense emotion and excited meter and movement.[89]

This astrophic passage may be unexpected because other prayer forms have a strophic form. Here the irregular form is probably appropriate for the excited movement of the singers, for astropha often accompany mimetic stage action.[90]

Kommos (306–478)

306–14: anapaests

315–23: str. a		$-\cup\cup-\cup\cup-\cup-$	ibycaean
332–39: ant. a 316		$\cup\cup\cup-\ \cup--$	cr ba
		$\cup--\cup\cup-\cup-$	glyc
	335	$-\cup\cup-\ \cup--$	ch ba
		$\cup-\cup\cup-\cup-$	telisillean
	320	$-\cup\cup-\ \cup--$	ch ba
		$\cup--\cup\cup-\cup-$	glyc
		$*-\cup\cup-\ \cup--$	ch ba
324–31: str. b		$\cup-\cup-\ \cup-\cup-\ \cup-\cup-$	3 ia
354–62: ant. b 325	355	$-\cup-\cup\cup-\cup-$	glyc
		$-\overline{\cup}-\cup\cup--$	pher
		$\cup\cup-\cup-\cup--$	anac
		$\cup\cup-\cup-\cup--$	anac
	360	$\cup\cup-\cup-\cup--$	anac
	330	$*\cup\cup-\cup-\cup--$	anac
		$*\overline{\cup}--\cup\cup-\cup--$	hipponacteum

340–44: anapaests

345–53: str. g 345		$-\cup\cup-\cup-$	Aeolic
363–71: ant. g			colarion[91]
		$-\cup-\cup\cup-\cup-$	glyc
	365	$\cup--\ -\cup-\ \cup--$	ba cr ba
		$\cup-\cup-\ -\cup-\ \cup--$	ia cr ba
		$\cup--\ \cup--$	2 ba
	350	$\cup--\ \cup--$	2 ba
		$\cup-\cup\cup-\cup--$	enoplion
	370	$\cup-\cup\cup-\cup--$	enoplion
		$-\cup\cup-\ \cup-\cup$	ch ba

372–79: anapaests

380–85: str. d 380		$-\cup\cup-\cup\cup-$	hemiepes
394–99: ant. d	395	$-\cup\cup-\cup\cup-$	hemiepes
		$--\cup-\cup---$	?
		$-\cup\cup-\ \cup--$	ch ba

		∪−−∪∪−∪−−	hipponacteum
	385	−∪∪−∪∪−∪−−	alcaic
			decasyllable

386−93: str. e	410	∪−− −∪− ∪−−	ba cr ba
410−17: ant. e		−∪∪− ∪−−	ch ba
		−∪∪− ∪−−	ch ba
		−∪∪− ∪−−	ch ba
		−∪∪− ∪−−	ch ba
	390 415	*∪−− ∪−− ∪−−	3 ba
		−∪∪− −∪∪−	2 ch
		*−∪−∪−∪−	lec

400−4 anapaests

405−09: str. z 405		∪−− −∪− ∪−∪−	ba cr ia
418−22: ant. z		{ ∪∪∪−∪− −∪∪−∪− }	2 doch
		{ ∪∪∪∪∪−− ∪−∪∪∪− }	
	420	∪−∪− −∪−∪−∪−	ia lec
		∪−∪− −∪−∪−∪−	ia lec
		−∪− ∪−−	cr ba

423−28: str. ē		∪−∪− ⌣∪∪∪− ∪−∪−	3 ia
444−50: ant. ē	445	∪−∪− ∪−∪−	2 ia
	425	∪−∪− ⌣∪∪∪− ∪−∪−	3 ia
		∪−∪∪∪ ∪−∪∪∪	3 ia
		∪−∪⌣	
		∪−∪∪∪ ∪−∪− ∪−∪−	3 ia
	450	⌣−∪− −−∪− ∪−∪−	3 ia

429−33: str. th		∪−∪− −∪−	ia cr
451−55: ant. th 430		∪−∪− ∪−∪− ∪−∪−	3 ia
		∪−∪− −∪−	ia cr
		∪−∪− −∪−	ia cr
	455	∪−∪− −∪− ∪−−	ia cr ba

434−38: str. i		∪−∪− −∪− ∪−−	ia cr ba
439−43: ant. i 435 440		∪−∪− −∪− ∪−−	ia cr ba
		∪−∪− −∪−	ia cr
		∪−∪− −∪−	ia cr
		∪−∪− −∪− ∪−−	ia cr ba

456–60: str. k	Or:	∪–∪– –∪– ∪–∪–	ia cr ia
461–65: ant. k	El:	∪–∪– –∪– ∪–∪–	ia cr ia
	Cho:	∪–∪– –∪– ∪–∪–	ia cr ia
		∪–∪– ∪–∪–	2 ia
460|465		–∪∪– ∪––	ch ba
466–70: str. l		–∪∪–∪–	doch
471–75: ant. l		–∪∪– ∪––	ch ba
		–∪∪– ∪––	ch ba
		∪––∪∪–∪––	hipponacteum
470|475		∪––∪∪–∪––	hipponacteum

476–78: anapaests

Meter

Even though this is the most complex song in the *Oresteia*—Wilamowitz proclaimed it the most complicated in Greek poetry[92]—its meters, varied at the beginning, become simple and familiar as the ode develops.

In the kommos the corresponding strophes do not succeed one another but are interlocked as follows:

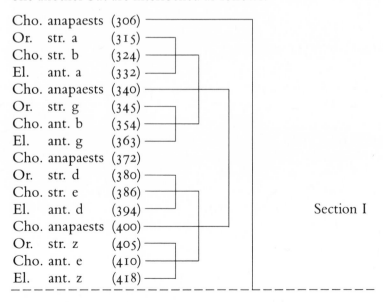

Cho.	anapaests	(306)	
Or.	str. a	(315)	
Cho.	str. b	(324)	
El.	ant. a	(332)	
Cho.	anapaests	(340)	
Or.	str. g	(345)	
Cho.	ant. b	(354)	
El.	ant. g	(363)	
Cho.	anapaests	(372)	
Or.	str. d	(380)	
Cho.	str. e	(386)	
El.	ant. d	(394)	
Cho.	anapaests	(400)	
Or.	str. z	(405)	
Cho.	ant. e	(410)	
El.	ant. z	(418)	Section I

Cho.	str.	ē	(423)	
El.	str.	th	(429)	
Or.	str.	i	(434)	
Cho.	ant.	i	(439)	Section II
El.	ant.	ē	(444)	
Cho.	ant.	th	(451)	

Or., El., Cho. str. k (456)
Or., El., Cho. ant. k (461)   Section III

Cho. str./ant. l   (466/471)
Cho. anapaests (476)   Section IV

In the first three strophic sets (306–79) Electra responds to
Orestes' song while the chorus interjects its strophic lyric or
anapaests. The meters in these initial strophes are varied,
establishing no ascertainable pattern or dominant metrical
motif; the basic meters are iambic, cretic, bacchiac, glyconic,
choriamb, and anaclast, with scattered lines of telisillean,
pherecratean, hipponactean, dochmiac, and enoplian. The
next strophe (380) tends to settle on dactylic meter, but in the
fifth strophe (386–93) the elements of the iambic meter begin
to appear clearly in the repeated combination of the choriamb
with the bacchiac. At this point there begins a movement toward an unresolved repeated iambic meter. Most of strophe z
is sung to iambic meter, and strophe ē consists entirely of
highly resolved iambic. But in strophes th, i, and k the meter
is clearly stated and reminiscent of the thematic meter of sin
and retribution from the *Agamemnon* and the parodos of this
play. In addition, this iambic is increasingly dull. In strophe ē
the iambic is the basic meter but no line repeats precisely the
pattern of another. In strophe th the unresolved iambic + cretic occur in all but one line; in strophe i the longer iambic +
cretic + bacchiac is repeated in three of five lines; finally,
strophe k opens with three identical lines that are very close
to the iambic trimeter: iambic + cretic + iambic. Thus
throughout this long song the movement is away from variation and the lively shifting of meters toward persistent repeti-

tion of a metrical pattern. The final two strophes, based on the choriamb and Hipponactean, turn the chorus away from the thematic meter as Electra and Orestes take the lead in expressing a strong call for vengeance.

Form

The complexity of this kommos derives to an extent from the variation of meters in the first half of the song; but far more intricate is the continuing alternation of singers. Toward the end of the kommos problems mount in assigning lines to the correct speakers and hence the assessment of the musical form becomes even more difficult—especially in the final stanzas at 456–75. Yet even in the face of such confusion it is possible to describe the intent of the poet in composing this long song and to suggest suitable staging. The kommos is introduced by a passage of anapaests that are echoed in the closing section of three anapaestic lines. This meter acts as a frame defining all the elements of the enclosed song as a separate musical entity, which the chorus calls a hymn of the gods of the underworld (475).[93] It is noteworthy that the poet wanted his audience to see the whole kommos, with its interchanging of singers and its varied meters, as one unified song.

As is evident from the arrangement of the interlocked strophes, the kommos falls into four basic sections. The first section is defined internally by a tightly woven pattern of individual songs (315–422) divided into two symmetrical halves by a stanza of anapaests. Each of the four times Electra sings, she echoes the music and content of Orestes' stanzas, and the chorus alternately sings strophic lyric or anapaests between their songs. Anapaests are not generally a strophic meter, but in the choral stanzas Aeschylus has made this more linear meter approximate strophic correspension;[94] the anapaestic section at 340–44 is similar in metrical pattern to the five-line unit at 400–4, and each of these units falls between the strophic pairs sung by Orestes and Electra in each half of this first section. After the lackluster parodos of the slave women, the kommos offers hope that the music-making

ability of this chorus has been restored to a level at least reminiscent of the early songs in the *Agamemnon*. Not only are
they singing to a varied meter and adhering to a strict symmetry, but they are also creating order within a complex pattern of interchanging singers.

In the second part of the kommos (423–55) the chorus
seems to be attempting the same kind of intricate order, but it
does not quite succeed, as can be seen in this pattern:

Corresponsion Pattern

Cho.				a
El.				b
Or.	⌐	ē		c
Cho.	⌐ i		th	c
El.				a
Cho.				b

The parts are unbalanced and unequal; Orestes has only one
strophe, Electra two, and they do not sing in corresponding
lyrics. Even the pattern of corresponding strophes does not
offer the fine symmetry of the first part; critics have noticed
this odd pattern and have tried to restore order by shifting
Orestes' lines to a position following antistrophe th, thus
creating the pattern *abc abc*, an interlocking symmetry that
would recall the balance of the first section.[95] A basic justification for this shift of lines is the necessity of restoring order,
but in this trilogy, where there are ample signs that Aeschylus
is developing order and disorder in musical form as a theme,
such an argument rests on a weak foundation. Better to leave
the text as it stands and initially, at least, to attempt an interpretation of the disorder.

The placement of 434–38 depends on one's perception of
how the thought is being developed. Those who have trans-
ferred the lines find Orestes irresolute and wavering; Electra
and the chorus feel the need to strengthen him by their list of
past crimes and atrocities, and he then pledges to pursue his
goal with an "unbending vigor" (455).[96] But this adjustment

of the traditional text (a text that admittedly shows serious disturbances of line order at 70, 165, and 225–30) is complicated by problems both big and small. The main question concerns the motivation for the kommos if Orestes has really made up his mind before his arrival at Argos—as he clearly states in his speech at 269–305. An answer to this question rests on an assessment of the tone of Orestes' speech at 405–9 and the chorus's response, especially in the corrupt lines 415–17, and on a determination of what goal Electra seeks at line 418.

Given that all critics agree that at 434–38 Orestes expresses decisiveness and resolution, one must ask whether he has any chilling doubt that must be allayed before he confronts the deed. Lesky argues that the command of Apollo is not operational in the kommos because Aeschylus wants to show the personal anguish of Orestes in making his own decision. According to such an interpretation the characters in the kommos are balancing the issues of divinely mandated punishment against their fear of full personal responsibility and their natural desire to avoid such a crime. By the end of the play this problem is made visually clear for all as the Erinyes chase Orestes offstage because he has followed Apollo's command. If Orestes wrestles with this decision in the kommos, he does attain a tragic stature, but the technique of separating the two sides of his dilemma by confining the command of Apollo to the first scene (269–305) and the personal decision of Orestes to the kommos is uncomfortable—indeed, unparalleled in Aeschylean drama.[97] Lesky counters by stating that archaic style generally separates complex situations into their components and looks at them first from one side and then from the other before uniting them into a comprehensive view. There are, however, few traces of such archaic separateness in the structure of the *Oresteia*, which is generally regarded as the least archaic of Aeschylus' dramas.[98] This interpretation presenting a more tragic Orestes seems to originate in the desire to move the offending lines and thus to restore formal order to the kommos.

If the lines are retained in their manuscript location (and there is no indication in the manuscript that they have been moved nor any good explanation as to how or why they were moved), then the kommos is part of the exposition of Orestes' decision in order to show how many factors—material, religious, personal, psychological—are involved in the strong inertial push compelling him to avenge his father's murder. The audience learns from Orestes' statement in the first scene and, even more, from the emotional statements in the kommos how solid his decision is. Such an interpretation is similar to the manner in which other Aeschylean characters present their decisions and finds parallels in the passage in *Seven against Thebes* where Eteocles defends his decision on varying grounds against the chorus—although in the *Choephoroi*, since there is unity among the participants, there is no need for the inflexible opposition inherent in the epirrhematic form. A closer parallel is the responsive and sympathetic song shared by Cassandra and the chorus (*Ag.* 1114–77). The kommos in the *Choephoroi* continues and supports the first scene, introducing elements from all sides to portray the complexity of the choice that Orestes has already made. At 405–9 he calls on the power of the dead to come to aid his endeavor, asking Zeus where people with such minimal resources (*amechanos echonta* and *atima*) can turn for aid; he is not despairing but rather acknowledging that he will carry through even with the scant powers he can gather. The slave women call this a a pitiable cry (*oikton*), acknowledge that they have been dispirited at times too, but end the stanza in what seems an encouraged state;[99] and Electra asks how they would get through to the dead (*tuchoimen*).[100] It is noteworthy that this interpretation places both the chorus and Electra in the weaker position. They repeat details from the past but Orestes summarizes all in his statement at 433–38 about the dishonor to his father and makes his assertion at 438.[101] The chorus, showing spirit, finally urges him to the deed. In such an interpretation Orestes remains adamant as he brings the weight of his inner will to bear on the choice and leads Electra to the actual invocation of their father's spirit in lines 479–509.

I favor this view of the kommos because it has parallels to the normal Aeschylean technique of presenting characters who defend rather than debate their decisions. In this section of the kommos the singers maintain a complex song, but their optimism is misguided, for the murder of Clytemnestra brings only a demand for more blood. Aeschylus appropriately adds an element of disorder to this ode, and by again disappointing the audience's expectation prompts consideration of the cause of such disorder. It is significant that in strophes e and z, just before this section, the iambic meter has begun to reassert itself.

The third section consists of a strophic pair, with each of the three conspirators speaking separately within the strophe and then repeating the corresponding lines in the antistrophe (456–65). In one sense this is a sign of close collaboration: the three now join in one strophe singing precisely the same iambic line; yet there is also a mark of developing disunity: this is the first time in the play that the characters break the form of the strophe by singing individual lines.[102]

There are two difficulties in assessing the musical form of the final section of the kommos (466–78). First, although the meter suggests that the kommos is framed as a musical unit, the prayer of Orestes and Electra continues in spoken iambics until line 509.[103] The chorus should not rise to a grand conclusion only to have the words of the children continue in the same vein; the scene seems to call for a diminishing role for the slave women as they shift the impetus for the murder to the children and take a secondary position as accomplices for the rest of the play. There are also markings in the manuscript that may indicate that the antistrophe is sung by a different voice than the strophe.[104]

Although the assignment of lines in this section remains uncertain, it seems clear that the anapaests (476–78) must be given to the chorus because of the reference to the children; most editors assign the lyric lines (466–75) to the chorus also.

It would be possible to see the strophe as a summation of the family's problems and the antistrophe as a corrective concluding statement: "Ah, yes, *but* the cure for these woes is in the house. . . ." However, because the necessary word *but* is not in the text, the antistrophe must be read as the continuation of the same thought pattern: there have been and will be woes in this family's history, another of which is the cure within the house—but a cure that will itself require a horrible deed.

It seems that both strophe and antistrophe are different approaches to the same incident. The first stanza is an emotional outcry at the suffering to be caused by the crime; the second, a detached statement of the necessity pressing on Orestes and Electra. Given the signs of formal irregularity in the final third of this song, the need to conclude the music even though the prayer continues, and the markings in the manuscript, I suggest that the chorus splits into two sections, one for each stanza, and moves into the background or to the side of the orchestra, leaving Orestes and Electra alone near the tomb.

Such an assignment of parts implies two coordinated stage effects. First, if Aeschylus is continuing to use his audience's expectations of a unified chorus, then it is appropriate to have this chorus split as a further sign of its continuing problems in organizing its song. Yet because the slave women will never have the shattering experience of the old men in the *Agamemnon*, they do not totally collapse. Their music continues in a balanced strophic arrangement, and the whole chorus may join in on the final anapaestic lines. The women, however, end their lyric as two groups, and this split in the musical form would be reinforced in their choreography. Second, the prayer of the two children builds in intensity, and the scene reaches its conclusion after the end of the music.[105]

If this conception of the ending is correct, then there is a musical theme running through the whole kommos: the progressive disintegration of the order that was promised by the complex patterning of the first section. The second section conveys an inability to repeat the patterning; the third section shows the splitting of the traditional lines, and the fourth section continues the musical dislocation in the chorus's role as it divides into two separate groups. Finally the full chorus joins for the closing three anapaestic lines, which serve to mark for the audience the ending of a complex musical unit although the thought continues in the speeches of Electra and Orestes.

The distortions in musical form reinforce deeper themes in the play. Numerous elements of the past are woven together in the kommos: the atrocity of the slain king, the claims of justice, the shame of the house, the mutilation of the dead Agamemnon, the forced exile and deprivation of Orestes, and, finally, the shabby treatment of Electra.[106] All point to the need for another murder; blood is demanded for blood. When the kommos is finished all three conspirators have convinced themselves of the rightness of their cause and their method. They all think that they are singing a new song for new days, but, their words describe the methods of the harsh old world; both the repetition of the meter from the *Agamemnon* and the similar breaking of the traditional strophic form continue to underline this fact.

The First Stasimon (585–651)

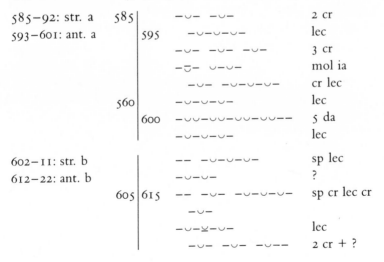

		—∪—∪∪—∪—	glyc
		—∪—∪∪——	pher
610	620	⏒——∪∪—∪—	glyc
		—∪—∪∪——	pher
623–30: str. g		∪—∪— —∪—∪—∪—	ia lec
631–38: ant. g		*∪—∪— —∪—∪—∪—	ia lec
	625	—∪—∪—∪—	lec
		∪—∪— —∪—∪—∪—	ia lec
	635	∪—∪— —∪—	ia cr
		*∪—∪— —∪—∪—∪—	ia lec
		∪—∪— —∪—∪—∪—	ia lec
	630	∪—— —∪—∪——	ba ithy
639–45: str. d		∪—∪— ∪—∪—	2 ia
646–51: ant. d	640	∪—— ——∪— ∪——	ba ia ba
		*∪—∪— ∪—∪—	2 ia
		—∪—∪—∪—	lec
	650	∪—∪— ∪—∪—	2 ia
	645	—∪—∪——	ithy

Meter

The first stasimon marks the juncture between the two halves of the play, a type of intermezzo separating the planning and the execution of the murder. Its theme is the righteousness of the coming revenge when seen in the perspective of the bloody deeds of women in myth. This method of argumentation is not far removed from that of the chorus in the *Agamemnon*: by analyzing events in mythological history it identifies forces that are permament. But there the old men were honest thinkers and frank speakers who readily admitted the problems in their thinking; here the slave women have already decided on the necessity of the murder and are only seeking justification.

The chorus cites three cases as precedents for the coming crime; in fact, however, all are poor parallels and none justifies the act of murder.[107] Althaea, Scylla, and the Lemnian women are offered as examples of the depth and destructive-

ness of women's guile. Althaea killed her son in revenge for
the slaying of her brothers but she seems to have escaped
punishment. Although she suffered a personal loss, the force
of justice did not demand revenge on her.[108] Scylla cut the
lock from the forehead of Nisus while he slept and betrayed
her city. Yet where is the avenger? Her end is a metamorpho-
sis accomplished by the gods with no human intervention:
poetic justice, but scarcely a precedent for justifiable homi-
cide.[109] The women of Lemnos killed their husbands, yet no
massive revenge was delivered upon them.[110] These three
precedents purporting to justify the coming murder are thus
largely inapplicable.[111] In none of these cases did a human
have to take the role of avenger and kill another person,
much less a person as closely related as his mother. On the
basis of these stories Orestes should not kill his mother but
should let her live out her life until the gods decide to take
their vengeance. Worse yet, if these cases do provide any precedent relevant to the present situation, Orestes is only asking for suffering and vengeance himself by undertaking such
a crime. Yet in the final two stanzas the chorus draws the expected moral: Justice, Zeus, Destiny, and the Erinyes all demand murder. The orderly method of reasoning employed
by the old men in the *Agamemnon* is here only weakly imi-
tated; the slave women's thought is flawed when they adopt a
series of inapposite cases as parallels to the present situation.

   An analysis of the meters supports this interpretation. The
first two strophes, which rank women's overwhelming passion high among the evils loose in the world, are sung predominantly in lecythia. Out of eight lines in the first strophe
at least four are standard lecythia; one other line is questionable but is very close to the lecythion form. The other three
lines are composed of cretics and dactyls. The second set of
strophes, concerning Althaea and Scylla, are sung in a variety
of meters with no dominant theme; the ending of each strophe
is an alternating glyconic/pherecratean (priapean) meter. In
the third pair of strophes the predominant meter is the lecythion, but there is a noticeable presence of the iambic meter;

out of eight lines there are five lecythia, each introduced by one iambic metron. Appropriately this strophe tells the audience that Clytemnestra's killing of Agamemnon is the real event to be compared with the mythical examples. The final two stanzas, drawing the moral from these stories, is sung to clear iambics and bacchiacs. Three out of six lines are identical unresolved iambic dimeters. The basic metrical and musical pattern of this ode thus offers three stanzas of varied meter with an emphasis on the lecythion, concluded by two strophes of strongly iambic meter.

It is important to note the subject sung to each of these rhythms. When the chorus sings of the horrors and atrocities wrought by both Clytemnestra and her mythological predecessors, they introduce the meter associated with the theme of Zeus's order, a meter that has scarcely appeared in this play. The final two stanzas, which are filled with words like Dike, Zeus, Themis, Sebas, Aisa, and Erinys—the words of patterned justice—are sung to the familiar meter of sin and retribution. Once again the wrong meter accompanies each set of words. The slave women try to justify the crime about to take place but they do it badly. Their conclusion really points toward the continuance of bloodshed and violence in the house. They can sing the music of order, but they put it in the wrong place, and when they do speak of the patterned universe with cosmic justice, they sing the music of sin and retribution.

Form

After the dislocations in musical form in the parodos, the first interlude, and the kommos, it is not surprising that the music throughout the rest of the play is not consistently organized in balanced strophes; the eight matched strophic stanzas of this stasimon make it the most symmetrical song in the *Choephoroi*. This stasimon is in a position similar to that of the ode at *Agamemnon* 975–1033. There a symmetrical ode established the idea of order and balance that was to be destroyed by the action in the following scenes. If there is an equivalent to an act division in the *Choephoroi*, this stasimon provides it. Now that the conspirators have met and their plotting is complete, they all leave the stage to prepare for their roles. During this lull the chorus sings this ode.

In the *Oresteia* Aeschylus is writing about a higher type of justice that men will come to understand and accept in the last play, but this form of justice is not even mentioned by the current inhabitants of the house of Atreus. The slave women are misguided in yearning for the continued killing that has come to characterize the house, and Aeschylus uses music to indicate the deficiencies in their wishes by filling the rest of his play with songs that are formally jarring or disturbing to the audience; but he does establish a norm through this long stasimon. He restores the traditional form of the tragic chorus, which had disintegrated at the murder of Agamemnon. By the very form of the music the women show their deep conviction that this murder is restoring the orderly working of justice and of Zeus in the universe, and the poet provides no clues in either word or form that would undermine the firmness of their statement.

This stasimon provides an effective bridge between the two parts of the play. It gathers and organizes many of the themes and motifs already presented: the horrors abroad in the world, the gloomy quality of daily life, the conflict between passion and reason, the presence of justice, and the demands of the dead. It picks up the theme of musical form established in the *Agamemnon*: the reinvigorated chorus expresses trust that all can return to normal living. But the stasimon also effectively introduces the second part of the drama. The arguments used by the chorus sound hollow and are sung to the "wrong" meter, yet the slave women will be genuinely surprised when their supposed agent of justice is driven from the stage. The formal order that seems to be present in this stasimon will begin to come unstrung as soon as the chorus sings again. In this ode, which seems straightforward and regular in form, Aeschylus is putting his audience in a better position to appreciate the coming musical effects.

The Second Interlude (719–29): anapaests

The rest of this play is composed of many short episodes; a character enters, speaks his or her few lines, and then disappears—usually behind the doors of the palace, where the real action is taking place. As a result the chorus finds itself alone onstage four times in the space of some four hundred lines (653–1075). Even Aeschylus with his love of the chorus undoubtedly found it excessive to write full strophic stasima for each of these occasions, and he twice uses short anapaestic interludes that allow the chorus to fill the time before the next event. One might argue that the audience would perceive at least the first of these interludes as the opening of a stasimon and would experience the same type of thwarted expectation that occurred at *Agamemnon* 1342. There, however, Agamemnon's death cries provide a violent interruption of their song. In the *Choephoroi* the chorus itself has the first word as it notices the entrance of the nurse. The quietness and ease of transition from song to episode do not permit a sharp disappointment of expectation, although the anapaests might arouse the expectation of a fuller strophic ode.

The second half of the play is undeniably jagged in movement: people are constantly coming and going, the climax approaches in a series of short steps, and the action is retarded in pace while the suspense builds. If there is any definable musical effect in this short interlude, it is probably that of staccato movement.[112] Music would increase the audience's awareness of the piling up of short scene upon short scene, because the songs that are sung each time the stage is empty punctuate the action so that it cannot flow from one scene to the next in a more integrated structure.[113] Because the action of the play no longer involves the chorus as principle actor, the slave women provide the entr'actes in musical accom-

paniment to the real action of the play, which has moved inside the palace and is hidden behind the doors.

The Second Stasimon (783–837)

783–89: str. a		–∪– –∪– –∪–	3 cr
794–99: ant. a		–∪–∪–∪–	lec
	785 795	*–∪– –∪–	2 cr
		*–∪–∪–∪–	lec
		–∪∪–∪–	doch
		∪∪∪–∪∪∪∪∪	?
		–∪–∪––	ithy
790–93:		∪∪–– ∪∪–	2 ion
ephymnion a		∪∪–– ∪∪–– ∪∪––	3 ion
(NOT REPEATED)		∪∪∪–∪–∪–	lec
		–∪∪– ∪––	ch ba
800–6: str. b	800	–∪–∪–∪–	lec
812–18: ant. b		–∪– –∪∪∪ –∪–	3 cr
		–∪–∪–∪–	lec
	815	–∪∪∪∪∪–––	?
		–∪–∪–∪–	lec
	805	–– –∪–∪–∪–	sp lec
		∪–∪– –∪–∪–∪–	ia lec
807–11:		∪∪∪– ∪∪∪– ∪∪––	2 paeonic ion
ephymnion b			
(NOT REPEATED)		∪∪∪– ∪∪∪– ∪∪––	2 paeonic ion
		–∪∪– ∪∪––	ch ion
		–∪∪–∪–	hemiepes
		–∪∪–∪∪–∪––	alcaic deca-syllable
819–26: str. g		–∪– –∪–	2 cr
831–37: ant. g	820	–∪–∪–∪–	lec
		–∪–∪–∪–	lec
		–∪– –∪– –∪–	3 cr

835	∪−∪− ∪−∪−	2 ia
825	∪∪∪− −∪−∪−∪−	cr lec
	−∪−∪−∪−	lec

827–30:	∪∪−− ∪∪−− ∪∪−−	3 ion
ephymnion g	∪∪−− ∪∪−−	2 ion
(NOT REPEATED)	∪∪−− ∪∪−−	2 ion
	−∪− ∪∪∪− ∪−−	2 cr ba

Meter

The second stasimon is a prayer for the success of the plot.[114] Because this theme is continuous in the second half of the play, perhaps the entrance of the nurse at 730 should be seen as only a momentary diversion from the prayer. Once she has gone, the chorus resumes the song it has "begun" in the anapaestic stanza. Thus the use of music and dance reinforces the choppiness of both the scenes and the choral odes at the end of the play.

Compared with other strophic lyrics in the *Oresteia*, the meter in this song is remarkably unsettled. There is a movement from strophes composed mainly of lecythia to strophes containing some iambic meter, but this shift is by no means as clear as that in the second stasimon of the *Agamemnon*;[115] the interjection of the mesodes further diminishes the usual reinforcing effect of strophic repetition. The lack of a predominant meter is the more surprising in view of the chorus's attempt to create a formal order. All strophic sections are seven lines; all the mesodes are five lines. In addition, the first three lines of each strophic stanza employ a similar meter; the first two strophic pairs contain three cretics and two lecythia (although the order is not the same), and the third strophe begins with two cretics followed by two lecythia. Probably the music is at least reminiscent, if not identical, at the beginning of each strophe, thus directing the audience's interest to the further development of this pattern in each new stanza. Lecythia, with the related ithyphallic, seem to recur throughout the first strophe. The first mesode contains one lecythion, but otherwise its meters differ from those in the first strophic pair. The second strophic stanza continues the lecythion mixed with iambic; the following mesode introduces the paeonic and ionic but has no dominant meter. The final strophe continues the mixing of iambic/cretic with lecythia.[116] Then follows a mesode of seven ionics with a closing line of iambics. This prayer for vengeance, then, starts with a strong statement of the lecythion meter, but despite the reiteration of this meter in the opening lines, the song continually intersperses iambics. It appears that the choruses in both the *Agamemnon* and the *Choephoroi* have wanted the music to remain on the lecythion theme but have usually heard it drift to the iambic or at least be diluted by iambic by the end of the song. The ionic *a minore*—common to the mesodes—has been heard in an extended pattern only once before, at *Agamemnon* 690–95, answered by a corresponding passage at 708–13. There the subject matter was the bloodshed and grief caused by the crime of Helen and Paris. It may be significant that the continuous ionics in the third mesode occur while the chorus tells Orestes not to mind Clytemnestra's cries of "My child!" but to complete the deed that will prove potentially as damning as that of Paris. A repetition of the music would underline the connection, but there is no evidence to insist on this musical reminiscence.

Form

One of the most highly organized songs in the *Oresteia*, the thanksgiving ode in the first stasimon of the *Agamemnon* (355–474), consists of an anapaestic introduction, firmly stated iambic meter in the strophes, and matching glyconic coda sections repeated six times at the end of each strophic stanza. The prayer of the slave women strives for similar ornateness and complexity through the balanced number of lines and the repeated similar meters opening each strophe, yet the effect is one of confusion rather than order. Most noticeably, the presence of the noncorresponding mesodes breaks up the unity of the prayer, in contrast to the organizing influence of the coda sections. The five-line mesodes are so placed that they interrupt the strophic pattern: *aba cdc efe* versus *abab cbcb dbdb* in the *Agamemnon*. Some critics have suggested that each mesode should be repeated after the antistrophe, but this strategy would create more order than the playwright wanted, if one may judge by the structuring of the music throughout the trilogy.[117]

Furthermore, because the mesodes neither develop any of the meters of the strophes nor strongly reinforce a meter of their own, they serve only to destroy the dominance of any meter that might be successfully established through the immediate repetition of an antistrophe. Both meter and form thus present a chorus which is tangled and confusing in comparison to the Hymn to Zeus in the *Agamemnon*. The slave women have a concept of form but fail to develop that concept. To the extent that they move toward the iambic, the music defines their words; in praying for the justice of Zeus they are praying for more bloodshed, as they state explicitly in the word *phonion* at the end of their song.

The Third Interlude (855–68): anapaests

A small song again marks the end of a brief scene, contributing further to the generally rapid and jagged movement in the second half of the play and filling the short time necessary for Aegisthus to enter the house and to be slain.

In addition, the song is reminiscent of the *Agamemnon* both because of its meter and placement and because of the scene that it introduces.[118] In both plays a person appears standing over two bodies whom she/he has slain in the hope of achieving release from suffering by working in the name of justice. At *Agamemnon* 1331 the chorus sang a series of anapaests that would have developed into another ode if it had not been interrupted by the death screams of Agamemnon. Here the slave women sing a series of anapaests that are interrupted by the screams of Aigisthus, and although the chorus seems to remain united, music does stop—or almost stops. Upon hearing the cry of Aigisthus the women sing one highly resolved iambic and three cretics before returning to iambic trimeter. The brief lyric beginning would lead the audience to anticipate a song of joy now that the hated tyrant is dead, but this expectation is immediately thwarted. The parallel to the *Agamemnon* is quite precise and equally ominous for the characters. There the chorus was paralyzed by utter confusion; here the slave women announce that they will stand aside because they are uncertain about events in the house. They have not felt uncertainty before the event, but now they want immunity if any part of the plan has miscarried (872–74). Characters throughout the trilogy are gripped by fear and helplessness, and music again shows that the same type of inactivity and uncertainty is beginning to infect this chorus. The anapaests with the following iambic and cretics are a part of the musical pattern in the *Choephoroi* that conveys a sense of all being not quite right, of continuing disorder, and of a chorus unable to construct the correct song despite their longing to do so.

The Third Stasimon (935–71)

935–41: str. a	935	⏑⏑⏑–⏑– –⏑⏑–⏑–	2 doch
946–52: ant. a		⏑⏑⏑–––	doch
		⏑⏑⏑–⏑– ⏑⏑⏑–⏑–	2 doch
		⏑–⏑– ⏑–⏑–	2 ia
	950	⏑⏑⏑–⏑–	doch
	940	⏑–⏑– –⏑–	ia cr
		⏑⏑⏑–⏑– ⏑––⏑–	2 doch
942–45:		⏑⏑⏑–⏑– –⏑⏑–⏑–	2 doch
ephymnion a		⏑⏑⏑–⏑– –⏑⏑–⏑–	2 doch
(NOT REPEATED)		⏑⏑⏑– ⏑–⏑–	cr ia
		⏑––⏑–	doch
953–60: str. b	965	⏑⏑⏑–⏑– ⏑⏑̲–⏑–	2 doch
965–71: ant. b		⏑⏑⏑–⏑– ⏑⏑⏑–⏑–	2 doch
	955	⏑⏑⏑⏑̲⏑–	doch

	$\left\{ \begin{array}{l} -\cup\cup-\cup- \quad -\cup\cup-\cup- \\ \cup--\cup- \quad -\cup\cup-\cup- \end{array} \right\}$	2 doch
	$\cup--\cup- \quad \cup--\cup-$	2 doch
	$\cup--\cup-$	doch
960	$\left\{ \begin{array}{l} -\cup\cup-\cup- \quad \cup--\cup- \\ \cup--\cup- \quad \cup--\cup- \end{array} \right\}$	2 doch
961–64:	$\cup\cup\cup-\cup- \quad \cup\cup\cup-\cup-$	2 doch
ephymnion b	$\cup\cup\cup--$	?
(NOT REPEATED)	$\cup\cup\cup-\cup- \quad \cup\cup\cup-\cup-$	2 doch
	$\cup-\cup- \quad \cup-\cup-$	2 ia

Meter

As Orestes leads his mother into the palace to kill her over the
body of the fallen Aegisthus, the chorus sings this exultant
song of triumph because evil is ended and justice reborn. The
meter echoes that of the women's earlier short prayer for an
avenger (152–63); there the dochmiac betrayed their excitement at the mere hope of revenge just before Orestes was discovered; now they express their jubilation in the longest series of dochmiacs in the *Oresteia*.

Aside from the fact that the dochmiac seems to have been
the appropriate meter in which to express extreme happiness
or wretchedness,[119] it is also possible that in this trilogy the
dochmiac assumes a thematic function as the meter that accompanies murders. Each time dochmiacs have been heard
they have been closely associated with a murder that is about
to be committed or has just been committed in the name of
justice. The disturbed chorus of old men used the dochmiac
in their scenes with Cassandra and Clytemnestra, scenes that
surround the murder of Agamemnon. It is probable that
Aeschylus placed similar music in parallel positions in both
plays to emphasize further the basic similarity in the actions;
both the acts of Clytemnestra and Orestes are violent and are
judged to be equally deserving of punishment.[120] Through
such music the poet reminds his audience that little fundamental change has occurred in the second play.

Form

Just as the dochmiac meter allows virtually endless variation and renders difficult any attempt to establish a clearly repeated metrical formation, so also the form of this ode is continually shifting and difficult to predict. The pattern is the same as in the second stasimon: *aba cdc*. The lack of stanzas corresponding to the *b* and *d* sections has again led critics to supply a repetition of each mesode after its antistrophe, but here, too, an attempt to achieve symmetry is not in accord with the patterning of music throughout the play. It is more sensible to consider how the audience would hear the odes: because the meter of the mesodes continues that of the strophes, it is impossible to distinguish where the strophes end and the mesodes begin unless one is reading a text. Thus it would be difficult for the audience to anticipate the ending point for each antistrophe, and the break is strong when the music suddenly stops. In form this is a highly asymmetrical stasimon.[121]

The Final Scene (972–1076)

Choral anapaests

1007–09	1018–20
— — — — ∪∪— — —	— — ∪∪— ∪∪— ∪∪—
∪∪— ∪∪— ∪∪— —	∪∪— ∪∪— ∪∪— —
— — — —	— — — —
— — ∪∪— ∪∪— —	— — ∪∪— ∪∪— —

The end of the *Choephoroi* is a study in disappointment. Orestes thinks that in slaying his mother and Aegisthus he is an agent of justice; but he occupies the same position on the stage that Clytemnestra did in the last scene of the *Agamemnon*, and before the scene is over he will be driven offstage by the avenging Furies.[122] Clytemnestra enjoyed her triumph for about the same length of time. The chorus has repeatedly stated its trust that justice will be done and the state set free from its troubles; but before the end of this scene the women will realize that another death is demanded. Their final words acknowledge that they are witnessing yet another beginning for the house rather than an end. Complementing this disappointment is the lack of musical development. In the *Persians* and the *Suppliants* there is a long musical procession offstage, and such an ending will occur in the *Eumenides*. Given the building excitement of the dochmiac stasimon, the audience could have expected such a conclusion in the *Choephoroi*, but musically the last scene is a disappointment.

The dochmiacs of the chorus are abruptly curtailed by the appearance of Orestes over the two bodies, an instantaneous answer to the chorus's prayer. He states his justification with conviction and exhibits his evidence, though without the triumphant joy expressed by Clytemnestra. But the chorus is definitely not happy with the results and feels in no mood to continue the spirit of its previous ode: "Woe for the awful deeds. You have been killed in a hateful death. Alas! Alas! Suffering blossoms even for the survivors" (1007–09). Orestes is shocked at losing the women's support so quickly and asks urgently whether they no longer believe that Clytemnestra was guilty in view of physical evidence; but even he must admit that the act is painful and, if a victory, a highly qualified one (1010–17). The chorus can only echo his unhappy sentiments by speaking of the unhappy condition of all men (1018–20).

Both choral responses to Orestes are four-line anapaestic stanzas. Given the exultation of the previous dochmiacs, this is dispirited music for the long-awaited moment of triumph. The only music found to suit the occasion is a brief anapaestic stanza as the women turn from the joy and fiery enthusiasm of the dochmiac stasimon to a less emotional meter and a more reflective tone. Their final statement at 1065–76 is equally joyless, and the play ends on an unresolved, questioning note: "Where will it end? When will the wrath of destruction, stilled to sleep, come to an end?"

The disappointment conveyed by the music in this scene is

reinforced by a sign that the chorus attempts a kind of formal closing response to Orestes but fails. As has been noted earlier, even though the anapaest is not essentially a strophic meter, there are moments in the trilogy when the chorus tries to order its anapaestic stanzas into an imitation of a strophe/antistrophe structure. In this closing scene the four-line anapaestic units do almost correspond; the last three lines in each stanza are so precise in their corresponsion that it is impossible to avoid the feeling that Aeschylus was allowing the slave women to act like a formal chorus, but the stanza is so short and the meter so unpromising that they seem overwhelmed by discouragement and soon lapse into spoken dialogue.

More striking than the sullen, puzzled statements of the chorus is the increasing activity of Orestes as he realizes the weakness of his defense and then sees the Furies advancing. The chorus moves from excited song and motion to a slower and shorter song, and from there to spoken lines; Orestes moves from a speech of justification, which is formal in tone, to a more emotional defense and an expression of despair and from there to more clipped sentences and short shrieks as he rushes offstage. By the end of the scene Orestes has the more animated speeches and movement as the chorus becomes prosaic in its utterances and exits to a staid marching meter. It is fitting that they leave the stage making no summary statement, but asking questions.

The musical scheme of the *Choephoroi* is fully dependent on the music of the *Agamemnon*. The musical effects and thematic meters are not as strongly established on their own in this play, but because the original audience saw the three plays sequentially there was no need for the second play to stand on its own. Consequently, a successful production of the *Choephoroi* as a single play is difficult.

The predominant meter is the lyric iambic, which accompanies the subject of retribution for crime in the *Agamemnon*.

The chorus of slave women enters to this meter. When they try to sing colorful, animated, or varied rhythms, they inevitably revert to the old iambic theme. When they try to use the meter that is related to order and harmony, the lecythion, they also eventually sing in iambs. Even when they start a ritual song that begins six times with a lecythion pattern, they are drawn ineluctably into the familiar iambics. Thus the music consistently works against and undercuts the words of the conspirators. They inevitably sing of justice to the music of vengeance.

Although this chorus is not plagued by the same chilling doubts as the chorus in the *Agamemnon*, it has a surprising amount of trouble in singing an ornate and organized song as the old men did in the earlier parodos. The slave women's songs are often short, and in their long songs some element in the form thwarts their attempts at symmetry and makes patterning or anticipation almost impossible. Unlike the chorus in the second stasimon of the *Agamemnon*, they seem unable to express themselves in nonthematic meter. In the last half of the play the slave women sing a fully organized and balanced ode only to find themselves unable to do so again as the action of the conspirators nears completion. Instead they sing several short songs that tend to break up the action, and the anapaests they use raise no expectation of corresponding sections and offer only the hope of development into a longer, more ornate lyric. After the murder they lose their ability to sing while Orestes is driven offstage—their minds perplexed, their excitement brusquely checked, and their music abruptly calmed.

The musical design of the play underlines the simple fact that the world has not yet been reordered. Throughout the play the women delude themselves with thoughts that all is working out splendidly, yet when they try to coordinate their songs into a pattern, confusion results. The *Choephoroi* continues to reveal the universe as harsh and willful. Signs of orderly music in the traditional manner hold promise of a return to harmony, but that will be achieved only in the final play; for the moment, the music undercuts the hopeful utterances of the characters. In the action of the *Choephoroi* there is no end, no return of justice, no freedom from unhappiness, and very little harmony.

The design of the music in the first two plays is similar in many ways. In the middle of each play the chorus performs once in an ordered and symmetrical way, deviating from this musical norm for the remainder of the drama. In both plays mesodes, epodes, and ephymnia break up order and symmetry, and a death scream immediately stops the chorus's music-making. Although many elements besides the music indicate both the similarities and the differences between the parallel actions in the *Choephoroi* and the *Agamemnon*, it is important that the audience perceive a continuation of the basic themes of the first play, which become deeper and more complex in the second. Agamemnon, Clytemnestra, and Aegisthus are among the most perverse people on the tragic stage and fully deserve each other as members of one of tragedy's first love triangles. They are all so personally invested in palace intrigue that it is impossible to present their story without acknowledging the immense stake that each of them had in seeing his or her own definition of god's desire fulfilled. Orestes, on the other hand, is an innocent who would have stayed far away from Argos if he had not been compelled to return. The world in which he lives remains that of the *Agamemnon*; the characters and their motivations have changed, rendering the situation at the end of the second play more bleak, uncontrolled, and threatening than in the *Agamemnon*. The strongest indication on the stage that the same forces continue to live is found in the music, the thematic rhythms, and the continued inability of the chorus to define any unified or ordered pattern by which men can understand their lives. In the *Eumenides* men will again be able to orchestrate choral music, but only when they have a world to sing about that in itself is harmonious.

EUMENIDES

The Two Parodoi (143–77, 254–75)

First Parodos
140–142: spoken lines

143–48: str. a	—	— ⏑⏒–⏑– ⏑⏑⏑–⏑–	2 doch
149–54: ant. a	—	—150 ⏓–⏑– ⏕–⏑– ⏑–⏑–	3 ia
145		⏑⏑⏑–⏑– ⏑⏑⏑–⏑–	2 doch
		⏑––⏑–	doch
	—	––⏑– ––⏑– ⏑–⏑–	3 ia
	—	⏑–⏑– –⏑– –⏑–	ia 2 cr
155–61: str. b 155—	—	⏕–⏑– ⏑–⏑– ⏑–⏑–	3 ia
162–67: ant. b		⏑––⏑– ⏓–⏑–	doch ia
		⏑⏑⏑–⏓–	doch
	165	⏑⏑⏑⏑⏑⏑–	doch[123]
160		⏑–⏑– –⏑– –⏑–	ia 3 cr
		–⏑–	
		⏑⏑⏑⏑⏑⏑ ⏑⏑⏑⏑–	2 ia
169–72: str. g	—	⏑–⏑– ⏕–⏑– ⏑–⏑–	3 ia
173–77: ant. g 170	175	⏑⏑⏑–⏑– –⏑⏑– ⏑––	doch ch ba
		⏑⏑⏑–⏑– ⏑⏑⏑–⏑–	2 doch
		⏑–⏑– ⏑––⏑–	ia doch

Second Parodos
244–53: spoken lines

254–75: astrophic	—	⏑⏑⏑–⏑–	doch
	255	*–⏑ * * ––⏑–	?
		⏑––⏑– –⏑⏑⏑⏑⏑–	2 doch
	—	*⏑–⏑– ––⏑–	2 ia
		⏑⏑⏑–– ⏑––⏑–	2 doch
	260	⏑⏑⏑–⏑– ⏑––⏑–	2 doch
	—	⏑–⏑– ⏑–⏑– ––⏑–	3 ia
		⏑–⏑– –⏑–	ia cr
		⏑⏑⏑–⏑– ⏑⏑⏑–⏑–	2 doch
	—	––⏑– ––⏑– ––⏑–	3 ia

265	∪∪∪−∪− ∪∪∪∪∪−	2 doch
	−−∪− −−∪− −∪−	2 ia cr
—	−−∪− ∪−∪− ∪−∪−	3 ia
	∪−∪− −∪− −∪−	ia 3 cr
	−∪−	
—	−−∪− ∪−∪− ∪−∪−	3 ia
270	−∪∪−∪− ∪∪∪−	doch cr
	−∪∪−∪−	doch
	∪−∪− −−∪− ∪−∪−	3 ia
—	∪−∪− −−∪− ∪−∪−	3 ia
	∪−−∪−	doch
275	−∪∪−∪− ∪−−∪−	2 doch

The *Eumenides* does not begin with harmonious, pleasant music. The screams of the priestess, the strident rasping of Clytemnestra, the groans and moans of the Furies are the dissonant sounds characteristic of the early scenes. In addition, there are two parodoi in this play and each falls short of the audience's expectation in both music and form. The first "entrance song" is odd in any case: the members of the chorus awaken to find themselves already onstage and the play so far under way that they must run to catch it. Rather than presenting the music and dance of a properly arrayed and assembled chorus, the scene offers the splutterings and stretchings of loathsome monsters awakening one by one. The voices are split as each Fury on waking adds her bit to the song, and the chorus is finally gathered only to be chased offstage. In terms of the traditional choral form this entrance is a shambles. The second parodos, the Furies' entrance into Athens, is no better. They enter as a pack of hunting dogs spilling into the orchestra, searching randomly here and there for their prey.

For this chorus meter strongly reinforces form. Iambodochmiac is used frequently by Aeschylus and the later tragedians for scenes of excited emotion or high tension.[124] Here it effectively characterizes angry confusion and frantic disorder with haphazard, groggy movements. The second parodos is composed of the same two meters, with the iambic measures less resolved and more clustered, and thus stated all the more clearly. Because the Furies sing of vengeance as they seek retribution for sin in both parodoi, it is appropriate that a large proportion of their song consists of the iambic:

> You must give me in payment the right to suck red clots
> from your living limbs. I would have my nourishment
> from you—a hideous drink.   (264–66)

The very formlessness of this ode is even more effective in characterizing the chorus. In fact the whole first part of the *Eumenides* is composed of frustrated attempts to create order. No other Greek tragedy introduces so many short and causally independent scenes within 235 lines:

> The priestess is repelled from the temple (1–63).
> Apollo sends Orestes to Athens (64–93).
> Clytemnestra arouses the chorus (94–139).
> First parodos—choral song as Furies awake (140–178).
> Apollo sends the chorus away (179–234).
> Change of scene to Athens (at 235).

All these scenes are relevant to the plot but none is so important that a later section of the play would be unintelligible without it. The playwright summarizes the confusion in his characters' world by introducing in individual scenes the antagonistic champions (Apollo and Clytemnestra), their agents (Orestes and the Erinyes), and the clash of forces from the first two plays (Apollo versus the Erinyes). Thus the opening of the play presents in both form and content the disarray in the universe.

For example, the scene with the priestess is so unnecessary to the plot that she is never seen nor mentioned again. She enters listing in orderly succession the gods who have ruled over Delphi and then prays to the deities of the place that her prophecy may be even more felicitous for the Greeks; she is a pure, holy, devoted servant of the radiant Apollo. But the strong feelings of order and piety that she conveys are shattered at her first glimpse of the Furies. This woman, the most delicate character in the *Oresteia*, is repelled violently from the temple, unable to walk as she tells of the gory sight within. In the opening scene of the *Agamemnon* the watchman's suspicions as well as his joy set the tone; similarly, at the beginning of the *Eumenides* the violent ripping of a diaphanous veil of innocent piety and harmony portrays vividly the ominous presence even in a divine sanctuary of the unexpected, the sudden, the grotesque, and the horrible.[125]

The sleeping chorus most forcefully presents this formlessness. The Furies do not enter; they are discovered in sleep so deep that several characters have come and gone without disturbing them. The ghost of Clytemnestra has to berate them six times to elicit more than a sleepy groan. Then they rise one by one, stretch, and slowly organize themselves. While they are waking and arranging themselves into a proper tragic chorus, they sing the parodos, such as it is. Their individualized and extraordinary stage action throws disorder into the usually ordered form of strophic song. The chaos that underlies their music is made visual when they are driven out of the temple and sent off to Athens before they have a chance to act like a normal "entering" chorus.

The evidence for sound and music in this scene reinforces this concept for staging. As the chorus wakens slowly, the text provides tantalizingly vague indications of subverbal sounds.[126] Although the difference between a *mugmos* and an *ogmos* is unknown, these sleepers mutter two *mugmoi*, then two *ogmoi*, and finally, just before breaking into intelligible speech, a *mugmos diplous oxys*; both words are translated by "whimpers" and "groans." Their groaning becomes louder as they show more physical signs of awakening. Finally one of them utters the first intelligible line in a half-sleep. After Clytemnestra delivers her vindictive charge, one member of the chorus raises her head, notices that Orestes is gone, and starts to waken others; she, at least, speaks a recognizable trimeter. Then one by one the members of this chorus begin to rouse one another and enter the orchestra.[127]

At this point one manuscript indicates that the lines of lyrics should be split among individuals rather than sung by the chorus as a whole. The Medicean manuscript shows line 140 spoken by the chorus of Erinyes but a scholiast adds "one of these," and as the song progresses there is clear support in the situation and words for splitting the choral parts: the opening words of the short iambic section (140–42) describe one Fury awakening another, and, of course, the other is not speaking. Individually spoken lines seem to continue into the strophic lyric, where there is almost a conversation: "Oh! Alas! We have suffered, my friends. . . . Surely I have suffered much and all in vain. . . . We have suffered horrible pain. . . . I have lost my quarry" (143–48). The paragraph markings in some editions seem to present the right spirit if not the precise distribution of these lines and one scheme has been indicated on the scansion chart.[128]

This must be one of tragedy's most untraditional and imaginative uses of the chorus. If Aeschylus wanted to show that the formalism of his chorus was still broken and that these gods of justice were unable to create a harmonious and ordered musical form, he could have done it in no stronger way than by opening with this parodos. The words begin as inarticulate groans; the music is sung to a standard meter for frenzied and tense emotion. The song seems to be split among various members of the chorus, and they may never sufficiently organize themselves to sing a unified strophe. Their dance mimics the groggy movements of a person fighting off a deep sleep. Finally, when they have roused themselves and are ready to act like a chorus, they do not enter the beginning of the drama; they leave the stage in disorder.[129] This impression of disorder is all the stronger because of the strophic form of their song, which imposes an external framework of order and normality on meters appropriate for astrophic song. In addition, individual members of the chorus sing separately rather than in unison, as is customary in strophic lyric.

The increasing disorganization in musical form in the trilogy becomes even clearer from a comparison of these parodoi with those of the previous two plays. In the *Agamemnon* the chorus entered as the traditional marching chorus singing anapaests, and then, after taking its position, performed a long stasimon. In the *Choephoroi* there were no anapaests, but the chorus entered in a procession singing a unified lyric song. In the *Eumenides* the initial appearance of the chorus—ugly, stupefied, clumsy in movement, and disoriented—embodies the chaos surrounding Orestes. In terms of theater this parodos is a master stroke, representing visually and aurally the formless quality of a world of violence and force.[130]

After the chorus is driven out of the temple by Apollo, the scene shifts to Athens, where Orestes is appealing to Athena. No sooner has he finished his prayer than the Erinyes enter portraying themselves as a pack of hounds close on the trail of a fawn. The occasion presents the chorus with the opportunity for a proper entrance song, but this is the chorus that never was, and they still lack the ability to sing a formal parodos.

This passage (244–75) is divided into two sections by the meter. The coryphaeus enters speaking iambic trimeters and leading the others. Ten lines does not allow much time for the whole chorus to arrive through the side entrance, but inasmuch as there is no formation, they may come on quite rapidly, several at a time, without waiting for each other.

There are, however, indications in words and phrasing that individuals in the chorus speak some lines of the lyric as they scatter throughout the orchestra sniffing out their victim. Some editions divide the lyric into two-, three-, or four-line units, which are indicated on the scansion chart. These units read easily as speeches of individuals or separate groups responding to one another as they individually search for and discover Orestes:

> —Look! Look! Seek everywhere lest the mother-slayer escape going away secretly and not pay for his crime.

—He has wound himself around the statue of the immortal goddess taking her as his defense and wishes to go to court to escape his debts.

—But this is impossible! A mother's blood on the ground cannot be taken away; alas, the sacred stream poured on the ground is gone!   (254–63)

These are not the deliberate speeches of a unified chorus moving from topic to topic in an orderly fashion; these are remarks of individual Furies who slowly come to perceive the situation in a series of responses to one another.[131] They are no more ordered in this scene than the broken chorus after the death of Agamemnon in the first play.

Such stage direction explains the lack of a strophic structure for this song. The Furies sing random lines containing no particular pattern and are free to move as individuals in the orchestra, inasmuch as their movements do not have to be repeated to an antistrophic stanza immediately thereafter. They search out their victim and then close in on him as separate entities rather than as members of an organized chorus who must always be conscious of the group nature of their dance.

Both of these parodoi join with the other early scenes of the play to present an impression of thorough and vicious chaos, a reflection of the true state of the universe before the trial that is to restore order and balance under the reign of Zeus in cooperation with the Eumenides. If the dramatic chorus is a vestige of the basic ritual out of which tragedy developed, then this chorus is a total denial of the order, the structure, the music, and the dancing of the early form. The rebirth of musical order in the reconstitution of the chorus will accompany the establishment of permanent world order, the blessing for which the early rituals were performed.

The First Stasimon (307–96)

307–20: anapaests		
321–27: str. a	$-\cup-\cup-\cup-$ $--$	lec sp
334–40: ant. a	335 $-\cup\cup$ $-\cup-\cup-\cup-$	da lec

	— — —∪— —∪—	sp 2 cr
	—∪——∪——	?
325	—∪— —∪—	2 cr
	—∪— —∪—	2 cr
340	—∪—∪—∪—	lec

328–33:		∪∪∪— ∪∪∪—	2 paeonic
ephymnion a		∪∪∪— ∪∪∪—	2 paeonic
(Repeated 341–46)	330	∪∪∪—∪∪——	pher
		—∪—∪—∪—	lec
		—∪—∪—∪—	lec
		—∪—∪—∪—	lec

349–53: str. b	360	*—∪∪—∪∪—∪∪—∪∪——	5 da
360–66: ant. b 350		*—∪∪—∪∪—∪∪—∪∪——	5 da
		———∪∪——	3 da
	365	———∪∪—∪∪—∪∪—∪∪——	6 da
		*—∪—∪—∪—	lec

354–59:		—∪—∪—∪—	lec
ephymnion b	355	∪∪∪— ∪∪∪—	2 paeonic
(NOT REPEATED)		∪∪∪— ∪∪∪—	2 paeonic
		∪∪∪— ∪∪∪—	2 paeonic
		∪∪∪— ∪—∪—	paeonic ia
		—∪∪— ∪—∪—	ch ia

367–71: str. g		—————∪∪—∪∪——	5 da
377–80: ant. g		—∪∪—∪∪—∪∪—∪∪——	5 da
	370	—∪∪—∪∪—∪∪—∪∪	4 da
	380	— — —∪—∪—∪—	sp lec

372–76:		∪∪∪— ∪∪∪—	2 paeonic
ephymnion g		∪∪∪— ∪∪∪—	2 paeonic
(NOT REPEATED)		∪∪∪— ∪∪∪—	2 paeonic
	375	*∪∪∪— ∪∪∪—	2 paeonic
		—∪—∪∪——	pher

381–88: str. d		∪—∪— —∪—	ia cr
389–96: ant. d	390	∪—∪— —∪—	ia cr
		∪—∪— — —	ia sp

385	— — ∪ — ∪ — ∪ —	2 ia
	∪ ∪̽ ∪ ∪ ∪ ∪ ᷉∪ ∪ —	2 ia
	∪ — ∪ — ∪ — ∪ — ∪ — ∪ —	3 ia
395	᷄∪ ∪ — ∪ ∪ — ∪ ∪ — —	4 da
	— ∪ — ∪ — ∪ —	lec

Meter

In the iambic and anapaestic introductory sections to this stasimon the Furies clearly state their intention of singing a hymn. The previous formally announced song by a chorus in the trilogy was the old men's hymn of praise in the *Agamemnon* when they heard that Troy had fallen (*Ag.* 355–474). There the chorus sang as a unit to a quite clear and repeated iambic meter with glyconic coda sections tying the six strophes even more closely together. Here it is necessary for the Furies to announce their hymn because the elements of disorder are so prevalent that the audience would quite reasonably begin to doubt their continuing desire to maintain such a form; in contrast to glyconic codas in the *Agamemnon*, the refrains here are so sporadic that they discourage the impression of unity.

The meter of this song appears desultory. Only in the final strophic pair is a familiar meter—the iambic—established. The first set of strophes moves from lecythia to dactyls to iambics; the first ephymnion is a mixture of the fourth paeonic (∪∪∪–) and lecythion. If any meter is stated clearly it is the lecythion, but it is repeated only in the three successive lines at the end of the first ephymnion. The second and third set of strophes are almost pure dactyls, and their ephymnia are largely in the fourth paeonic. The fourth set of strophes is composed of clearly stated iambic and there is no ephymnion. Thus the basic movement of this chorus is from the tentative initial statement of the lecythion to dactyls to iambics. Simultaneously there is an increasingly strong statement of the fourth paeonic (itself a resolved form of the cretic).

The striking feature of choral song up to this point in the

Eumenides is the lack of an insistent repeated meter. Although the Furies sing a mixture of iambic and dochmiac in the two parodoi, they are unique among the choruses in the trilogy in having not yet identified themselves with any firm thematic meter. In this Binding Song they sing gory and grotesquely vindictive words: they openly seek to obtain human sacrifice, mental derangement, family disaster, crippling assault, pollution, defamation, and endless pursuit to the grave and beyond. But the meter that accompanies this very plain talk is not the expected iambic until the very last stanza. In the ephymnion there is a type of cretic, but it is far from the clear form that has been persistently present in the repeated, drumming iambics of previous strophes and ephymnia. Aeschylus seems to have chosen a resolved form of the cretic to lessen his stress on the iambic meter until the very end of the song; as a result his audience might perceive that the chorus, though vindictive and true to the gorier themes of the previous plays, by not organizing its song around that one meter offers the hope of developing beyond the narrow limits of this musical theme.[132]

In the *Eumenides*, mortals will move out of chaos into a world that is better ordered and offers more hope. It is therefore appropriate that the music of the play should not fall quite as insistently or as automatically into the iambic meter of retribution. To be sure, the Erinyes are not weak in their belief or in their demands for vengeance; they mean every word they say. At the moment of their arrival in Athens it appears that the cycle of sin and punishment is going to continue, but in fact it will be stopped before the play is over. The music shares in leading the audience to this new dispensation; the meter of sin and retribution is present, but it is never pressed with intensity. In the *Choephoroi* the insistence on the iambic rhythms was appropriate because it called attention to a static situation that allowed little hope of change in spite of the supposedly careful thought and planning of the conspirators; but in the *Eumenides* liberation and innovation are paramount themes—and this change in theme is echoed in the metrical design of the first three choral songs. The use of the iambic is sufficient to show that the moral demands of gods and men remain the same, but its dilution hints at change; by this shift in emphasis Aeschylus prepares his audience for the rise of another meter in the next stasimon that will continue to grow through the end of the play as the thematic accompaniment to the establishment of a new order.

Form

When the chorus announces its hymn, the audience has every right to expect that this previously sleepy, sprawling, disheveled group will finally emerge as a representative of the tragic chorus. It could be argued that the story demands that the Erinyes in their early scenes be constantly in motion peering into far corners and scattered widely over the orchestra. At this point, however, there is no element of plot that should weaken their unity; they are now in position, have found their victim, and should be ready to present their case. And indeed the Erinyes here state that they will join in a choral dance (307–11).

Their hymn begins with a highly formal organization. The Furies form themselves and announce their principles in anapaests and then move to their incantation in strophic lyrics. Such an introductory section has occurred earlier in the prayer of the old men (*Ag.* 355–66) and before the long kommos in the *Choephoroi* (306–14). The first sections of the incantation are regular: a strophe with an ephymnion is followed by the corresponding antistrophe and a repetition of the ephymnion. The second strophic set has strophe-ephymnion-antistrophe, but there is no manuscript support for a repetition of the ephymnion either in this place or after the next strophic pair. Repeated ephymnia were added after each of these strophic units by later editors; however, as in other passages the text should probably remain as the tradition gives it.[133] The pattern of this hymn would then be: *abab cdc efe gg*—in other words, there is no predictable pattern at all. The attempts of critics to bring order into this hymn demonstrate how disjointed such a song seems to readers; how much more chaotic it must have seemed to an audience, for whom music and dance would have reinforced the impression.

Another possible disordering feature in this song is the distribution of lines. If ephymnia b and g are not added to the manuscript version of the chorus, there are twelve lyric stanzas for twelve potential speaking roles. Although such line assignments are only possibilities, there is an interesting parallel to be drawn to the broken chorus in the *Agamemnon* (1346–71). There twelve individual members of the chorus each took two lines and then were interrupted by the appearance of Clytemnestra as an agent of destruction; here there are potentially twelve individual parts, and the chorus is interrupted by the appearance of Athena as an agent of compromise and understanding. Indeed, the progression of thought in this song makes the twelve-part distribution of lines at least possible, for the ode is not composed of statements that develop logically, with each point depending on the last. Rather the Erinyes make a series of individual assertions about their prerogatives and methods, avoiding the complex speculation on the future or evaluation of patterns from the past that are familiar from the odes of the old men in the *Agamemnon*. This lack of connection is shown most clearly by the distressing ease with which the repeated ephymnia can be inserted by scholars without disturbing the sense of individual stanzas or of the whole ode.

Even in this ritual song there are signs of severe disorganization. There is no reason why the Furies should be unable to sing a unified hymn, but they fail. They neither sing to thematic meter nor sing together nor even maintain a pattern in their song. The Furies remain the most disorganized chorus in Greek tragedy as each of these disordering elements is presented both aurally and visually to the audience.

The Second Stasimon (490–565)

490–98: str. a	490	—∪–∪–∪–	lec
499–507: ant. a	500	—∪– —∪– —∪–∪–∪–	2 cr lec
		—∪– —∪–	2 cr
		—∪– —∪–∪–∪–	cr lec
	495	—∪–∪–∪⏒	lec
	505	—∪∪∪∪ —∪–⏒	2 troch
		∪∪∪–∪–∪–	lec
		—∪–∪–∪–	lec
508–16: str. b		—∪–∪–∪–	lec
517–25: ant. b		—∪–∪–∪–	lec
	510	—∪–∪–∪–	lec
	520	—∪–	cr
		—∪–∪–∪–	lec
		—∪–∪–∪–	lec
		—∪–∪⏕∪–	lec
	515	—∪–∪–∪–	lec
	525	—∪–∪–∪–	lec
526–37: str. g		—∪– —∪–	2 cr
538–49: ant. g		—∪–∪–∪–	lec
	540	—∪– —∪∪–∪∪–∪∪	cr 3 da
	530	—∪∪–––∪∪––	4 da
		—∪–∪–∪–	lec
	545	—∪∪–∪∪–∪∪–∪∪–	4 da + –
	535	—∪∪––	2 da
		∪–∪– —∪–	ia cr
		—∪∪– ∪––	ch ba
550–57: str. d	550	∪–∪– —∪– ∪–∪–	ia cr ia
558–65: ant. d		—∪– ∪––	cr ba
	560	∪–∪– —∪– ∪––	ia cr ba
		∪–∪– —∪– ∪–∪–	ia cr ia
		∪–∪– ∪–∪– ∪–∪–	3 ia
	555	∪–– —∪– ∪––	ba cr ba
		—∪∪– ∪–∪–	ch ia
	565	—∪∪– ∪––	ch ba

Meter

After the mixture of meters in the first stasimon, the order and clarity of the second signal something new. The first two strophes are almost completely lecythia: in the first strophic set, six of eight lines, in the second strophic pair, eight out of nine. The third strophe marks a transition between the two thematic meters with a mixture of lecythia, iambs, cretics, and bacchiacs. The fourth set of stanzas is iambic. Thus the movement is from a strong statement of the lecythia through a strophe of indeterminate pattern to iambic. Most remarkable is the return of the repeated lecythion, which has not been heard with such emphasis since before the Cassandra scene (*Ag.* 975–1033).

The reappearance of this meter underlines a fundamental change in the presentation of the Furies. Previously they were characterized as egocentric daemons of fear and blood. In this ode they do not change their nature, but they dwell more on justifying their role as protectors of world order. Athena has just admitted that there is a legitimate issue between the Furies and Orestes that is not easy to decide, and as she departs to select a jury of citizens to help her in this subtle case, the Furies develop this theme by explaining that they are divinities of justice who perform a necessary function in protecting the rights of the individual within the family.[134]

The Furies are goddesses of the early family and clan structure basic to agricultural society. No innocent person need fear their vengeance, but one who disregards them will lead a miserable existence, for they will haunt the very ground he walks upon and cultivates for his family's food and comfortable burial. They can even threaten to loose pestilence and death on Athens if their claims are not recognized. In this rugged and frightening way they maintain justice within their limited sphere.[135] It is therefore appropriate that they sing this statement of their ordering function to the lecythion meter. The chorus in the *Agamemnon* hoped for the ordering force of a high god, but in the absence of this lofty type of divinity, society needs a basic type of authority, like the Furies, who will protect the primeval ties of the family—and they quite rightly sing to the meter of order. Measured against the Olympians in this trilogy, these goddesses are fair and honest though rough, and commendably concerned for mankind. The general recognition of the fairness of their claim will lead to a new order accompanied by new music at the end of the play.[136]

In this ode the lecythion is strong but does not last; it fades in the third stanza, and the familiar iambic beat emerges in the fourth set of strophes. To this iambic meter the Furies sing the fate of the man who chooses to ignore their prerogatives: he founders, crashes into the rocks, and drowns unlamented and ignored. This kind of vengeance against the sinner leads to an ethic based on fear, and the appropriate music for such retributive justice is the iambic rhythm.

This stasimon precedes the trial scene and provides a necessary corrective to the earlier frightening, vindictive, egoistic presentation of the Furies. To prepare the audience to find sufficient justification for the action of the Furies to convince half of the jury, the music fittingly provides ambiguous signals by incorporating large sections of strongly stated lecythion and iambic.

Form

This stasimon has a counterpart in the other two plays of the trilogy. Each contains a highly ordered ode that separates the action into two parts (*Ag.* 975–1033 and *Ch.* 585–651). Before this song in the *Eumenides* the Furies have been pursuing Orestes as he seeks protection and release; after this song come his defense and acquittal. In the other plays the formal ode dividing the action has been deceptive as a guide to the future dramatic development, for the choruses thereafter have difficulty in music-making. In contrast, this moment introduces the increasingly orderly and symmetrical songs that will characterize the rest of the play. As the possibility of finding a new organization for the world begins to grow after the intervention of Athena, so also the chorus begins to re-form its singing to the optimistic meter of order. In this play the Furies do have a fair claim against Zeus, and as they state this claim, the meter and form, the music and dance begin to reveal the order and thematic music that will be fully displayed at the end of the trilogy.

The Finale (778–1047)

Repeated Stanzas (778–880)

Stanza I (778–92 =
808–22)

		∪—∪— ∪—∪— ∪——∪—	2 ia doch
		∪—∪— ∪—∪— ——∪—	3 ia
780	810	∪—∪— ∪—∪— ∪∪∪∪—	3 ia
		∪——∪—	doch
		—∪—∪—∪— —∪—∪—∪—	2 lec
		*∪——∪∪	doch
		∪∪∪—∪—	doch
785	815	——∪— ∪∪∪∪— ∪—∪—	3 ia
		∪∪∪∪∪∪—	doch
		∪—∪— ——∪— ——∪—	3 ia
		∪—— ∪——	2 ba
		∪—— ∪——	2 ba
790	820	∪——∪∪∪	doch
		∪—∪∪—— ∪——∪—	2 doch
		—∪∪— ∪——	ch ba

Stanza II (837–46 =
870–880)

	870	∪∪∪—∪∪	doch
		—	
		∪∪∪—∪∪∪ ∪∪∪———	2 doch
		∪∪∪—∪—	doch
		—	
840		∪——∪— ∪—∪∪∪∪	doch
		—— ——	2 sp
	875	—∪∪—∪— ——∪∪—	doch + ?
		—∪∪———	doch
845		∪∪∪—∪— ∪——∪—	2 doch
	880	—∪∪—∪— ∪——∪—	2 doch

Kommos (916–1020)

916–26: str. a			—∪— —∪—∪—∪—	cr lec
938–47: ant. a			—∪—∪—∪—	lec
			—— —∪—∪—∪—	sp lec
		940	∪—∪— ∪—∪—	2 ia
			—∪—∪——	ithy
	920		—∪—∪—∪—	lec
			—∪—∪—∪—	lec
			—∪—∪—∪—	lec
		945	∪—∪— ∪—∪— ∪—∪—	3 ia
	925		——— ———	2 mol
			—∪—∪—∪—	lec

956–67: str. b			—∪— —∪—	2 cr
976–87: ant. b			—∪—∪—∪—	lec
			—∪—∪—∪—	lec
	960	980	—∪∪—∪∪—∪∪—∪∪——	5 da
			∪————	ia [137]
			—∪∪———	hemiepes [138]
			—∪∪—∪∪—	hemiepes
			—∪∪—∪∪——	da
	965	985	—∪∪—∪∪——	da
			—∪—∪—∪—	lec
			—— —∪—∪—∪—	sp lec

996–1002: str. g			—∪∪—∪∪—∪∪—∪——	praxillean
1014–20: ant. g		1015	—∪—∪—∪—	lec
			—∪—∪—∪—	lec
			—∪—∪—∪—	lec
	1000		—∪—∪—∪—	lec
			—∪—∪—∪—	lec
		1020	—∪—∪—∪—	lec

Exodos (1033–47)

1033–35: str. a		—∪∪—∪∪—∪∪——	4 da
1036–39: ant. a		———∪∪—∪∪—∪∪——	5 da
	1035	———∪∪———	3 da

1040–43: str. b	1040	$\left\{\begin{array}{l} \text{---}\cup\cup\text{-}\cup\cup\text{--} \\ *\text{---}\cup\text{---}\cup\text{--} \end{array}\right\}$	da
1044–47: ant. b			
	1045	$\text{-}\cup\cup\text{---}\underline{\cup\cup}\text{--}$	da
		$\text{-}\underline{\cup\cup}\text{-}\cup\cup\text{-}\cup\cup\text{-}$	da
		$\cup\cup\text{-} \quad \cup\cup\text{-} \quad \cup\cup\text{-} \quad \text{-}$	paroemiac

Meter

The ending of the *Eumenides*, the finale following Orestes' acquittal, falls into three sections divided by meter. First the Furies pour out their feelings of insult and outrage while Athena attempts to console them. After the Furies decide to accept Athena's offer of conciliation, they sing with her their mutual promises to Athens. Finally there is a procession of Furies (now changed to Eumenides), women and children of Athens, Athena, and the jurymen offstage to end the play.[139]

The repeated songs of the angered Furies in response to Athena (778, 808, 837, and 870) are emotional expressions of outrage and self-pity with no recognition of the arguments in the trial. By their sterile repetition of shock and hurt they prove the emptiness of their case in that they are unwilling to see any justification for the six citizen votes against them. While they retreat immediately to threats of indiscriminate destruction, Athena through the establishment of the court and the promise of cooperation in the future offers a chance for a new beginning with guarantees of the very rights that the Furies demand. Athena answers their bluster in calm, reasoned, generous words—and they refuse to hear her.

Their meter underlines their intransigence. Their repeated songs are composed almost totally of iambics and dochmiacs. If the Furies acted as they threaten to do, they could renew the cycle of sin and retribution by violating the rights and feelings of some other god, who would then have to pursue them or their earthly agent. It is therefore appropriate that the meter associated with retribution is heard; yet dochmiacs dominate and become even stronger in the second repeated stanza. This music of excitement and frenzied activity has been associated with the Furies since their first appearance onstage, when they sang their words of angry vengeance; in the previous two plays it has been associated with the approach of the next murder. Here it anticipates the possible launching of a pestilential attack by the Furies.[140] Their music is thus still related to the old order of violence and takes little notice of the new concept of justice dawning before their eyes. Both meter and words summarize everything that the Furies have represented up to this time, and both are easily modulated as Athena brings them to speak rationally in response to her calm persuasion.

After Athena has convinced the Furies to accept a new position, their words and music are emphatically different from the song of violence and wrath; now they sing of blessings and prosperity for Athens (916–1020). Calling on Zeus the all-powerful, they prophesy a world of harmony, fertility, health, law, happiness, peace, and divine cooperation. They now sing in a slower, more stately way to the lecythion meter. In the first set of strophes this meter is repeated unresolved in seven out of eleven lines; in the second strophic pair there are repeated lecythia in four lines, with five lines of dactyls and one of cretics. In the final set of strophes the first line is dactylic, but the next six are identical lecythia. There is no doubt that the lecythion is the dominant music of this ode, which concludes a long scene beginning at 490. The lecythia in the ode before the trial scene (490–565) were overcome before the end of the song, and the familiar iambic theme of retribution became the prevailing motif in the final stanza. After the judgment the meters were iambic and dochmiac, but Athena finally stilled this music through her calm and rational words. Now, however, the lecythion grows stronger and more insistent as the Eumenides sing of endless blessings that they will shower upon Athens in cooperation with Zeus and Athena.[141] The other notable meter in these strophes is the dactylic, which lends epic dignity to this new hymn and preludes the exodos, where dactylic rhythm predominates.

Form

After the votes of the jurors have been counted and Orestes has been acquitted, the Furies angrily sing a lyric strophe expressing their feelings of insult and dishonor, and threatening pestilence and death for Athens. Athena answers their strophe with a speech in iambics, whereupon they repeat word for word the same threatening strophe. Again Athena answers in iambs, and then this pattern with repeated lyric stanzas recurs. Each time, Athena answers their song with increasingly persuasive speech; finally the chorus stops singing and questions Athena more closely.[142]

This scene with its interplay between song and speech is related to two other scenes in the *Agamemnon*. When Cassandra is singing her frenzied lyrics, the old men of the chorus answer in iambics, but she soon disturbs them by her words and they also begin to sing lyrics. Later, when Clytemnestra uses calm iambics to try to explain her reasons for killing Agamemnon, the old men are agitated and answer her in lyrics. Eventually they arouse Clytemnestra to a singing contest. The scene with the Furies moves in the opposite direction. Athena is speaking good sense, and the Furies are clearly emotional and uncomprehending as they claim to have been completely dishonored (although in fact they have lost by only one vote). Athena is persuasive and conciliatory as she promises them a place in Athens where they will receive honor from the citizens. There is not much to be said against her proposal—and the Furies offer the most ineffective kind of resistance. They do not reason back at her. They add nothing new to their case against Athena and the Olympian gods. They simply repeat, word for word, the same impassioned outburst. When Athena answers, offering them a share in her rule and devotion from the people of Athens, the chorus again refuses to consider her words and bursts into a song of self-pity. Athena strengthens her offer by promising even greater honors, and the chorus again repeats the same blustery protest. No spectator could claim that Athena is treating the Furies badly; indeed, quite the reverse is true. Finally, when Athena does bring them to spoken iambs, there is communication and they quickly reach an agreement. Whereas in the previous plays the aim was to heighten the impression of anxiety by movement from words to music, here Aeschylus portrays growing conciliation by moving from music to speech. As Athena's reasoning overcomes the Furies' feeble, irrational outbursts, so also her speech overcomes their emotional music.

Once persuaded and having accepted their new position, the Furies pour forth blessings upon Athena in three strophes. In response Athena answers in anapaests. The form is similar to the end of the *Agamemnon*, where Clytemnestra responded in anapaests to the old men's lyrics as she tried to justify her deeds; there the imbalances in musical form reinforced their inability to reach agreement. Here both Athena and the chorus agree on order and harmony as they sing to celebrate their newly won unanimity. In the *Agamemnon* singers competed; here they complement one another. Appropriately, Athena's singing shows signs of increased order over the song of Clytemnestra. Clytemnestra never managed to sing a series of anapaestic stanzas in an arrangement that would show a close similarity to choral corresponsion, although she did achieve a modest success in her initial pair (Ag. 1462–67 and 1475–80). In contrast, Athena responds to each of the lyric stanzas of the chorus in anapaests except for the last where she organizes the final procession in spoken iambics; thus she makes five anapaestic responses. She sings the middle three of these (948–55, 968–75, and 988–95) as eight-line stanzas in which the second and seventh lines are monometers ($\cup\cup-\cup\cup-$) and the final line is paroemiac ($\cup\cup-\cup\cup-\cup\cup--$). Thus she brings the anapaestic meter close to being in strophic responsion,[143] and she frames her response with anapaestic sections of eleven and twelve lines (927–37 and 1003–13), providing an approximate symmetry to her song. Here the chorus has no problem with ephymnia or wandering meters; its strophes

are sung to a basic thematic meter and lack the jarring junctures and additions that characterize the debate with Clytemnestra. This conversation in orderly musical balance continues through the end of the play. It is impossible to know
whether the melody of Athena harmonized with or echoed
that of the Eumenides whereas the music of Clytemnestra
clashed with that of the old men, but given the close association of musical form to content in this trilogy, it is a strong
possibility.

The long finale (778–1047) is almost all music and dance.
When Athena and the newly created Eumenides have finished
their song and their farewells, Athena speaks over the music
and organizes the procession to escort the Eumenides to their
new home (1021–31). The Furies, on changing their attitude
and becoming Eumenides, also change their costumes from
drab black to a bright red and are finally led offstage to their
new seats of honor by an escort of Attic women carrying
torches. From being the most chaotic and unkempt chorus in
Greek drama, the Eumenides become a proper formal chorus
as they are reconciled to their new position of honor. Under
the guidance of Athena and with the music of their escorts
they are led offstage to a dactylic meter. The final line of the
singers in the last two strophes is an anapaestic marching
meter appropriate for a formal exit;[144] but the dominant dactylic meter in this final song of the trilogy recalls the first
choral music in the parodos of the *Agamemnon*. There dactyls
told of the omen of the eagles eating the pregnant hare; now,
however, there is no imbalance, no lack of symmetry, no unexpected change in the music. The final scene is complex, in-
volving a number of characters each singing their own song,
but the harmony and the order of the musical form exemplify
and embody the new dispensation that has been established in
the universe. The play appropriately ends with the joyous
and sincere cry of victory—ὀλολύξατε.

CHAPTER 3

THE MEANING OF MUSIC
IN THE *ORESTEIA*

The musical design of the *Oresteia* provides important clues to the correct interpretation of the trilogy. As pointed out earlier, both the plays themselves and ancient secondary testimony offer evidence that Aeschylus was deeply interested in writing plays that required careful attention to scene design, choreography, costume design, and play directing.[1] He himself personally supervised many of these aspects of production in the premiere performances of his plays. The exercise of such complete directorial control leads easily to the assumption that Aeschylus made every theatrical element then available contribute significantly to his dramatic concept. Thus an analysis of any one feature will necessarily help modern readers and directors to define the intent of the poet in the other features and in the whole play. Music and music-making have a role in every Greek tragedy, but in the *Oresteia* Aeschylus has given his chorus a larger role with long, impressive songs that are closely related to the events of the episodes; in addition, an extensive series of metaphors and images about sound and music focuses attention on the actual singing and dancing of the chorus.[2] Given the importance of music-making in the *Oresteia*, it is reasonable to conclude that a correct assessment of its musical design can provide a powerful key to the interpretation of the trilogy.

Five basic organizing principles in the *Oresteia* are directly derived from the analysis of musical forms in the previous chapter.

First, the trilogy centers around two major opposed themes, each persistently joined to distinct metrical patterns.

The connection between meter and theme is established early in the *Agamemnon*: the theme of the overarching and powerful justice of Zeus (lecythion) versus the theme of continuing crime and necessary punishment (iambic).[3]

Second, music is a truer guide to the direction of men's thoughts than are their words, for few of the mortal characters understand what is happening in their world. This case is clearest when the chorus in the third stasimon of the *Agamemnon* falls into confusion trying to find a satisfactory and consistent position between the two contrasting themes—and both are expressed through music.[4] In addition, the continual breakdown in musical form throughout the *Agamemnon* reveals that the old men's thought pattern in response to events keeps pushing them to conclusions that they resist.[5]

Third, the return of the lecythion meter in full force at the end of the *Eumenides* signals the removal of this confusion as words of justice are sung to the meter associated with justice. When Athena persuades the Furies that there is a better way to resolve conflicts in the future, the emergence of the new understanding is marked by a shift in the meter and an increased order in the musical form.[6]

Fourth, the trilogy presents a steady decline in the chorus's ability to sing and dance up to the middle of the third play. The chorus of the *Agamemnon* consists of ambitious and proficient singers who seek enlightenment and understanding but are sufficiently rigorous and honest to acknowledge problems in their own thoughts. The chorus of the *Choephoroi* represents a decline in this mental acuity, accompanied by a corresponding loss in the expressiveness and variety of the musical forms. This decline continues into the *Eumenides*, reaching its low point with the sleeping chorus. Ambitious music-making is restored only toward the end, when the Erinyes accept a position within the new order.

Finally, at the end of the trilogy the recurrence of dactyls recalls the dactylic prophecy of Calchas in the first part of the parodos of the *Agamemnon*. There a prophet who foretold frightening events for the house was completely correct.

With similar certainty the dactylic ode of the ladies of Athens tells of the coming unity of Zeus and Moira with the new Eumenides and the citizens of Athens. This dactylic meter is thus an appropriate conclusion to a play in which a new vision of the future has been made clear to all, but in itself it is not the thematic meter that identifies the issues around which the play has been built. The dominant meter emerging strongly toward the ending of the trilogy is the lecythion, which replaces the heavily iambic songs of the women in the *Choephoroi* and of the Erinyes in the first part of the *Eumenides*. The restatement of this meter suggests that the triumphant conception that permits the confident final procession is the shared belief in the dominance of Zeus as a god who seeks justice for all and who will work in cooperation with both gods and mortals to establish on a firm basis a new and orderly reign.

Each of these assertions is based on themes in the drama that can be identified by the development of the musical design in its meter and in its form. Individually none of these statements is totally new, but the interaction of these ideas suggests a general interpretation of the trilogy that differs from the judgments of many scholars and, even when it agrees in its outlines with previous opinion, provides a new dimension to this ancient drama through the appreciation of the basic thematic concerns portrayed through music.

The *Oresteia* was conceived by a poet accustomed to view events developing across vast spaces and through long periods of time. There are obviously many large themes involved in the *Oresteia*, among them the founding of the polis, fate and free will, and the curse on the family of Atreus.[7] But the musical design of the play gives prominence to two major organizing themes: the justice of Zeus and the necessity of exacting punishment for crime. Although these themes need not be irreconcilable, they are in conflict at the beginning of the *Agamemnon*. A play that opens with a father slaughtering his daughter in order to pursue Zeus's will and with a chorus unhappy that so many men have died in a holy war waged for the sake of one promiscuous woman reveals the playwright's concern with this fundamental conflict from the outset. Somehow Zeus demands such awful acts that common sense cries for vengeance, and yet without such acts there would be no justice; befuddlement and confusion are so widespread and profound that characters easily choose to rest their dilemmas in the hands of Zeus. Their attitude is: "If he wants it that way, then he must know why. We trust in him and we believe that he is there. He has to be there—because if he does not exist, these acts of bloodshed have no explanation."[8] Because this Aeschylean faith in *pathei mathos*, the doctrine that Zeus brings learning to mortals through their sufferings, is basic to the trilogy, it is important to acknowledge that it is stated initially as the belief of the chorus rather than as the certainty of the playwright.[9] The chorus immediately qualifies its attitude toward this belief by expressing misgivings about the pain and violence through which Zeus and his fellow gods are leading men:

> There drops in sleep before the heart
> A pain reminding us of suffering.
> Grace comes from the gods, I think,
> But with violence. . . .   (179–82)[10]

In the first two plays Agamemnon at Aulis, the herald, and Orestes share this ambiguous attitude about Zeus's ability to assign punishments that teach rather than torment men. But there are two characters in the *Agamemnon* who should be able to provide a firm understanding of Zeus's rule: Cassandra and Clytemnestra. Of course, myth guarantees that Cassandra is not in the slightest confused about the nature of the world in which she lives. She knows that she is being led to Argos to be slaughtered and that her city has been leveled despite continual prayers to the gods; appropriately, she has no words to waste on the enfeebled construction that makes the expedition to Troy a pursuit of justice. But then myth also guarantees that Cassandra cannot be a source of information for the characters in the play, because she is never to be believed. The audience hears her words and sees her suffering, and to them she offers the only explanation that can make sense of a collection of perplexing and painful events: the universe is not being managed for the betterment of mankind. Cassandra herself is a clear visual representation of a god's injustice.[11] The audience can accept her visions, but the characters, including the chorus, must wait a few more scenes before seeing the grim truth for themselves.[12]

Clytemnestra, however, should be a source of confidence for the other characters in the play once her beacon speech has established her credentials as a competent planner and manager. Yet even Clytemnestra has problems maintaining her icy self-control when the chorus cannot be made to accept her assessment of the killings and delivers such telling blows against her arguments that she is unable to find an adequate defense. The old men's minds reel in bewilderment because they can foresee only more and more bloodshed. And Clytemnestra ultimately agrees—to an extent—as she humbly concedes that she wants only the small reward of release:

> I am willing to swear an oath with the god of the Pleisthenids and to be content with the present situation even though it is hard to endure; but in the future he will go from this house to another family and exhaust them with killings in their house. It is sufficient for me to have a small share of my possessions if only I have driven the murderous madness from the house.   (1568–76)

Where has this highly competent, self-assured woman gone astray in her reasoning? At 1384–87 she reveals candidly, for the first time in the play, what she has been thinking about:

> I struck him twice, and with two groans his limbs went slack, and as he fell I struck him a third blow—a votive thank-offering for Zeus beneath the earth, the savior of dead men.

In this statement Clytemnestra identifies Zeus, that high god of Olympus in whom the chorus has put such confidence, with a god of the underworld who seeks vengeance on murder within the bloodline—or so we are to learn in the *Eumenides*.[13] In the *Agamemnon*, all of whose characters have an inordinate trust in an Olympian Zeus as the enforcer of justice, such confusion is understandable; indeed, it is the root of the chorus's belief that Zeus directs all the various divine agents involved in seeking justice. But this trust is also the root of the misunderstanding and confusion that plagues the characters in the *Agamemnon*, because Zeus simply is not the god of the dead nor does he exercise control over the Furies, the true gods of dead men under the ground in this trilogy.[14] Clytemnestra has unwittingly been serving these black underworld divinities in pursuing vengeance for a father-daughter murder. When Agamemnon entered the palace, she prayed to Zeus the Accomplisher (973–74), but she was about to perform the task that was the direct concern of the Furies, namely avenging murder within the bloodline. Because she thinks that she is doing the work of Zeus, she is unable to understand that Zeus can ask for vengeance against her; yet the chorus can see that the divine system comprising Zeus and the Furies as well as numerous other divinities does not allow murders to go unavenged. Because of her basic misunderstanding even Clytemnestra, the most confident character in the play, becomes confused. Only after her deed does she realize that she too has been depending on a divinity that she has created in her own mind,[15] and thus she is willing to seal an oath with the spirit ruling in the house rather than insisting on the divinely inspired righteousness that she initially claimed. After the loathsome Aegisthus has fully cheapened her cause in his brief scene,[16] she is even willing to admit that she is caught in a system that is larger than her understanding or control and that her confidence has been shattered:

> In no way, dearest of men, let us work further evil; these before us are many to reap, a painful harvest. There is enough of suffering. Let us not be bloody. Go now to your homes, old men, before you suffer for your actions. We must accept these matters as we have them. If it

> should happen that we might say "enough of these trou-
> bles," we would welcome that, for we have been sadly
> stricken by the heavy heel of the *daimon*.   (1654–60)[17]

Only the chorus can feel confidence in stating the new and
grimmer understanding to which all the characters have come:

> The robber is robbed; the killer pays the price. The law
> remains while Zeus remains on his throne: the doer suf-
> fers; for this is ordained. Who would cast the cursed
> seed from the house? The race is glued to ruin. (1562–66)

In the course of the *Agamemnon* much confusion is corrected, but the dawning of this clear understanding is not a
happy event. Confusion has arisen because mortals have been
too willing to assume that in pursuing the proper punishment
for crime they are acting in the cause of a higher justice, the
justice of Zeus. At the end of the play each of the characters
onstage realizes that the justice of Zeus is a dream created by
humans who—knowingly or unknowingly—cloak the pursuit of their own desires with the mantle of Zeus's authority.[18]
Accompanying the growing awareness of the chorus that in
their world Zeus does not lead men through suffering to
learning is the steady decline of the lecythion and the increasing insistence on the iambic meter. By the end of the drama
music has died out completely; in a bloody and imperfect
world, individuals have perpetuated the cycle of killings and
vengeance to the point where the chorus can see no end and is
consequently unable to speak vigorously for, or even medi-
tate upon, the pursuit of justice for all men.

The *Choephoroi* begins on the same bleak note. The chorus
is composed of slave women who witness a kind of raw justice being imposed upon wrongdoers, yet they have learned
the necessity of accepting such fates, whether just or unjust,
repressing their own personal hatred in their hearts. The
characters in this play are both hesitant to act and confused in
their own desires: the slave women seek to rid themselves of
masters whom they find tyrannical and cruel; Electra, though

weak in action, fully joins these women in their hatred and is willing to be advised by them in perverting the offering that she brings to Agamemnon's grave; and Orestes is determined to kill Aegisthus and Clytemnestra even though such an act violates one of the primal taboos.[19] Each of these conspirators expects murder to be a cleansing act sanctioned, approved, and protected by Zeus and Apollo. Apollo has given this message clearly to Orestes, and throughout the play all characters trust that Zeus is fully supporting the necessary killing of Clytemnestra. They even interpret this command in terms extremely flattering to Zeus as they equate him with a god who seeks cosmic justice, linking his name with that of the underworld gods with whom Zeus should be working in order that man's idea of perfect justice prevail (394–99, 405–9, 641–51). Yet at the end of the *Choephoroi*, as in the last scenes of the *Agamemnon*, mortals become disillusioned with their conception of Zeus. Orestes is not radiantly triumphant as he stands over the two bodies, but he is careful to justify himself by referring to their deed and producing his evidence, the robe in which Clytemnestra wrapped her husband before striking him; he admits, however, that his victory seems polluted. Almost immediately he sees the Furies and is driven from the stage. The chorus, shuddering and foreseeing unhappiness for Orestes, closes the play wondering if there will be—or can be—any end to the evil and bloodshed in the house. The principle difference between the first two plays in regard to the major themes of justice and punishment lies in the motives of the murderers. Clytemnestra and, to a far lesser extent, Aegisthus are caught in a complex web of motives that allows them to believe they are doing just deeds in joyfully pursuing their own personal desires; but Orestes and his fellow conspirators are reluctant killers. Orestes' crime, however, despite the difference in motivation, is merely another instance of man's savagery toward his fellow humans; consequently the meter of crime and punishment dominates the musical scheme of the *Choephoroi* even in passages where the chorus sings about a higher concept of justice. In addition, the continuing disruption and disorder in the musical form provide indications that the conspirators do not understand their relentless insistence on vengeance.

As the plot of the *Oresteia* develops, the root of the problem confronted by the chorus in the *Agamemnon* becomes clearer. The relationship between mortals and gods is so soured and inadequate that there is no prospect for improvement under the current regime nor is there a chance that humans will work together effectively, especially when their efforts can always be undercut by the interference of a god who operates in accord with the code of conduct tolerated in the reign of a clumsy Zeus. In the *Eumenides* the gods themselves appear onstage to fight out directly the issue that has been veiled in human actions in the earlier plays. The conflict of the trilogy's two major themes is presented not only orally but visually in the confrontation of the Furies and Apollo. When the Pythia comes on stage, she describes the orderly process by which the gods endowed Delphi with sacredness and holiness. But this serene history is soon forgotten when she finds the loathsome Furies asleep in Apollo's sanctuary, and throughout the next several scenes the Furies attack the justice of Zeus, here represented by Apollo. Their pursuit of justice is rugged and uncompromising, yet they perform a necessary function in protecting those who ask for their aid even if only in their limited area of inquiry. Because their interest is not cosmic justice but the proper pursuit of individual punishment against specific crimes within the bloodline, their early songs are appropriately sung to an almost unrelieved iambic meter. They have no doubts about their cause; they sing this music loudly and clearly. But at the end of the play, when they begin to see that they can cooperate with the Olympians in achieving a broader form of justice, they change their meter.

In the *Agamemnon* Zeus tries to play the role of the king god, and mortals want to view him in this role, but events make them lose faith in their high god; they see behind their image a whimsical, mad god who makes vigorous self-assertions under the guise of justice and who uses men to perform ugly deeds. Men have been suffering and dying to save this god. In the new dispensation, however, Zeus will remain the king god but will take a wider view of justice. He will respond to the concerns of the Furies whenever he sees justice achieved by a simple murder for murder within a kinship group. He will take account of Artemis' disgust when she feels that the hare slaughtered by the two eagles is an omen unworthy of the goal of the Trojan expedition. He will try to devise a means of punishment for crimes that also permits mortals to feel that justice is serving all parties. Most important, he will trust men to maintain a court of law in which the community through its representatives will attempt to resolve issues of crime and punishment among themselves.

The fundamental issue affecting interpretation of the *Oresteia* is whether Zeus remains constant while the world learns the advantages of his rule or he develops from the cruel tormentor of mankind, evident in *Prometheus Bound*, to a benevolent aider of society.[20] A major difficulty in discussions on this issue is disagreement on the nature of the Aeschylean chorus, which makes many of the general statements about Zeus's interest in justice. The foregoing analysis of metrical and musical patterning has shown that the chorus is not purely the mouthpiece for the final thoughts of the poet; it is a character within its play. As such, the audience's perception of Zeus's reign is derived from the chorus's statements which are only the reports of men caught up in an evolving action and looking with hope or fear toward the future. That the actual nature of Zeus's governance is different becomes apparent only as the characters in the play evaluate the events in the plot in order to understand Zeus's role more clearly. In fact a common theme in Aeschylean drama is man's difficulty in understanding the gods' intentions; characters—even choruses—can easily misread the signs communicating the gods'

plans. Critics, therefore, should always interpret choral statements in the context of the scene in which they occur.

The musical design of the trilogy adds evidence to the debate about a static or an evolving Zeus by focusing attention
on the necessary reconciliation of the two basic themes at the
trilogy's conclusion: Zeus's justice must embrace proper punishment for a crime. The Oresteian Zeus through his actions
seems always to be willing to seek justice even though the
universe is split among so many varied divinities that not all
can agree on any one solution. At the end of the trilogy Zeus
has gained such a large degree of acquiescence from gods and
men through Athena's device of the court that the universe
itself—gods and mortals—has developed rather than Zeus
alone. The meters of the trilogy imply that this development
does not involve fundamental change to a new posture but
rather an implementation of what men in the first play had
reason to hope could be true. According to this interpretation, Zeus may grow, but no more than all the other participants in the universe, and he need not change in nature.

In terms of the two major themes of the play, both men
and Zeus desire a just universe under the control of a high
god. How else can one explain Zeus's launching of the expedition against Troy and Apollo's pressure on Orestes to kill
his mother? Two factors in the Olympian scheme, however
—the instruction of men through harsh basic lessons and the
achievements of divine ends through the actions of men,
with a concomitant loss of direct control over the means and
degree of punishment—caused excesses and unfairness that
were viewed as new injustices. Consequently the problem of
defining the justice of Zeus lies with the second theme elaborated in the trilogy, that of crime and punishment. Men per-
ceived that specific acts punished specific crimes, and Zeus
often instigated these acts, but neither mortals nor Zeus
could have been pleased with the specific outcomes, especially in the case of Orestes. Orestes's "just" murder of his
mother presents a dilemma in which all participants desire

justice so fervently that they willingly accept the new means of incorporating mortals and gods into the reign of Zeus when Athena offers it. This new covenant requires from all an understanding of the nature of the crime and a recognition of other men's rights and interests in the administration of punishment. Zeus's acceptance of such a device requires no fundamental change; he is only fulfilling his own desire by extending to mortals participation in his reign.[21]

All men will benefit from the reordered reign of Zeus in four main areas. First, men are now given charge of their own affairs, especially in the establishment of the court of the Areopagus. No more will Clytemnestra find herself the only proper and available agent to seek vengeance for the sacrifice of Iphigenia nor will Orestes be driven to a murder that he does not want to commit. Instead, one's fellow citizens will decide the proper punishment for an offense and will accept responsibility for executing the penalty. In this way mankind will achieve independence from the constant intrusion of gods, provided that men administer justice fairly and well. In essence the establishment of the court of the Areopagus symbolizes the emergence of the organization of equal citizens called the city-state from a clan society dominated by a few families, the emergence of a community out of a society of individual units.[22]

Second, there is an increasing trust in the basic competence and goodness of both human and divine natures: the Furies decide to trust Athena as the spokesman for Zeus; Orestes entrusts his fate to the court, to Apollo, and to Athena; and men agree to trust each other's sense of justice in the courtroom process. This increase in the ability to inspire and receive the trust of others is new in the *Eumenides*. Clytemnestra does not trust Agamemnon, and he is portrayed as undeserving of trust, especially in the carpet scene. He professes to have a keen eye for picking those who are trustworthy (*Ag.* 830–44), but he cannot see how treacherous Clytemnestra has been. Clytemnestra's motherly qualities and trust in her son disappear in her first words on hearing that Orestes has returned: "Give me an axe!" (*Ch.* 889). Even Orestes speaks to Apollo with a cynical edge to his words:

Lord Apollo, you know how to avoid injustice, and since you know this, learn also how to avoid negligence. For your power to do right is the strength of your pledge.   (*Eum.* 85–87)

In contrast, trust pervades the end of the trilogy as various characters begin to perform acts of faith in giving up their personal prerogatives in the hope of finding a better system.

Third, the universe at the end of the *Eumenides* does not seem adverse to human progress; there is mutual respect for the rights and privileges of others. At the end of the trilogy men have pledged themselves to communicate freely and frankly with one another in assessing their feelings about rights and wrongs in the courtroom. The minority of voters receives guarantees that the justifiable features of its case will be heard and will even be acknowledged in the possibility of striking a compromise as a solution. Eventually government as a whole will be improved as more and more concerns are incorporated in the judgments made by the court. Earlier in the trilogy, Iphigenia, Agamemnon, Cassandra, Clytemnestra, and Orestes must have felt that their lives were tied to the plan of a god who did not allow them to fulfill their potential or to argue for their individual point of view; rather they were doomed because of their service to a higher force. Often they may have felt that they never understood the will or wishes of that higher force, and surely few of them had any choice about agreeing to serve. But at the end of the trilogy men are left to work out their own fates and to lead their city and their individual lives in directions that they themselves will determine as they attempt to seek justice for the greater portion of their fellow men.

Finally, knowledge of the world is possible. This is probably the most significant improvement in the new dispensation and is the reform on which most of the other changes are predicated. Once words and concepts take on a meaning that men can trust, free and open discussion becomes possible.[23] Artemis never believed that the expedition to Troy was an example of justice, even though men so defined it. Clytemnestra and Agamemnon were compelled to use words of irony or self-deception in order to achieve their goals. The whole key to the *Choephoroi* is concealment: Orestes and Pylades come in disguise and contrive a plan with the chorus and Electra. Words lose all meaning in the dealings between Orestes on the one side and Clytemnestra and Aegisthus on the other, yet by the end of the trilogy words regain their significance. Athena speaks in clear terms to the Furies, and the whole process of the courtroom allows each side to present its own position as well as to criticize the statements of others. Men and gods can now understand their responsibilities in implementing justice, and men have gained an institution in which each person understands his role.

These four elements are the principal characteristics of the new reign of Zeus. They are the signs of an age of community, which has emerged from an age of rampant individualism. Under the new dispensation, the justice of Zeus and the assignment of proper punishment for crime are no longer in conflict. With the brotherhood of humankind and the sovereignty of Zeus as equal foundations for the new society, both parties benefit even if both must work harder to make sure that their vision includes the concerns of as many of their colleagues and co-equals as possible in any decision.[24]

But the *Oresteia*, though highly relevant drama,[25] remains only a play. The new reign of Zeus so joyfully projected at the end of the trilogy is not guaranteed; it is only a hope. The plays presented a mythical story revealing to the audience a promise and hope that was theirs to grasp if they would. The story is simply too fantastic to be construed as an exploration of the actual genesis of the city-state; rather the *Oresteia* presents in concentrated, dramatic form the complexity of issues that underlies a working, active, and effective democracy. The principal belief presented in the trilogy is that people can rule themselves humanely, justly, and confidently provided that they care for and maintain their constitution and its values as prime concerns in every decision they take. But if they do not continually watch over the functioning of their democracy, then there is no guarantee that Zeus will preserve for them this form of government. The myth as told in the Oresteia shows how the forces of individualism will bring themselves to such discredit that men will cry out for reform and will—with the gods' aid—demand sufficient discipline and restraint from themselves that they will deserve and maintain a democratic government. Yet individualism is seductive, and if men do not continually curb their self-assertive tendencies in their day-to-day dealings, there is no barrier strong enough to prevent them from turning to individual activity at the expense of communal government. As they do so, society will increasingly resemble the world that existed at the beginning of the Agamemnon: expeditions and initiatives taken in the hope of serving a greater cause yet in fact favoring only a special group, people driven to seek their own desires because they are protecting themselves by the only means that they control, and a relationship between mortals and their gods so individualized that it cannot be reasonably discussed or even defined—it must be concealed.[26]

This interpretation of the Oresteia is reinforced by the musical scheme of drama. Just as music-making and choral dancing are activities that require a high degree of cooperation among many different individuals, so also the trilogy, as it moves to a highly musical conclusion, represents the growing harmony and cooperation between man and god, god and god, and man and man. Music and content fuse in the harmonious joining of the two themes, the justice of Zeus and the assignment of punishment for crime. At the beginning of the trilogy proper punishment is determined in each individual case without the interests of criminal, judge, jury, and community being involved; people's views of the same act of punishment range from praise for the height of justice to condemnation for the depth of mindless and vindictive revenge. The severity of punishment is either defined as humane, on the grounds that the criminal would be educated, or is seen as a form of sadistic self-satisfaction. The theme of necessary punishment for crime is established at the beginning by the iambic meter. This meter is employed with increasing insistence as justice appears to be increasingly the pursuit of a limited and individualized goal. The iambic remains virtually the exclusive meter of the *Choephoroi* and characterizes the Furies in their hunt for Orestes. Yet there persists the hope of a fitting punishment delivered by the only adequate force in a large and complex world, the high god Zeus, who can view the concerns of individual men in their proper perspective. The old men in the first play fervently believe in the existence of such a god and have a vision of the blissful progress of the universe under such a ruler. They are not naive; they know that there is suffering in the world, but they have a vision of a brighter and more hopeful world to come. They sing about their faith to the lecythion, but events keep revealing inconsistencies in their theory. Finally they must relinquish their belief and confront the inevitable conclusion that their hoped-for god is only a dream. Yet at the end of the trilogy the lecythion reappears in a repeated, clear form as a dominant meter of the final scene. This reappearance does not occur at the simple restatement of a conclusion that was prophesied earlier; rather there is a change in the terms in which mortals view their universe. The old men hoped for a high god who would manage and balance the affairs of the world with sensitivity for men's rights, but the development accomplished in the trilogy surpasses their hopes. Men now will be trusted to manage their own affairs and will receive every encouragement from the high god and his colleagues to maintain justice for the betterment of all.

The attainment of knowledge is the fundamental achievement portrayed in the *Oresteia*: what is actually knowable, how we can come to know it, how we can have confidence that our individual perceptions are in fact knowledge, and what means the world possesses for correcting false belief and modifying inaccurate information so that we can gain knowledge. Of all the characters who roam through the confusing universe of the *Oresteia*, only Cassandra really *knows*. Men assert illusory beliefs as though they were knowledge and adopt courses of action because, in their limited view, these seem correct, expedient, or unavoidable—but they are not certain where wisdom lies in making such choices. Even Zeus and Apollo, Artemis and the Furies do not act in accord with fixed principles, but rather seem only to react to individual crises. Only Cassandra understands the nature of the universe in which she lives; she has learned from experience the crassness of the gods and the self-delusion of men. But Aeschylus realizes the double potential of the universe for a bleak and bloody life of individualism as well as for a more satisfying life of cooperative society. He has a vision of a democratic society which will be sought and can be attained by all men. And it is through his music that he reveals his theme clearly, even though his characters are openly confused or deluded. This element of his dramatic design points consistently toward the goal of a beneficial reign of Zeus. In the course of the trilogy music exposes the infatuation of visionaries, the confusion of lost men, and the delusion of the self-righteous. Music is a truer guide to the beliefs of the singers than are their words. Inevitably, then, any production of the *Oresteia* must join music, dance, and word to convey the full range of meaning in any one scene.

The fusion of oral and visual elements is never more vital than at the end of the *Oresteia*, when the justice of Zeus becomes the justice of mankind. In this culminating the use of music and music-making as both verbal and visual metaphors, the whole populace of Athens is represented in the harmonious song that accompanies the procession of the converted goddesses to their new home on the slopes of the Areopagus. To the insistent dactyls of the exodos both gods and mortals leave the stage to enter the city where all the hopes expressed in the fragile dramatic structure can be realized. Dactyls were the meter used by Calchas at the beginning of the trilogy to prophesy discord. At the play's conclusion Aeschylus' strong musical statement of a favorable society for free mortals and benevolent gods likewise remains only a prophecy, but one that can be just as real as the one heard and lived through by the members of the house of Atreus.

CHAPTER 4

MUSIC IN THE OTHER
AESCHYLEAN PLAYS

The fact that the *Oresteia* is the only fifth-century trilogy to have survived relatively intact has made it both a treasure and an object of unduly reverential awe. The challenge for interpreters is to value the *Oresteia* at its proper worth, but not to be so dazzled by its luster and power that they are blinded to the particular features and idiosyncratic methods of Aeschylus' other plays. Music and music-making were concerns to a greater or lesser extent to all fifth-century Greek tragedians, although among the surviving plays only the *Oresteia* presents so long a dramatic unit containing such a high percentage of choral lyric lines. Aeschylus' other plays contain examples of similar usage of choral music and dance. In itself this evidence is often so slight or ambiguous as to appear meaningless, but viewed in relation to the metrical structure and the form of the choral odes in the *Oresteia*, some individual elements of music-making in the other plays seem either to have served as models for the trilogy or at least to be so similar that they are best understood as features of a consistent Aeschylean style.

PERSIANS

The *Persians* is Aeschylus' only other complete surviving play, and although it is not sufficiently long to permit the clarity or fullness of analysis possible in the *Oresteia*, there are a striking number of similar musical and sound effects incorporated in its design. First there are a number of words describing the music or the sounds that must have been audible during the performance. These call to mind the stage directions *mugmos* and *ogmos* in the *Eumenides* (117–29) or the interjected cries of Cassandra and the chorus in the *Agamemnon* (1072–1172, 1448, 1455, 1489 = 1513, 1538). Yet in the *Persians* these sounds are so fully incorporated into the music of the chorus that they are often repeated in corresponding places in antistrophes and are once attached to a refrain, thus becoming less like random sound and more similar to the structurally important *ailinon* refrain in the parodos of the *Agamemnon*. Such cries are: *oa* at 117 and 122; *otototoi* at 268 and 274; *popoi/totoi* at 550–51 and 560–61; the combination of *pheu*, *ee*, and *oa* corresponding in the stanzas at 568–75 and 576–83; *ee* at 651 and 656; and the full refrain line closing the stanzas at 663 and 671.[1]

Because in the latter three passages (256–89, 532–97, and 623–80) the odes are related to ritual song types, the lament and the invocation, such sounds are probably an indication that the chorus was imitating such music in its dance and song. At line 280 the chorus urges itself to raise a wail for the lost Persians, and this section contains several wailing sounds (257, 268, 270, 274, and 283). At 546–47 the chorus states that it will join the other mourners of Persia, including the queen, in raising a lament. This ode contains several striking musical effects: repetitions that correspond verbally and probably musically at 550–52 and 560–62; and the repeated cries in the second strophic set (568–70 and 576–78). Such repetition and the corresponding interjections are customary in ritual lament.[2] The song at 628, accompanying the libations that Atossa pours on the grave to invoke the dead Darius, is called a hymn (625). At 636 the chorus members refer to some sort of cries which they have been uttering. Because these are not evident in the text, it is probable that there were sound effects, now lost, accompanying the whole invocation scene; some of these may be represented in the interjections at 652 and 657 and reflected in the refrain line at 663 = 671.[3] And, of course, the final recessional scene of the play is a highly musical lament with repeated cries, antiphony, and refrain accompanied by the customary breast-beating, hair-tearing, and robe-ripping by both Xerxes and the chorus (1002–77).[4] These song forms are appropriate to the characterization of the chorus and the situation, and are similar to the elements of hymns, cult songs, and laments included within the musical structure of the *Oresteia*;[5] in the *Persians*, however, these song forms are even more clearly defined by the chorus through explicit introductory statements, the interjection of appropriate sounds, and accompaniment by customary gestures.[6]

In addition to this mimetic function, sound and music characterize the opposition of the Persians and the Greeks.[7] As the messenger reports the disaster at Salamis, the Greeks are marked in many ways within his narrative as the winners:[8] god was against the Persians and for the Athenians, Xerxes was duped by the clever Greeks, and his men were driven to battle in fear of his dire threats, but the Greeks fight willingly (345–47, 355–63, and 369–73). But this contrast between the two sides is probably at its clearest in the description of the differing sounds from each army (384–432, 462–71). First, the Greeks greet the dawn with a loud cry, which the surrounding lands echo like a song of triumph. The messenger calls this cry a paean, the song Greeks sing rushing eagerly into battle accompanied by the blast of the trumpet. His description culminates in the words of the Greek battle shout:

> Children of Greece, go forth! Free your country, free your children, your wives, the shrines of your ancestral gods and the tombs of your fathers. Now is the battle for all.   (402–05)

From the Persians there is no music or organized chanting, only a babble of Persian speech that eventually modulates to the moans and shrieks of the dying as the night comes on. Xerxes makes no comment; he only groans.[9] Even when the Greeks speak a stream of incoherent words, a *rothos* like the Persians, they do it in accord and are successful in their attack (462). Such descriptions are a characterizing technique familiar from the *Oresteia*; the House of Atreus hosts a reveling band that sings its own discordant songs, Cassandra sings like a poor nightingale and later is reported to have sung her swan's song, the cries of victor and vanquished stand out clearly in the city of Troy (1186–93, 1140–45, 1444–46, and 321–25).

This one-act play is so much shorter than the *Oresteia* that it is difficult to assert strongly that there is a developing scheme in the progression of meters. There does seem to be, however, a thematic connection with two specific meters, which can be suggested because there is a clarity of metrical forms similar to that in the *Oresteia*.[10] The lyrics of the par-odos consist almost entirely of drumming ionics, which then fade to the lecythion mixed with some iambics at the close. It is generally assumed that the ionic was an oriental meter, which was employed heavily in the entrance song because Aeschylus wanted to make his audience aware that the play was set in the Persian court.[11] In later odes ionic meters appear sporadically,[12] and costumes and Persian words give a non-Greek coloration throughout the play. The iambic, however, is the predominant meter in which the chorus laments the ex-isting woes of Persia. When the messenger enters with the unexpected bad news of the Persian defeat (249), the chorus interjects a series of short lamenting stanzas in iambics, simi-lar to the meter of the final section of the kommos closing the play after Xerxes has told the chorus in detail of the losses to Persia. The first stasimon (548–97) also contains a large por-tion of iambic, appropriate for a lament; but when the chorus turns to the political implications of the defeat at Salamis in the final two stanzas, it employs an insistent dactylic meter. The invocation ode (634–80) seems a song of high musical coloration because of the repeated interjections and refrain line mentioned above, but it is difficult to find any firm direc-tion in the variety of meters contained in the song.[13] The in-tensity and directness of the chorus increase throughout this ode but lead to no obvious concluding summary or general-ization. As the elders shift their address from the gods to the

king, begin to bewail their personal losses, and express open
affection for Darius, the tone of their appeal becomes noticeably more urgent. Thus as the meters refuse to settle on any
one strongly asserted pattern, the song develops an ever
more intense tone until the ghost of the king suddenly appears, interrupting their music. In contrast, the third stasimon (852–907), in which the chorus celebrates the military
and political successes of Darius, is largely dactylic, appropriately echoing both the meter and political content at the end
of the first stasimon. The final kommos (931–1077) begins
with a variety of meters but at line 1002 settles on a basic iambic meter, similar to the meter of the first stasimon, as the
chorus laments the Persian dead. Thus in both the iambic and
dactylic meter there seems to be a thematic association with
laments and political concerns respectively; this alignment is
similar to the thematic associations of the iambic and trochaic
meters in the *Oresteia*, but there is not the development of
music used for the inappropriate song nor a resolution of either theme. The single play is really too short for such development, and because there is no conclusion on a note of harmonious and joyful reconciliation, there is no occasion to
resolve the meters. Rather at the end of the play the Persian
elders are so exhausted or overcome with mourning that they
cannot continue a formal ode and they leave the stage with
cries of unorganized mourning. Such a conclusion strengthens the impression of Persia's debilitating disorder—both political and theological—and consequent decline.

Departures from the expected symmetry in musical form
reinforce this impression of increasing disorder. The mesode
in the parodos has remained an obstinate problem for scholars who seek to regularize it by dividing it into strophic
stanzas or to locate it after line 114; it probably should be retained in its traditional position, where it not only fits better
syntactically but also portrays the confidence of the chorus,
which finds no reason for worry even when the queen tells
them her frightening dream.[14] This mesode provides the
theological basis for the expedition to Greece. It is ironic that

a god's deceptive seduction has enticed the Persians into undertaking and supporting an invasion that will be destructive for them, but, as they state, it is impossible for a man to escape from such a snare without injury. The snare, the trap, and the net too high for leaping recur in the *Oresteia* as the devices of justice, as does the old men's attempt to fool themselves into thinking that such rules apply to others but not to them.[15] These Persians are devoted and patriotic; yet even though they see nothing wrong with their theory, the events of the play will compel them to learn a harsh lesson. By placing this theological section in a mesode, or in a strophe without the expected antistrophe, Aeschylus signals to his audience that there is something incomplete or unsettling in the chorus' thought at this point.[16] The audience, knowing the result of the war, would realize how ironic the chorus's words are—and how characteristic of Persian pride.

Such disappointed expectation in formal structure occurs three more times in the play. The first provides a striking stage effect: the ghost of Darius rises from his tomb, and with a dignified address cuts the chorus off in the midst of its catalogue of woes (681).[17] The elders fall speechless from awe and fear before a ghost and a king who in life inspired reverence by his very being. But a further reason for this epode is the mirroring scene created at the end of the next choral ode (852–907), where the chorus sings of the glories of Persia under Darius until it is interrupted by Xerxes' entrance. Darius rose in the trappings of a monarch; Xerxes is in rags. Whereas Darius has come to be of service, Xerxes enters despairing because he has failed the Persians and himself. This intentional contrast between the two entrances is complete, and the similarity of an abrupt termination of the chorus's song when Xerxes appears adds a strong reminder of the old king's entrance.[18] The achievement of reminiscence by the unexpected disruption of a musical form is further developed in the *Oresteia* when the entrance of Orestes standing over his victims recalls the similar entrance of Clytemnestra in the *Agamemnon*. In the first play Clytemnestra enters to interrupt the disjointed suggestions of the broken chorus; in the *Choephoroi* Orestes enters before the chorus has a chance to repeat the ephymnion (*Ag.* 1372 and *Cho.* 972).[19] The conclusion of the *Persians* also employs a device that Aeschylus uses in an extreme form at the end of the *Agamemnon*. There the chorus leaves with no music; here the chorus shares strophes with Xerxes in joint lamentation. But its lines become shorter as the song becomes increasingly antiphonal, and the words turn more to repetitive imitations of a wailing lament. Given the lack of content in the elders' words and the grief that drives them into hysterics of mourning, it is fitting that their song ends abruptly with an epode, a stanza with no balancing antistrophe. It is not a moment to be crowned with a normalizing, orderly exit song; the lyric simply ends as the mourners escort Xerxes offstage with dismal laments, the last music heard by the audience.[20]

The *Persians*, which Aeschylus wrote about halfway through his career, thus contains signs that he was already working on ideas for musical forms that became important organizing elements in the more developed musical design of the *Oresteia*.

SEVEN AGAINST THEBES

A production of the *Seven against Thebes* requires careful attention to sound and music. The play begins with the sounds of war and the disorganized music of frightened women and concludes with a carefully structured lament; war and its confusion are gone and the sorrowing for lost men takes their place.

A few direct references to musical forms probably give a clue to the tone to be sought in staging, but these occur only late in the play. At line 825, after the chorus openly wonders whether it should raise a shout of triumph or sing a lament, it settles on a song for a tomb, called an unfortunate song of the spear (835–39). While the women watch the entrance of Antigone and Ismene, they are singing the hymn of the

Erinys and the hateful paean of Death (866–70). This song contains several cries of lament (875, 881, 892–93). At the end of this long lament the women report that the family curse has raised the shrill song of triumph because it has won the war (953–55). In this ode the women perform a ritual lament over the bodies of Eteocles and Polyneices,[21] but within the formal elements of the lament they metaphorically define the events of the play in musical terms.[22] Outside this one ode there is little explicit or implicit allusion to song forms,[23] but the strong statement here that the history of the house can be seen as an extended song is an important clue to the correct interpretation of the musical forms throughout the play.

Music has a general function in heightening contrasts between characters. The play opens with a statesmanlike address by the king, Eteocles, to his subjects urging them to be of good cheer and courage in defending Thebes. A scout enters, gives his report of the enemy's activities outside the walls, and then departs to continue surveillance as Eteocles prays for victory for his city. Such an opening shows the king in control, the general directing his troops, the chief priest of the town in communication with the gods—all is in order. But this serenity is instantly undercut by the chaotic entrance of the women, who pour onto the stage panicked and despairing. They can hear the noise of enemy troops outside and see the dust raised by the enemy army. They urgently beg their gods for help even though Eteocles is there watching—and for him their despondency is a dispiriting sight. The contrast is between Eteocles, continually called the helmsman of the ship, and the women, who fear that despite his preparation and strategy Thebes will be destroyed if the gods do not take an active role in the coming battle. And, of course, in this difference lies the key to the play. Eteocles would like nothing better than to be the successful general, but he will discover that the gods are controlling his fate.[24] He is under the curse pronounced by Oedipus, and even though he carefully matches his champions to the enemy warriors at six of the seven gates, he finds that he has been acting to fulfill the curse when he

must himself go to the seventh gate.[25] This contrast in attitude is immediately evident through the initial music of the
chorus. The normal entering chorus would have anapaests
followed by strophic song or would simply enter to strophic
lyric; these women sing no strophes as they enter and use a
predominantly dochmiac meter, which accompanies frenzied
and emotional movements.[26] They use a great many words
for the sounds outside the wall that motivate their frantic entrance: *hoploktyp'*, *boan*, *bremei*, *orotypou*, *ktypon* (twice), *pa-
tagos* (83, 84, 85, 86, 100, and 103). Thus sounds of warfare
from offstage break into the entrance song of the women,
which may be sung by sections of the chorus rather than the
usual united, orderly entrance songs most clearly seen in the
Persians, the *Suppliants*, the *Agamemnon*, and the *Choephoroi*.[27] This characterizing use of music is seen later in the
opening of the *Eumenides*, where the sleeping Furies grunt
and groan before the confused waking song (117–77).

The *Seven against Thebes* does not seem to develop its
themes through an association with specific meters; rather
disorder in sound and form continues to be contrasted with
order, which is portrayed in unified and balanced choral
song. After the initial characterization of the chorus through
their stormy entrance, the women begin strophic song for a
prayer to the gods (109–80); even though the noise of the
siege forces is sufficiently loud to unsettle the women in the
second strophic pair (149–65), they continue in strophic
stanzas. Then Eteocles tries to calm them by asserting his authority. He speaks as they sing in iambo-dochmiacs, the same
meter as the opening of the entrance song, but now they respond in short balanced strophes; eventually he leads them to
spoken dialogue in stichomythia and finally to a formal choral ode in meters more typical of strophic lyric.[28] This modulation from disorder to increasing order and reasonableness is
the reverse of the effect created in the Cassandra scene, where
the frenzied singer leads speakers to song. The development
in musical form makes clear Eteocles' success in curbing the

frenzy of the women and in bringing them to peaceful behavior despite the fearful words that they persist in speaking.[29]

In the long shield scene the chorus plays a formal role in separating the sections in which champion is paired with challenger. Six times they sing a five-line comment in a strophe/antistrophe structure after each choice of Eteocles. But when their king chooses to accept the role to which the curse has led him, they do not sing but speak in iambics to mark the beginning of a new action;[30] the switch in the direction of the play at this moment is marked by absence of another strophe. Eteocles can no longer play the role of general for the city and accepts his individual role as the son of Oedipus. As the women argue against his decision their musical form closely repeats that of the first scene of the play (78–368):

Song with signs of disorder[31] or unexpected speech by emotional chorus	(78–180, 677–82)
Epirrhema with Eteocles speaking three-line statements and the chorus responding in balanced strophes (iambo-dochmiac)	(203–44, 686–711)[32·]
Stichomythia	(245–63, 712–19)
Exit of Eteocles	(286, 719)
Ode with no signs of disorder in form	(287–368; 720–91)[33]

Thus the two major themes of the play are reinforced through musical form in the scenes surrounding the shield scene. The first part of the play, lines 1–652, shows the conduct of a king in ordering his city. His thoughts are concerned with events here and now as he maneuvers to see that his troops win the battle. In the second part of the play (653–791) the characters look to the past as they are forced to acknowledge the living force of the curse. But the two parts are really all the same action although the characters themselves are never aware of this fact until too late:[34] Eteocles in calming the women and seeking to organize the war effort is in fact fulfilling the curse by trapping himself in his own war plans. The identity of these seemingly separate actions is reflected in the musical form, which is repeated even though the subject matter of the play seems to be developing in a cause-and-effect, linear way. The formal lyric closing each section summarizes that part of the play and allows time for a new action offstage that will start off the next scene: in the first ode (287–368) the women state their fear of the impending invasion and plead for the gods' aid; the second ode (720–91) analyzes events from the distant past leading to the fate that their king may suffer.

It is appropriate that the messenger enter immediately—almost brusquely—as the surprising fulfillment of their worst fears: "I am afraid that a swift-moving Erinys may accomplish its goals" (790–91). His unannounced, unprepared for entrance represents that quick and decisive working of the Erinys.[35] Such will be the dismaying experience of the chorus in the *Agamemnon*, which expresses hope for the future only to have it dashed immediately by the death cries of Agamemnon (1331–47); and similar is the distress of the chorus in the *Persians*, which sings of the former glories of Persia under Darius immediately before being interrupted by the entrance of Xerxes in rags (852–906).

The final section of the *Seven against Thebes* begins with the long and complex lament mentioned earlier (822–1004); in this section the continuing juxtaposition of order and disorder in musical forms makes visible onstage the problems that confront the city of Thebes at the end of the play. The women begin to sing a formal ode with introductory anapaests in which they wonder whether they should shout out for joy or lament their fallen kings. They decide to mourn for the kings and have completed two strophic stanzas in an iambic meter reminiscent of the second stasimon (720–91) when they see the procession bearing the two bodies coming onstage (848–60).[36] The entrance of the procession prevents the chorus from continuing in strophic stanzas as would be normal given the length of formal laments elsewhere. The appearance of two new characters, Antigone and Ismene, begins the final action of the play (861); the interruption of the strophic song of the chorus, the astrophic lyric iambics (848–60), the new anapaestic introduction to accompany the processional entrance of the sisters (861–74), and the announcement of a more formal lament (863–65) are all indications of a new beginning to its song.[37] When the women finish the ode, the sisters take up the antiphonal lament as the procession begins to move offstage; but suddenly the herald interrupts, creating another nonstrophic conclusion to their lyric, canceling their plans and sending disorder into the conclusion of the play. Antigone refuses to obey the decree of the city councillors. The chorus sings one section together as all its members wonder what course to take now; then they split into two groups, each following one of the sisters as they go to separate burials. This type of split ending is seen again in the exodos of the *Suppliants*, and the device of the split chorus occurs several times in the *Oresteia*—all in places where the words indicate a lack of concerted direction in the action of the group (as at *Ag.* 475–87 and 1348–71, *Eum.* 140–77 and 245–75).[38]

Thus the chorus of Theban women begins a formal lament but is interrupted and must start over; Antigone and Ismene are similarly interrupted by the entrance of a new character. In this part of the play singers question what they should do, make up their minds, and then are blocked; it seems difficult to complete a formal ode. In addition, the entire final third of the *Seven against Thebes* (792–1078) is built around a reversal of the basic musical pattern that has organized the action twice before in the play:

Formal ode followed by entrance of messenger/herald	(875–1004; cf. 286–368, 720–91)
Stichomythia	(1042–53; cf. 245–63, 712–19)
Disordered song	(1054–78; cf. 78–180, 677–82)

This parallel structure is not precise, for it lacks the epir-rhematic section, but in broad terms the chorus, which has twice begun with disordered music at a moment of crisis and has then moved to a formal song, now begins with a formal lamentation ode and concludes in an irreconcilable confrontation between the divided citizens of Thebes.[39] The occurrence of such a split at the end of the *Suppliants* is acceptable to critics because it leads to another play within the same trilogy, but here the effect is more striking and difficult because there is no unified ode to end the whole trilogy; this final play introduces a chorus in disarray and ends with a new crisis causing further disorder. In the first and second sections of the play, musical form frames the stages in the development of dramatic themes. At the beginning of each section the chorus of women is unsettled by threats to their city and its ruler, but by talk Eteocles reduces their frenzy to a calmer state. They close each section accepting, if not understanding, the decision that Eteocles has made and has just left the stage to execute; the sign of this more reflective attitude toward the developing crises is the women's ability to sing a formally balanced strophic ode. Thus twice musical form follows, enhances, and frames the action by directing the audience's attention to the movement from disorder to order in the emotions of the characters and the potential of the situations. But the poet reverses this pattern in his musical design as he looks forward to the continuing tragedy of Thebes, the city whose fortune is repeatedly dominated by the strong-willed descendants of Labdacus.[40] And, as the chorus makes clear in its lament (822–47), the history of the house is being told through contrasting musical forms.

Such repetition of musical forms to identify contrasting scenes occurs at the parallel interruptions of strophic odes by Darius and Xerxes in the *Persians*. The abrupt and unprepared entrances of characters like the messenger and the herald are familiar from the same scenes. In addition, the contrast of music with speech to convey the emotions of contrasting characters is found in the scene between the messenger and the chorus in the *Persians* (249–89). There the scene does not seem to lead to further musical development, but Aeschylus may have come to realize the potential in this type of epirrhema as an element in a larger musical movement. Of course, in a study of dramatic style it is compelling that all of these elements in the design of musical form are found in more complex configurations in the *Oresteia*, especially in the interruptions of choral song by Clytemnestra and in the Cassandra scene.

SUPPLIANTS

The *Suppliants* has been discovered to have a surprising number of parallels to the *Oresteia*, though seemingly not in the area of music and music-making.[41] Superficially it displays several typically Aeschylean musical features. There are three odes that are stated to be song forms: the first, second, and third stasima are introduced as prayers (521, 625–29, and 772–73). There is an extended epirrhematic section and a kommos, forms that also appear in the scene with Cassandra, in the chorus's debate with Clytemnestra, in the middle of the *Choephoroi*, and in the Furies' angry dispute with Athena; in addition, there is a unifying coda section in glyconic/pherecratean meter at the close of a series of three strophic pairs (630–97), a structure found in the first stasimon of the *Agamemnon*. But there appears to be no serious interest in developing music to accompany or frame principal themes, actions, or metaphors of the drama.[42] In fact there are relatively few references to music or musical form. It may be that the predominant role of the chorus in this play encourages Aeschylus to focus the imagery and theatrical devices on areas other than music-making. It is undoubtedly easier to have the chorus provide commentary through music when individual actors are carrying the plot.[43] One could also speculate that the music in this play is quite normal in order to prepare for more striking effects when the chorus discovers its trust in Zeus to be overconfident and its own reasoning inadequate in the later two plays of the trilogy.[44] With only the first act of the trilogy extant, it is difficult to define the author's method of organizing his last two acts, but it does appear that this play is not as heavily involved in adaptations of musical form and coordination of theme and music as the other dramas of Aeschylus.

Although musical form does not seem to develop in any organic way throughout the play, there are some variations on tradition that enrich their particular scenes. The parodos is a highly formal entrance song beginning with anapaests, the normal "marching" meter that introduces the orderly entrances of the *Persians* and the *Agamemnon*. Such an opening is appropriate for the maidens, who, though fugitives, are not actually being chased onstage by their pursuers but are only gathering themselves after debarkation for the next phase of their plan. They even have the time to sing a long balanced strophic song once they have arrived onstage.[45] Yet at the end of the last three strophic pairs they add ephymnia. Probably such additions are to be viewed as enhancements to the ordering power of the chorus as they sing an ambitious song, but the manuscript gives no indication that the final ephymnion was repeated even though most editors repeat it in the text.[46] Each of the other ephymnia, even when repeated, follows the sense of the preceding stanza. After the final strophe containing their threat to kill themselves, they describe how hated they feel in fleeing Hera's continuing vengeance against Io and her descendants. In the final antistrophe they close with a forceful prayer, calling upon Zeus not to abandon them because he would then be deserting his own progeny and would be condemned as an unjust god. To repeat their words about Hera's anger at this point does not suit the context either emotionally or in terms of their characterization, which stresses trust in Zeus's protection. The only argument supporting the repetition of the last ephymnion is the need for symmetry once this form has been established for the audience in the previous strophic pairs; but the *Agamemnon* and *Choephoroi* offer examples of this disappointment of expectation where the poet uses musical form to indicate to his audience that some element in the words and situation is not quite right.[47] In this case the maidens' trust in Zeus will prove to be misguided when they are forced into marriage in the second play. In addition, it has been noted that the extremism that leads them to misinterpret the will of Zeus is reinforced in the ambiguity of their language and of the imagery used throughout the play;[48] and, of course, this point is made even more forcefully when the chorus splits into two groups at the end of the play in disagreement about marriage.[49] But these are the only two indications through musical form that the words and hopes of the chorus are excessive. All their other music is quite precisely balanced and fulfills the formal expectations of the audience.

The extended epirrhematic scene in this play moves from song to speech, as opposed to the static characterization through song versus speech in the *Persians*. In the first scene (335–489) the maidens attempt to convince Pelasgus that he should offer them protection. The scene begins with stichomythia, then the chorus sings combined iambic and dochmiac in six paired stanzas while the king answers each of five times in five iambic trimeter lines. This balance is interrupted when Pelasgus gives his "diver" speech stressing the need for correct judgment in response to their insistence on justice (407–17). Then the maidens turn to two strophic pairs containing their maximum threat: dragged from the altars they will leave the king and his children a heavy penalty to pay for neglecting the just appeal of suppliants. In response the king can only assure them that he appreciates the dimensions of the dilemma and will convey the full implications of any decision to his townspeople. Finally there is a sharp exchange in stichomythia in which the suppliants threaten to hang themselves upon the gods' statues if they are not protected—and this seems to resolve Pelasgus to accept the women.

This is a tightly reasoned scene.[50] The king speaks in moderate terms as he debates with himself the proper course of action; the women do not rouse him to hysterics or to temper—nor is that their intent. They do, however, bring the full pressure of the situation to bear upon him by amplifying their threat to him and to the town as they sing increasingly intense and formal musical passages. The arguments they offer depend upon long-term considerations of human pity, Zeus's command that men will protect suppliants, and the king's responsibility to maintain the justice of Zeus. The king's responses are more conditioned by practical considerations of potential war, the desire to gain general support for a decision, the need for understanding the legality of the Egyptians' demands, and the king's obligation to protect his people and state. The basic positions are stated in the first section of stichomythia: the chorus asks for asylum on the basis of Zeus's justice, and Pelasgus acknowledges the possibility of war if he does not assess correctly the claims on either side of the case. As the chorus moves into individual strophic stanzas its language becomes more poetic, its sentences longer, and its demands more earnestly stated and therefore more pressing. Pelasgus feels increasingly cornered as he tries to explain the difficulties of their request. When he expresses only good wishes, they ask for justice; but justice will be a public pursuit if war comes, and he insists on consulting with the people. The suppliants assure him that no king need be so noncommittal and advise him to avoid pollution; they continue to stress their inability to receive equitable or reasonable treatment from the Egyptians and press for a decision in accord with justice. Such pressure causes the king to call out in an impassioned appeal for clear vision on behalf of his city; in so doing he breaks the balanced form of the scene (407–17). But this call for understanding only spurs the suppliants to push their case harder in a strophic ode in which they raise their language of ethical concern and potential sacrilege to its highest point yet in the debate: they have been driven out impiously, the Egyptians threaten the use of force and display their *hybris*. Justice will be violated if they are hauled by the hair from the gods' altars, and the citizens of Argos will have to pay a price to enforce justice either now or later. And now the king sees that he cannot avoid pain for himself or for his people; he can only hope that all will turn out well. He has come to realize the full extent of the threat that these dangerous suppliants press upon him. To complete his thinking the women of the chorus resort to stichomythia for one brief passage to make clear to the king that they will hang themselves on the gods' statues if he refuses aid.

This is not a scene of frenzy or excitement; it is an intensely rational scene of increasing pressure. It is appropriate that the suppliants' musical forms become longer and their appeal more forceful as they insist that the king recognize the full implications of their petition; and it is equally appropriate that the king not sing in response to them. The contrast of music and speech shows the opposition of the two sides through dramatic form. But the return to speech and the closing of the scene by a dialogue with Danaus is a sign that Pelasgus, who now understands the problem that confronts him, sees clearly the necessity of dealing with it.[51] In this scene he is portrayed as the reasonable and responsible king who will protect the women later in the play. Music is thus used in this scene as a reinforcement to the increasing levels of the chorus's argumentation against a king who never sings and ends the scene on the level of speech. It is a scene of persuasion and understanding with music appearing as an accompaniment to the verbal progress of the scene rather than leading a life of its own throughout the rest of the drama.

In the kommos between the Egyptian herald and the chorus music also reinforces the stage action but again develops no continuing thematic importance. In this scene (825–951) the herald tries to lead the chorus to speech from its excited music but is sharply interrupted and made to face the reasoned force of Pelasgus. The herald comes onstage to rush the maidens away with little grammar and much repeated emotionalism. Although his precise words are hard to determine, he does not seem to sing strophes but rather assembles a mixture of meters for his brusque commands and threats. At line 872 he begins iambic speech and his grammar becomes clearer (possibly Aeschylus feels that the audience has come to know his dialect well enough that he can return this character to normal Greek speech) as he simply states the plain facts for the women: they will not escape; they will be dragged to the ships if necessary, for he does not respect the statues of their gods; and they will be taken back to Egypt. Previously, when the herald entered, the chorus interrupted its prayer to Zeus to cry out in what can only be called an astrophic stanza. The effect of this chaotic cry is similar to that of the broken chorus in the *Agamemnon* when the death cries of Agamemnon reduce the chorus to confusion. But the suppliants have heard the strong vote of the people, have seen their father rush after aid, and have the statues of the gods to trust in. They quickly unite to sing a series of strophic stanzas in reply to the herald, calling down destruction on him and the Egyptians. When he turns to speech, they turn to formally balanced cries for help from the gods and Pelasgus but augment their musical form with a repeated ephymnion attached to their third strophe and antistrophe. This form has been used in the parodos to create a sense of order that is then broken, and it is more extensively employed in the *Oresteia*. Here the chorus begins to sing a form that implies a high degree of unity and order. When at 903–10 the herald begins to lay hands on one of the maidens, they start to sing in lyric iambics, but he interrupts; they begin again in the same meter and are again interrupted by the herald, who now threatens to drag them away.[52] They remain faithful to balancing their music while the herald seeks to stifle their song through his rough interruptions and responses.

This scene does move from song to speech—but here abruptly—with the entrance of Pelasgus. He and the herald exchange blunt lines in stichomythia that ends the maidens' need for song and quiets the harsh threats of the herald. The musical direction of the scene thus stresses the helpless horror as well as the concordant faith of the suppliants but also shows the power of Pelasgus as a forceful and reasonable king who is able to look out for the well-being of his people. Although this is also a musical scene, like the earlier one it expresses no greater theme beyond the dramatization of Pelasgus opposing the Egyptians' threat of force.

If there is any larger musical effect identifiable in this play, it may be found in the song of blessing for Argos at 625–709. The suppliants ask that no plague come upon the city "arming an Ares who is without chorus and without lute, the father of tears—a battle cry among the people" (678–82). Rather they pray for singers to provide "songs of blessing at the altars" and that "a chant accompanied by a harp come from holy mouths" (694–97). The chorus is the protagonist in this play, and appropriately much of the play is music. The women are coming to a new land with hopes for a different life; many of their odes are prayers, and it may be that the great amount of ordered music-making is to be seen as the appropriate accompaniment for the striving of the fugitive. Their role as suppliants provides appropriate motivation for group singing and dancing—as the chorus says in its ode: prayers for peace and prosperity should call forth sounds of praise from holy mouths. But there is also the wish to avoid the strife that ruins choral music.[53] Only slight signs of coming disagreement are present in the parodos and in the momentary splitting of the chorus in the exodos. None of the musical effects identified in the play is without parallel elsewhere in Aeschylean drama, but their slightness and subtlety probably testify to the fact that musical variation does not play the major role that it does in the other plays, especially in the *Oresteia*.

PROMETHEUS BOUND

It is difficult to assess the musical design of the *Prometheus Bound* because the evidence seems to point simultaneously in two directions.[54] Certain features of its musical structure have quite precise parallels in Aeschylus' other plays; other musical elements are unique in the surviving plays—but then, so are the short anapaestic sections that serve as surrogates for a full ode in the last half of the *Choephoroi* or the multiscened opening of the *Eumenides*. In many ways the *Prometheus Bound* is an anomaly, and the musical design of the play provides no exception.[55]

First, there are scarcely any words for music or sound and no use of traditional musical forms such as prayers, cult songs, or laments, in the design or motivation of the choral odes. Indeed, there is little direct motivation of the songs of the chorus that would be similar to the Persians' announcement of their lament or Atossa's encouragement of the chorus to join in the invocation (*Pers.* 546–47 and 619–22). The Oceanid chorus lets each scene end and then fills in with a song that, though not irrelevant to the scene, provides only general comment and does not aid the development of the dramatic themes.[56] The chorus does not even seem to be very aware of its music. Only at line 553–60 does it acknowledge that its current song is different from its previous marriage song.[57]

The lyric meters of the chorus are not diverse, being overwhelmingly iambic, dactylo-epitrite, choriambic, or anapaestic, and these often in unvaried repetition.[58] Given that these account for about 80 percent of the choral meter in the play,[59] it is clear that there is no other play as uninspired in the choice of meters except the *Choephoroi*; but in the latter the insistence on iambic meter is an element in the whole musical movement of the trilogy.[60] Such could also be the case here, but evidence about the other plays of the trilogy is so scanty that no formal statement can be made about the larger musical structure.

The first musical moment is the monody of Prometheus, which is sung to an odd mixture of anapaests and iambics with a small lyric inset at lines 114–17.[61] Not only is it unusual to have a character alone onstage for such a long time, but there is no Aeschylean precedent for a solo monody by a main character. The watchman and the Pythia are both onstage alone, but they do not sing and are certainly not major characters. Yet there is good dramatic motivation for each of these three characters to be alone, and both the watchman and Prometheus are eager to stress how long and lonely their vigils are.[62] And even though there are no parallels for the monody of Prometheus, the astrophic structure of the long song may be appropriate for the dismal condition of the lonely sufferer, who does not seek traditional strophic form for his words.

Then the chorus of Oceanids enters with no anapaests; they sing strophes between which Prometheus interjects stanzas of anapaests. Again there is no parallel for this type of entrance in Aeschylus.[63] Furthermore, the only Aeschylean parallels for the form of strophic lyric with interjected anapaests occur when Clytemnestra and Athena separately converse with the chorus in the *Oresteia* (*Ag.* 1448–1576 and *Eum.* 916–1020). There are, however, many ways in which these two major characters should be contrasted, and the repetition of musical form in the *Eumenides* serves to remind the audience of Clytemnestra's attempts at restoring order in the *Agamemnon*; but in the *Prometheus Bound* there is no indication of an impending contrast or a special design in musical effect. The basic issue is whether this passage is built on the basis of a traditional form for dialogue otherwise not present in Aeschylean drama or whether there is some unknown design at work.[64] At the very least, the form is unusual for Aeschylus, especially in the position normally occupied by the parodos.

But there are also features that are quite normal for the musical style of Aeschylus. For example, in the middle of each of the other surviving plays there is a perfectly symmetrical ode even though there are dislocations in the odes surrounding it. It is as though Aeschylus wanted to remind his audience in the middle of a play there is a norm from which the other odes are deviations. In addition, this ode divides the action into appropriate major sections. In the *Persians* a highly ordered ode of lamentation separates the messenger scene from the invocation of Darius and the entrance of Xerxes (532–97); in the *Seven* the preparation for battle and the selection of defenders are divided from the results of the battle by an equally symmetrical ode (720–91); in the *Suppliants* the prayer for Argos separates the obtaining of Argive aid from the arrival of the Egyptians (625–709); in the *Agamemnon* such an ode stands between the scenes preparatory to Agamemnon's entrance into the palace and the scenes leading to the murder (975–1034); in the *Choephoroi* the plotting section is separated from the execution of the plan by this type of ode (585–651); and in the *Eumenides* this ode (490–565) marks the beginning of the trial scene. In the *Prometheus Bound* such an ode at 526–60 separates the opening scenes with Prometheus, Oceanus, and the chorus from those with Io and Hermes.[65] Given that all other odes in the play show untraditional elements—epodic endings (397–435 and 887–907),[66] astrophic stanzas (687–95), and unprecedented forms (128–192)—there is arguable need for one ode representing the normal choral form in a world that is itself confused and unbalanced. But because the plot of the *Prometheus Bound* is only a series of visitations, no one of which causes the next, it is difficult to identify a development that is naturally composed of two parts. Thus the existence of such an ode is normal in an Aeschylean play, but the position of the ode is difficult to parallel elsewhere because the play itself is so anomalous in structure.

The other choral odes of the play all show signs of disorder—but then, rebellion and cosmic disorder are the subjects of the play. Both the first and the last stasima (397–435 and 887–906) close with an epode, but only the latter can be seen as parallel to previous Aeschylean epodes. Darius, Xerxes, the herald in the *Seven against Thebes*, and Clytemnestra all interrupt the traditional form of choral music, leaving an astrophic close. Similarly, at line 907 Prometheus does echo the final words of the chorus and can be portrayed as interrupting their song in order to correct their assertion of Zeus's irresistible and terrible power.[67] But at line 436 Prometheus opens the scene by offering excuses for his long silence, yet the epode form precedes. Is this a weak imitation of an Aeschylean form?[68] Or is it the epode form employed as a sign of the disorder rampant in the play? If so, it would be similar in its mechanical functioning to the odd astrophic lyric at 687–95, which is equally unparalleled in Aeschylean form.[69] Probably there is no answer to these questions, but it should at least be noted that the form of the music in this play, though in some cases similar to Aeschylean usage, often diverges from Aeschylus' practice in his earlier dramas.

In the Io scene there is a move from disorderly song to speech as this tortured sufferer is made to confront the long wandering before her but is also told of the hopeful resolution that will reward her toils. Her music moves jerkily from anapaests to astrophic iambics, and from this introduction to strophic dochmiacs, which modulate to lyric iambics between the speeches of Prometheus. Then she begins to speak in iambics with Prometheus. Scenes moving from song to speech occur in the *Seven*, the *Suppliants*, and the *Agamemnon*, but in those passages there are strong elements of the continuing dramatic theme to which the form is calling special attention. Here, because Io is being brought onstage only for one scene as another sufferer, the musical development presents the degree of her suffering rather than her character, and the effect is not further developed in the play. Perhaps this musical form is used thematically to call attention to the calming role of Prometheus' foresight and assurance, but only an examination of scenes in the missing plays of the trilogy would reveal whether this motif returns in the reconciliation between Zeus and Prometheus. In the Io scene alone the device seems shallow. When Io leaves the stage, she departs to cries, screams, and lyric anapaests. The movement from song to speech to song is appropriate, for Prometheus' counsel has really provided no remedy for her pains.

There is, however, a parallel to this musical form at the end of the play. First, the chorus bursts out with an astrophic, emotional outcry at 687–95. When Io leaves, the Oceanids sing a formal ode but then again lose their ability to make music as the destruction wrought by the earthquake provides the sound effects at the end of the play. The use of a nonmusi-

cal ending occurs also in the *Agamemnon* and has a similar
motivation here: before the crude show of force, there is not
much that orderly group singing and dancing can appropriately celebrate. The musical cycle of disorder-order-disorder,
which separately underlies the scenes with Io and the chorus,
is used in the musical design at the end of the *Seven against
Thebes*, although there the patterns are kept discrete, not interlocked as in the *Prometheus Bound*:

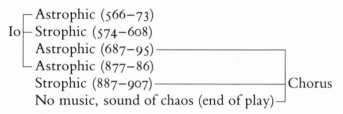

Io
- Astrophic (566–73)
- Strophic (574–608)
- Astrophic (687–95)
- Astrophic (877–86)
- Strophic (887–907)
- No music, sound of chaos (end of play)

Chorus

Notwithstanding strong doubts about the authenticity of
the *Prometheus Bound*, the musical design of the play provides
no element that is so un-Aeschylean that the case either for
or against is significantly reinforced. The arrangement and
structure of individual lyrics are in accord with Aeschylus'
practice in earlier plays; but there is also a shallowness in the
motivation and coordination of these patterns that seems odd
for Aeschylus.[70] Musical patterns in this play, though familiar
from other Aeschylean plays, often seem used for their own
effect and unrelated to the theme.[71] If the play's topic and
structure were not themselves so unusual, a case might be
made against Aeschylean authorship on the basis of musical
style; but given all the unusual features in the play, the musical form becomes only another anomaly.

Even though so few of Aeschylus' plays survive, they reveal a characteristic musical style. Beginning with the *Persians* there are musical forms composed to complement the
poet's dramatic themes, and in later plays these forms are developed and enriched until they become so deeply involved
with the presentation of themes that neither can be detached

from the other. Even the most aberrant play, the *Prometheus Bound*, reveals several features of Aeschylean musical form. Although the individual aspects of this style are difficult to define precisely on the basis of seven plays, half of which are fragments of a unified larger work, both the incorporation of aural effects into a total production through reference to traditional music and the control of his audience's expectations of symmetrical musical forms are fundamental in discussion of Aeschylean technique. Prayers, laments, invocations, and blessings occur in almost all the plays. In addition, characters are often presented through music. Xerxes, the women in the *Seven against Thebes*, the suppliant maidens, Cassandra, the old men of Argos, the Furies, Io—each of these roles contains significant sections of music that reinforce the verbal characterizations. There are also breaks in the formal structure of songs in the unexpected lack of the corresponding music to mesodes and astrophic stanzas as well as the abrupt ending provided by epodes when music seems to stop because it is interrupted. The movement of formal song to speech with intervening stages of astrophic song, anapaestic recitative, and stichomythia, and the corresponding movement from speech to song form the structural framework of several long musical scenes. Finally, there are places where the chorus seems to split into smaller groups or even individual voices in order to stress the inherent disorder or disagreement in the thinking of its members.

But probably the clearest indication of Aeschylean style remains the constant concern to make all the elements of the production contribute significantly to the total dramatic idea. Aeschylus not only wrote his plays; he saw them being produced in the broad theater of his mind and heard them with the keen ear that all great dramatists, composers, and musical writers must have. Undoubtedly he honed his talent by being an actor himself and by supervising carefully the details of the production as it was taking shape. Whether his choruses achieved their perfection of design during composition in the privacy of his study or during rehearsal will never be known, but the most important characteristic of Aeschylean music is the full development of the themes of his plays in the combination of words, meter, and form; music and dance became organic elements of the whole dramatic concept. And such theatrical unity is the hallmark of Aeschylean drama.

ABBREVIATIONS

AC	*L'Antiquité Classique*
Ag.	*Agamemnon*
AJP	*American Journal of Philology*
And.	*Andromache*
Ant.	*Antigone*
AT	U. von Wilamowitz-Moellendorff, *Aeschyli Tragoediae*, Berlin 1914
BICS	*British Institute of Classical Studies*
BRL	*Bulletin of the John Rylands Library*
C&M	*Classica et Mediaevalia*
Ch.	*Choephoroi*
CJ	*Classical Journal*
CP	*Classical Philology*
CQ	*Classical Quarterly*
CR	*Classical Review*
CSCA	*California Studies in Classical Antiquity*
DFA	A. W. Pickard-Cambridge, *The Dramatic Festivals of Athens*, 2d ed., rev. J. Gould and D. M. Lewis, Oxford 1968.
DTC	A. W. Pickard-Cambridge, *Dithyramb, Tragedy, and Comedy*, 2d ed., rev. T. B. L. Webster, Oxford 1962
Eum.	*Eumenides*
GB	*Grazer Beiträge*
GLM	G. Thomson, *Greek Lyric Metre*, Cambridge 1929
G&R	*Greece and Rome*
GRBS	*Greek, Roman, and Byzantine Studies*
Hipp.	*Hippolytus*
HSCP	*Harvard Studies in Classical Philology*

I.A.	*Iphigenia at Aulis*
JHS	*Journal of Hellenic Studies*
LMGD	A. M. Dale, *Lyric Metres of Greek Drama*, 2d ed., Cambridge 1968
MH	*Museum Helveticum*
OC	*Oedipus at Colonus*
OT	*Oedipus Tyrannus*
PCPhS	*Proceedings of the Cambridge Philological Society*
Pers.	*Persians*
PV	*Prometheus Bound*
REG	*Revue des Études Grecques*
RhM	*Rheinisches Museum*
SO	*Symbolae Osloenses*
Supp.	*Suppliants*
TAPA	*Transactions and Proceedings of the American Philological Association*
TDA	A. W. Pickard-Cambridge, *The Theatre of Dionysus in Athens*, Oxford 1946
Th.	*Thesmophoriazusae*
WS	*Wiener Studien*
YCS	*Yale Classical Studies*

NOTES

PREFACE

1. G. H. Gellie, *Sophocles: A Reading* (Melbourne 1972) 224.

INTRODUCTION

1. H. D. F. Kitto, "Rhythm, Metre, and Black Magic," *CR* 56 (1942) 99–108.

2. The best recent discussions are: M. Gagarin, *Aeschylean Drama* (Berkeley 1976); L. Golden, *In Praise of Prometheus* (Chapel Hill 1962); H. D. F. Kitto, *Form and Meaning in Drama* (London 1956); R. Kuhns, *The House, the City, and the Judge* (New York 1962); E. T. Owen, *The Harmony of Aeschylus* (Toronto 1952); K. Reinhardt, *Aischylos als Regisseur und Theologe* (Bern 1949); T. G. Rosenmeyer, *The Art of Aeschylus* (Berkeley 1982); G. Thomson, *Aeschylus and Athens* (London 1947).

CHAPTER I

1. The following books and articles are basic for a study of the production of Aeschylus' plays: P. Arnott, *Greek Scenic Conventions in the Fifth Century B.C.* (Oxford 1962); M. Bieber, *Die Denkmäler zum Theaterwesen in Altertum* (Berlin and Leipzig 1920) and *The History of the Greek and Roman Theater*, 2d ed. (Princeton 1961); E. Bodensteiner, "Szenische Fragen über den Ort des Auftretens und Abgehens von Schauspielern und Chor in griechischen Drama," *Jahrbücher für classische Philologie*, Suppbd. 19 (1893) 665 f.; W. Dörpfeld and E. Reisch, *Das griechische Theater* (Athens 1896), hereafter cited as D-R; N. G. L. Hammond, "The Conditions of Dramatic Production to the Death of Aeschylus," *GRBS* 13 (1972) 387–450; S. Melchinger, *Das Theater der Tragödie* (Munich 1974); A. W. Pickard-Cambridge, *The Theatre of Dionysus in Athens* (Oxford 1946; hereafter cited as *TDA*); O. Taplin, *Greek Tragedy in Action* (Berkeley 1978); E. Simon, *Das antike Theater* (Heidelberg 1972); T. B. L. Webster, *Greek Theater Production*, 2d ed. (London 1970); and A. D. Trendall and T. B. L. Webster, *Illustrations in Greek Drama* (London 1971).

2. *Vita* 11. F. Schoell's collection of testimonia concerning Aeschylus' life and poetry, in the preface to Ritschl's 1879 edition of the *Seven*, is the fullest; however, the collection in U. von Wilamowitz-Moellendorff's *Aeschyli Tragoediae* (Berlin 1914; hereafter cited as *AT*), is the most readily available and is therefore the one cited in this book.

3. A. Wartelle, *Histoire du texte d'Eschyle dans l'antiquité* (Paris 1971) chaps. 10–16, offers evidence for the continuing interest in Aeschylus from the Hellenistic period to the fifth century A.D.; there are many papyrus fragments showing a degree of popular appeal but he was often regarded as

an obligatory member of a canon or was cited as a powerful authority. See also I. Opelt, "Das Nachleben des Aischylos in christlicher Zeit," *Jahrbuch für Antike und Christentum* 5 (1962) 192–95.

4. *Vita* 5.

5. *Vita* 8.

6. W. B. Stanford, *Aeschylus in His Style* (Dublin 1942) 1–14.

7. The most impressive analysis of Aeschylean imagery is that by A. Lebeck, *The Oresteia: A Study in Language and Structure* (Washington, D.C. 1971); for a list of recent writings on imagery, see n. 38.

8. For bibliography, see chap. 3 n. 20.

9. *Vita* 16.

10. See *Vita* 14–16 and the references in Wilamowitz, *AT* 12–13.

11. Fragment 368 in H. Mette, *Die Fragmente der Tragödien des Aischylos* (Berlin 1939).

12. See Suidas, *s.v.* Aeschylos: "the first to introduce fearsome masks and to have his tragic actors wear them painted with colors."

13. *Deipnosophistae* 1. 21d. A. W. Pickard-Cambridge, *The Dramatic Festivals of Athens*, 2d ed., rev. J. Gould and D. H. Lewis (Oxford 1968; hereafter cited as *DFA*), several times (e.g., 198 and 205) notes that later commentators attribute inventions or innovations to Aeschylus on the basis of little evidence only because he is a revered figure in early tragedy. My discussion of his stagecraft draws only minimally on such unreliable sources. Generally I try to use the evidence of staging derived from the dramatic texts themselves. Cf. the skepticism of D-R, 203. Such statements, however, are evidence that Aeschylus possessed a solid enough reputation as a theater designer to be a credible "inventor" of stage devices and techniques.

14. The principal evidence for Aeschylus' use of painted scenery is Vitruvius 7, praef. 11, supplemented by the statement of Aristotle (*Poetics* 1449a16) that Sophocles introduced scene painting. If both accounts are true, then Aeschylus could have used scene painting as early as 468, possibly the year of Sophocles' first play (cf. Plut. *Cimon* 8.7); thus, painted scenery is possible for the *Seven against Thebes*, the *Suppliants*, the *Oresteia*, and *Prometheus Bound*, all of which offer good opportunity for painted backdrops (especially the *Eumenides* and *Prometheus Bound*); cf. however, the cautionary statements on the date of Agatharcus' work by F. Winter, "Greek Theatre Production: A Review Article," *Phoenix* (1965) 103f. Probably the earliest play to offer a large enough set for such painting is the *Oresteia*; see Pickard-Cambridge, *TDA* 1, 5, 8, 15, 34, and the most recent review of the evidence for a large stage building by Melchinger, *Theater der Tragödie* 83–111. Vitruvius reports that Democritus and Anaxagoras followed the commentary of Agatharchus on the scene he designed for Aeschylus in writing their treatise on perspective in scene painting. The staging of this play—whether it was the original production or a later revival—must have been sufficiently impressive that the two authors selected the production of an Aeschylean play as a guide for their own book. Scenes offering significant opportunities for a designer include, for buildings and monuments: the council chamber and the tomb of Darius in the *Pers.*; the statues of the gods in the *Supp.*; the palace of Agamemnon, the temple of

Delphi, and the courtroom scene in the *Eum.*; and (not a building but similar in scope) the rock of Prometheus, especially in regard to the final scene; for colors: the golden colors of the *Pers.*, the colored armor of the warriors in the *Seven against Thebes* (388–90, 494, 511–13, and 644) if any of this appeared on stage, the red carpet in the *Ag.*, the change to red robes in the *Eum.*, the colors for Oceanos and the Oceanids in the *PV*; and for stage levels: the tomb of Darius in the *Pers.*, the watchman's platform and the chariot of Agamemnon in the *Ag.*, the blocking of *Eum.* 1–234 and the positioning of actors in the remainder of this play, the rock of Prometheus and the position of the Oceanids and their father in *PV*.

15. See the evidence gathered by Pickard-Cambridge, *DFA* 180–96, demonstrating the flexibility in designing masks for any situation created by the playwright, and the discussion by I. Brooke, *Costume in Greek Classic Drama* (New York 1962) 75–81 and 101.

16. Cf. Aristotle's comment on the importance of controlled gestures, *Poetics* 55a22–34 and 61b26–62a14; the general comments on movement and gesture in Pickard-Cambridge, *DFA* 171ff.; and L. B. Lawler, *The Dance of the Ancient Greek Theater* (Iowa City 1964) 22–62.

17. It is also questionable whether "normal" music would be appropriate at *Pers.* 694–96 = 700–2, *Supp.* 825–902, and *Eum.* 117–77.

18. See above, n. 14.

19. See, for example, the discussion with pictures by Bieber, *Denkmäler*, and by Trendall and Webster, *Illustrations in Greek Drama*. Webster, *The Greek Chorus* (London 1970) xii, offers the best criticism of such evidence: "The pictures are not films or even photographs of the performance. They are what the artist remembered of the dance, translated into the prevailing conventions of his art and fitted into the space at his disposal."

20. *Vita* 15 gives the two actors regularly employed by Aeschylus as Kleandrus and Mynniskus, and Sophocles continuously used Tlepolemus (scholia to Aristophanes *Clouds* 1264). See the general comments by Pickard-Cambridge, *DFA* 167ff.

21. My friend and colleague Arthur Mayer reports having attended the first public showing of motion pictures in the United States in 1896: "Every book on the history of movies records that everyone in the theater at that first showing was frightened when a movie was shown of large waves breaking on shore but I can recall so clearly that no one was terrified at all. After all, the movies were being shown on a sheet hung up on the stage and no one could possibly have been under the impression that the waves were real."

22. See the evidence for interpolation of lines to make a later production more spectacular in D. Page, *Actors' Interpolations in Greek Tragedy* (Oxford 1934).

23. The most forceful contemporary case for this type of dramatic criticism is made by H. Granville-Barker, *Prefaces to Shakespeare*, 5 vols. (London 1927–47), in his introduction, e.g.: "What is all the criticism and scholarship finally for if not to keep Shakespeare alive? And he must always be most alive—even if roughly and rudely alive—in the theater" (I 4).

24. A comparison of the percentage of music in several individual plays of each playwright will make the point clearly. For Sophocles and Euripides we should include, among others, plays that either are well known (*OT* and *Medea*) or seem to be highly musical in content or effect (*OC* and the *Bacchae*). The figures for Aeschylus and Sophocles are from A. Gercke, "Die Prometheus-Trilogie," *Zeitschrift für Gymnasialwesen* 65 (1911) 173; those for the *Alcestis* and *Medea* come from M. Griffith, *The Authenticity of Prometheus Bound* (Cambridge 1977) 123; the others are my own: *Pers.* 43 percent; *Seven*, 43 percent; *Supp.*, 55 percent; *Ag.*, 41 percent; *Ch.*, 35 percent; *Eum.*, 34 percent; *PV*, 13 percent; *Ajax*, 19 percent; *Ant.*, 22.5 percent; *OT*, 16 percent; *OC*, 19 percent; *Alcestis*, 22 percent; *Medea*, 26 percent; *Helen*, 25 percent; *Bacchae*, 31 percent. Of course, numbers of lines are scarcely decisive, for some "musical" lines are much shorter than spoken ones. A more accurate comparison would involve timing several performances. Even these rough figures, however, support the basic claim that Aeschylus devoted more time to music and dance in his plays than did his two rivals.

It also seems clear from the chart in Kranz, *Stasimon: Untersuchungen zu Form und Gestalt der griechischen Tragödie* (Berlin 1933) 124–25, that Aeschylean songs contain a series of two through eight corresponding strophes rather than the one or two strophic pairs common in Sophoclean or Euripidean odes. Aeschylean structure thus would generally allow more opportunity for musical variation within each ode.

25. Cf. Arist. *Frogs* 911–20 and the recent discussion by O. Taplin, "Aeschylean Silences and Silences in Aeschylus," *HSCP* 76 (1972) 57–97.

26. *Vita* 9.

27. It is significant that the report stresses the action of the chorus: *sporaden . . . eisagagonta*.

28. See, for example, the recent study by W. D. Anderson, *Ethos and Education in Greek Music* (Cambridge, Mass. 1966); R. P. Winnington-Ingram, *Mode in Ancient Greek Music* (Cambridge 1936); and the latter's bibliography, "Ancient Greek Music, 1932–1957," *Lustrum* 3 (1958) 5–57.

29. E. Martin, *Trois documents de musique grecque* (Paris 1953), attempts to reconstruct the music to accompany Euripides *Orestes* 339–44 on the basis of the papyrus fragment first published by K. Wesseley, *Mitteilungen aus der Sammlung der Papyrus Erzherzog* V (Vienna 1892) 65–73, but much must be assumed about the notation on the papyrus to arrive at such a precise scoring. See also the discussion by E. Pöhlmann, *Griechische Musikfragmente* (Nuremberg 1960). See below, chap. 2, n. 10 for further discussion of the Euripides fragment. Less informative is the small fragment published provisionally by D. Jourdan-Hemmerdinger, "Un nouveau papyrus musical d'Euripide," *Comptes rendus de l'Academie des inscriptions et belles-lettres* (1973) 292–302.

30. Cf. the excellent study and bibliography collected by Lawler, *Dance of the Greek Theater*.

31. Striking examples are the apt comparison of the Persian army to a swarm of bees (128) and the deeply ironic metaphor of the steersman of the ship of state applied to Eteocles (2–3, 62–64, 208–10, and elsewhere). For

a complete analysis of the ironic use of a continuing metaphor see R. D. Murray, *The Motif of Io in Aeschylus' Suppliants* (Princeton 1958), especially in regard to the suppliants' misuse of the Io myth as a model for their own wishes (pp. 56–87).

32. Examples are Xerxes' entrance in his costume of rags, paralleling the glorious entrance of Darius (see below, chap. 4, pp. 157–8), or the purposeful repeated choice of a series of defenders by Eteocles in his attempt to dominate events as he is unknowingly fulfilling his fate. The *Oresteia* begins with the watchman talking about establishing choruses and dancing himself (*Ag.* 23 and 31).

33. Taking the reading of Kayser, which at least has attracted Fraenkel's approval. Certainty in restoring the correct reading seems beyond grasp.

34. Fraenkel, *Agamemnon* III 487f., and Kranz, *Stasimon* 20, comment on the reversal of roles in this scene, which is based on epirrhematic form: Cassandra does not reply to the chorus; she leads them.

35. Fraenkel, III 623ff., commenting on the combination of lyric and speech in the Cassandra scene, claims that Cassandra barely hears the words of the chorus, but I believe there is a growing degree of communication throughout the scene. First, she is silent when the chorus urges her to enter the house (1035–71). When she begins to wail in addressing Apollo, she is closely focused on a vision of her own fate. At 1090 she begins to be aware of the chorus's statements; J. D. Denniston, *The Greek Particles*, 2d ed. (Oxford 1959) 475, identifies the *men oun* in 1090 as adversative—"No. On the contrary"—and thus as responsive to statement of the chorus; cf. also *gar* at 1095. At 1100–29, unaffected by the chorus's troubled speeches, she describes her vision of Agamemnon's murder. At 1136 she turns to lamenting her own fate with little notice of the preceding speech of the chorus, but at 1146 she corrects the chorus's application of the nightingale simile. At 1167–72 she repeats the prophecy of her impending death in response to the chorus's question at 1162. At this point the scene moves quite naturally to speech and to the clearer communication of stichomythia. The comments of Denniston Page on 1072–1330 offer further support for this view.

36. Well described by H. Weil, *Études sur le drame antique* (Paris 1897) 270f.

37. For further discussion of the Cassandra scene within the musical pattern of the play, see chap. 2, pp. 58–68.

38. There have been many fine studies of the imagery in the plays of Aeschylus. Among the best are H. D. Cameron, *Studies on the Seven against Thebes of Aeschylus* (The Hague 1971); F. R. Earp, *The Style of Aeschylus* (Cambridge 1948) 93–149; B. H. Fowler, "The Imagery of the *Prometheus Bound*," *AJP* 78 (1957) 173–84; idem, "Aeschylus' Imagery," *C&M* 28 (1967) 1–74; idem, "The Imagery of the *Seven against Thebes*," *SQ* 45 (1970) 24–37; R. F. Goheen, "Aspects of Dramatic Symbolism: Three Studies in the *Oresteia*," *AJP* 76 (1955) 113–37; W. Headlam, "Metaphor, with a Note on Transference of Epithets," *CR* 16 (1902) 434–42; B. M. W. Knox, "The Lion in the House," *CP* 47 (1952) 17–25; R. Lattimore, especially his introduction to his translation of the *Oresteia* (Chi-

cago 1953); A. Lebeck, "The Role of Iphigenia in the *Agamemnon*," *GRBS* 5 (1964) 35–41; idem, *The Oresteia*; W. C. Scott, "Wind Imagery in the *Oresteia*," *TAPA* 97 (1966) 459–71; O. Smith, "Some Observations on the Structure of Imagery in Aeschylus," *C&M* 26 (1965) 10–72; and F. Zeitlin, "The Motif of the Corrupted Sacrifice in Aeschylus' *Oresteia*," *TAPA* 96 (1965) 463–508; and idem, "Postscript to Sacrificial Imagery in the *Oresteia* (*Ag.* 1235–37)," *TAPA* 97 (1966) 645–53. The recent book by E. Petrounias, *Funktion und Thematik der Bilder bei Aischylos* (Göttingen 1976), is a massive list of unsorted terms and is generally unhelpful.

39. Herodotus uses *lego* or *chraomai* to report oracles from various sources, but Thucydides introduces the oracle about the Dorian war with *aeido* (2.54.2). There are, however, a striking number of words or sounds of music (and often unpleasant music) associated with prophets and their prophecy in the *Oresteia*. Thomson, *The Oresteia of Aeschylus*, 2d ed. (Amsterdam and Prague 1966), comments on *Ag.* 156–57: *apeklagxen* "expresses the loud and excited tone of voice which marked the spiritual exaltation of the *mantis.* . . . This is the explanation of other words applied to the delivery of oracles, as *iachein* and *orthiazein*." Though noting the words describing oracles in the trilogy, Thomson does not identify the frequency of such words as an indication of Aeschylus' use of music and sound as metaphors.

40. See *Eum.* 332–3 and 345–6, where the hymn of the Erinyes is openly described as a hymn sung with no accompaniment of the lyre.

41. On the importance of this word as a sound word with a foreboding tone see W. B. Stanford, *The Sound of Greek* (Berkeley and Los Angeles 1967) 104f., who suggests the analogy "between the voice of Calchas and the cry of birds in the omen."

42. Compare the equally perverse funeral service of Agamemnon, at which Clytemnestra forbids wailing from those in the household and orders the chorus to have nothing to do with the service (*Ag.* 1551–59). In fact no citizens were allowed to be present and there was no lamentation; Electra was locked in her room where she could lament the dead king unseen (*Ch.* 429–33 and 444–49).

43. See the similar situation of the persecuted suppliants at *Supp.* 113–16.

44. G. W. Dickerson has kindly shared with me his figures on the characteristics of the spoken iambic lines in the *Agamemnon*. Defining a spondaic line as one in which the first two syllables of each metron are a spondee and a predominantly spondaic line as one in which this occurs in two out of the possible three cases, he finds that 60.4 percent of Clytemnestra's speeches are spondaic or predominantly spondaic, compared with only 43.5 percent for other speakers in the play.

45. See L. Deubner, "Ololyge und Verwandtes," *Abhandlungen der Preussischen Akademie der Wissenschaften*, Phil.-Hist. Kl. (1941) 1, which shows that there are aspects of ritual connected with *ololyge*. This connotation fits well with the sacrificial imagery surrounding Clytemnestra as presented by Zeitlin (see above, n. 38).

46. Kranz, *Stasimon* 127–37, discusses the cult elements in all the plays of Aeschylus. The particular song elements cited from the *Oresteia* are addi-

tional evidence for the general religious tone and quality of some Aeschylean songs revealed in the special insistence on musical cries and allusions to various forms of song. Plato, (*Laws* 3.700a–b) offers proof that there were fairly strict classifications of songs in terms of proper forms and melodies. Cf. J. A. Haldane, "Musical Themes and Imagery in Aeschylus," *JHS* 85 (1965) 37–40.

47. Cf. Fraenkel on 121: "Such *ephymnia*, refrains, belong to the oldest (and from a religious point of view the most important) elements of liturgical song . . . the refrain rounds off first the story of the *teras* (cf. 125) and finally the prophecy of the seer, and thus with its cry of alarm and its prayer for a happy issue it seems to heighten the effect of a promise of destiny."

48. See the discussion of the history of the Linos song by Wilamowitz, *Euripides Herakles*, 2d ed. (Berlin 1909) 293 ff.

49. L. J. Heirman, "Kassandra's Glossolalia," *Mnemosyne* 28 (1975) 257–67, finds a ritualistic invocation in her words but admits that the chorus (1075) as well as the audience would hear a lament.

50. S. G. Brown, "A Contextual Analysis of Tragic Meter: The Anapaest," in *Ancient and Modern: Essays in Honor of Gerald F. Else* (Ann Arbor 1977) 60–67.

51. W. Schadewaldt, "Der Kommos in Aischylos *Choephoren*," *Hermes* 67 (1932) 312–54. The direct call to Agamemnon really begins at *Ch.* 456; see especially A. Lesky's suggestions for staging to enhance the invocation of the dead, "Der Kommos der *Choephoren*," *Sitzungsberichte der Akademie der Wissenschaften, Wien* Phil.-Hist. Kl. 221 Abh. 3 (1943) 103 f.

52. Haldane, "Musical Themes and Imagery" 38 and n. 27.

53. See the discussion of a similar technique in the *Seven* by Haldane, "Musical Themes and Imagery" 36, and the treatment of the blasphemous paean in Aeschylus by D. Clay in "The Daggers at *Agamemnon* 714–15," *Philologus* 110 (1966) 128–32.

54. Other references to specific song types are the Linos song (*Ag.* 121, 138, 159) and the *ialemos* (*Ch.* 424; cf. *Supp.* 114).

55. On the presence of elements of program songs in Greek drama see the discussion by J. Rode, "Das Chorlied," 101–03 in W. Jens et al., *Die Bauformen der griechischen Tragödie* (Munich 1971).

56. W. Headlam, "The Last Scene of the *Eumenides*," *JHS* 26 (1906) 268–71, first discussed the association with the Panathenaic procession, but see further the note on 1027–31 in Thomson, *The Oresteia of Aeschylus*, 2d ed. (Amsterdam and Prague 1966) and in his *Aeschylus and Athens* (London 1940) 295 f.

57. See the discussions of the restoration of the true meaning of paean, *ololyge*, and incantation in the *Oresteia* by Haldane, "Musical Themes and Imagery," 37–40, and by C. W. Macleod, "L'unita dell' Orestea," *Maia* 25 (1973) 283 f.

58. Kranz, *Stasimon* 127 ff., emphasizes the religious quality of repetitions—words, refrain lines, and whole strophes.

59. *Nomos* is a difficult word to discuss with any precision because it can have such a breadth of meaning, but it should undoubtedly be included in

this discussion because it is used so frequently in the *Oresteia*. Most critics and translators—e.g., Sidgwick, Fraenkel, Young, and H. Lloyd-Jones, "Aeschylus, *Agamemnon* 416ff.," *CQ* 3 (1953) 96—see it as a general word for song or tune. But T. J. Fleming, "The Musical Nomos in Aeschylus' *Oresteia*," *CJ* 72 (1977) 222–33, takes it as a specific reference to the song form attributed to Terpander. In this case the number of references to the distorted or deformed *nomos* (whatever its exact meaning) joins this word and its compounds to the theme of the wrong song. Fleming shows how a further extension of meaning to the sense of "normal order" connects the murders in the house of Atreus as violations of such order to the distortions in music, which are described as *anomos* (*Ag.* 1142).

60. Cf. Fraenkel on 1186ff.: "The image of the *komos*, taken from the homely sphere of everyday life, has here assumed an unexpected and dreadful meaning. . . . The most joyous custom of Attic life is transformed into an object of horror."

61. Haldane, "Musical Themes and Imagery" 37, focuses on this function of the musical words in the *Oresteia*: musical symbolism "is used to throw into relief the irony of false victory and of the prayer thwarted by the curse, and it marks the passage of triumph into despair. It is most prominent in the *Agamemnon*, but is continued throughout the trilogy, finding its completion in the exodos of the *Eumenides*."

CHAPTER 2

1. E. T. Cone, "The Old Man's Toys: Verdi's Last Operas," *Perspectives USA* 6 (1954) 130, also quoted as the keynote in the fine study of operatic music by J. Kerman, *Opera as Drama* (New York 1952) 21 f.

The following books and articles are of special importance to the argument in this chapter: R. Arnoldt, *Der Chor im Agamemnon des Aeschylus Szenisch Erläutert* (Halle 1881); S. G. Brown, "A Contextual Analysis of Tragic Meter: The Anapaest," in *Ancient and Modern: Essays in Honor of Gerald F. Else* (Ann Arbor 1977) 45–77; W. Kraus, *Strophengestaltung in der griechischen Tragödie, I. Aischylos und Sophokles, Sitzungsberichte der Akademie der Wissenschaften, Wien* 231 (1957); W. C. Scott, "Non-Strophic Elements in the *Oresteia*," *TAPA* 112 (1982) 179–96; and R. P. Winnington-Ingram, "Ancient Greek Music 1932–1957," *Lustrum* 3 (1958) 6–57.

2. A. Wartelle, *Histoire du texte d'Eschyle* 46–48 and 152–57.

3. Wartelle, *Histoire du texte d'Eschyle* 152ff., discusses Aristophanes' service in having presented the colometry of lyric passages for readers whose innate sense of metric was disappearing. Papyrus fragments show that his colometry has been largely preserved in Byzantine manuscripts; cf. T. J. Fleming, "Ancient Evidence for the Colometry of Aeschylus *Septem*," *GRBS* (1975) 141–48 and the references cited therein.

4. The only extant music that may come from the fifth century is the papyrus fragments of Euripides *Orestes* 339–44 and *I.A.* 784–92; for the *Orestes* fragment see Wesseley, *Mitteilungen* 265ff., and the discussions by Pöhlmann, *Musikfragmente*, esp. 12–24, and idem, *Denkmäler altgriechischer Musik* (Nuremberg 1970) 78–82; for the *I.A.* see the provisional publication by Jourdan-Hemmerdinger, "Un nouveau papyrus musical" 292–302.

5. See the review of scholarship by Winnington-Ingram, "Ancient Greek Music" 6–57. The best recent discussion of the available evidence on the ethical and paideutic aspects of Greek music is W. D. Anderson, *Ethos and Education*.

6. For an especially clearheaded discussion of the importance of rhythm in Greek poetry see J. W. Fitton, "Greek Dance," *CQ* 23 (1973) 254–74. The most perceptive critic of the obstacles to understanding Greek meters for those whose ears and minds have been trained in a tradition of stress accent is A. M. Dale; her comments are especially relevant in "The Metrical Units of Greek Lyric Verse, I," *CQ* 44 (1950) 138–48; and in "Words, Music, and Dance," "Speech-Rhythm, Verse-Rhythm, and Song," and "Expressive Rhythm in the Lyrics of Greek Drama," all in her *Collected Papers* 41–60, 159–69, 230–47, and 248–58.

7. Not to mention the further complications in the possible relative values of short syllables produced by resolution; see the study by M. L. West, "A New Approach to Greek Prosody," *Glotta* 48 (1970) 185–94, and the discussion on rhythm by W. S. Allen, *Accent and Rhythm* (Cambridge 1973) 96–102. For precise figures on the frequency of such resolved forms in the three tragedians see D. Korzeniewski, *Griechische Metrik* (Darmstadt 1968) 55.

8. See A. M. Dale, *The Lyric Meters of Greek Drama*, 2d ed. (Cambridge 1968; hereafter cited as *LMGD*) 3 f.; Korzeniewski, *Griechische Metrik* 100; and D. S. Raven, *Greek Metre*, 2d ed. (London 1968) sec. 46.

9. T. B. L. Webster, "Tradition in Greek Dramatic Lyric," Broadhead Classical Lecture I (Christchurch, N.Z. 1969), has calculated that sixty-one basic metrical cola account for 90 percent of the lyric lines in tragedy.

10. *De comp. verb.* 19 expressly states that the melody of the strophe was repeated for the antistrophe, but our only direct evidence is the fragment from Euripides' *Orestes* (see above, n. 4), which at first glance seems to show that the music was similar; see the comparison of melody and accent by D. Feaver, "The Musical Setting of Euripides' *Orestes*," *AJP* 81 (1960) 1–15. But Dale, *LMGD* 204, denies the relevance of the accent markings: "Since strophe and antistrophe pay no attention to correspondence of word-accent, either the melody here must also have ignored word-accent or the melody of the strophe was not repeated in the antistrophe." She continues by describing our uncertainty on this point as "one of the most curious and deplorable gaps in our understanding of classical lyric" and inclines strongly to the view that melody did not take word-accent into account and that the music of the strophe was repeated. This would certainly be the case if, as Wartelle states, the musical notation accompanied only the strophe and the antistrophe was fitted to that melody (*Histoire du texte d'Eschyle* 47); see also Pöhlmann, *Musikfragmente* 17–29 and *Denkmäler* 82. Discussions of the applicability of the statements by Dionysius of Halicarnassus, *De comp. verb.* 11, to fifth-century music seem futile because we do not know the nature of the musical text he was using, but he certainly offers no reason for us to trust the reliability of accents as a guide to music; cf. W. B. Sedgwick, "A Note on the Performance of Greek Vocal Music," *C&M* 11 (1950) 222–26. For strong statements against the repetition of the

same music—unfortunately based heavily on a consideration of accents—see R. Giani and C. del Grande, "Relazione melodica di strofe e antistrofe nel coro greco, *Rivista di Filosofia* 59 (1931) 185–206, and W. J. W. Koster, "De Studiis Recentibus ad Rem Metricam Pertinentibus," *Mnemosyne* 3 (1950) 27–29.

I should also include in this discussion Dale's brief comment on the probability of repeated dance patterns (*LMGD* 213f.). Yet one must allow sufficient leeway in any such assertion for the significance of differences of content and tone between strophe and antistrophe in the passages she cites.

11. The rate of resolution in the normal stanza is not easy to calculate precisely. There is some doubt whether all cretic and bacchiac forms are syncopated iambics (cf. Dale, *LMGD* 16 and 108 ff.). Yet a comparison of the total number of feet in pure iambic and syncopated iambic lyric lines in limited passages in the *Oresteia* with the number of feet that show syncopated forms in those passages yields the following rates of resolution: *Ag.* 763–81, are 66 percent; *Ch.* 423–38 = 444–50, 58 percent; and *Ag.* 475–87, 53 percent. (For an explanation of the metrical appropriateness of these high rates of resolution, see the discussion of each of these passages later in the chapter.) Next come *Ch.* 22–41, 40 percent; *Ch.* 43–63, 33 percent; *Eum.* 778–92, 33 percent; and *Eum.* 381–96, 30 percent. In all other passages the highest ratio is 6 percent. Such figures support the observation of Dale, *LMGD* 81 ff., that resolution is used sparingly and carefully in Aeschylean iambics.

12. For a full discussion of such stanzas see Scott, "Non-Strophic Elements."

13. Dale, *LMGD 81*, states that Aeschylean lyric iambics "often have no, or very little, admixture of other metres, and the preponderance of the light *anceps* is striking; there are many stanzas which keep the short form throughout; others contain merely an occasional lengthening of the initial syllable or a colon."

14. See the patterns given by Kraus, *Strophengestaltung*, and by H. A. Pohlsander, *Metrical Studies in the Lyrics of Sophocles* (Leiden 1964), especially the latter's discussion of strophic construction, 172–90. Dale, *LMGD* 200 ff., contrasts the periodic structure of Aeschylus and of Sophocles.

15. Eur. *Electra* 503–46 vs. Aesch. *Ch.* 164–234; Eur. *Hipp.* 612 vs. Aristophanes *Th.* 275, *Frogs* 101 and 1471 (this was obviously a famous line; cf. Aristotle, *Rhetoric* 1416a28 ff.). There are also the close metrical parodies in the *Frogs* cited in Dale, *LMGD* 44 and 152 f., and the numerous lines that are therein quoted.

16. This is an effective technique of writers, musicians, and painters throughout the centuries. The clearest example in early Greek literature is Achilles' blunt rejection of the hypocritical speaker at *Iliad* 9.308–14; when Odysseus repeats the list of gifts offered by Agamemnon, he substitutes lines 300–06 for Agamemnon's more insulting 158–61. The change is especially striking because the Homeric audience is accustomed to hear verbatim repetition when a messenger reports (see *Iliad* 2.11–15, 23–43, and 60–70) and quickly hears any departure from the original message. Aeschylus plays upon a willingness to anticipate in lines such as *Supp.* 21–22

or some of Clytemnestra's ironic speeches, e.g., *Ag.* 611–12, 856–7, and 896–903—all of which must be heard to the end of the sentence before the real meaning supplants the supposed one. In addition, the words of Cassandra and Pylades acquire heightened significance and emphasis because they come after long silences. There is no general study of the use of anticipation in Aeschylean drama. The most recent statement concerning the manipulation of an audience's expectations is by Taplin, *The Stagecraft of Aeschylus: The Dramatic Use of Exits and Entrances in Greek Tragedy* (Oxford 1977) 92–98, who speaks only of specific expectations aroused by lines in the text. G. Arnott, "Euripides and the Unexpected," *G&R* 20 (1978) 49–64, expands the possibilities by discussing passages in which Euripides exploits conventions in order to disappoint deeply ingrained expectations.

17. I have used the Oxford text of D. Page (1972) as the source for all scansion patterns. According to standard usage in Greek texts I have identified successive pairs of strophes in the order of the Greek alphabet: str/ant a, b, g (for gamma), etc. Lines whose metrical form has not been adequately reconciled within the customary patterns of tragic lyric are identified by a question mark. Lines whose precise wording has not yet been fully discovered are marked with an asterisk.

More difficult are lines where there is a scholarly dispute over the proper line-end. Because our manuscripts vary in their arrangement of lines and because Triclinius offers a definite but still unsatisfactory colometry, editors continue to disagree over the precise scansion of a line; moving a final syllable from one line to the beginning of the next can significantly alter a scansion pattern. Such considerations, though important in this chapter, are not the primary subject here. I have followed the colometry of Page even in highly disputed passages because the problematic sections seldom involve the thematic meters: the iambic, the lecythion, and the dactylic. Thus my argument, which depends on the cumulative weight of usage, is not seriously effected by such specific uncertainties.

18. First noticed by J. T. Sheppard, *Aeschylus and Sophocles* (New York 1927) 20.

19. There is dramatic gain in Clytemnestra's early entrance, which is similar to the presence of Atossa while the disaster at Salamis is being described and to that of Prometheus while the extent of the world's sympathy at Zeus' outrages is being told; the presence of these characters focuses the spectators' attention and gives greater meaning to the narrative. Costumed in a vividly colored robe and remaining alone near the stage building in an attitude of prayer, Clytemnestra would attract the spectators' eyes while the chorus is singing; in addition, the design of the Greek theater, with the majority of the audience raised above the level of the orchestra and stage, made exactly this kind of simultaneous action possible. Clytemnestra at the altar visually suggests religion and its demands as the chorus sings 146–55, 218–27, and 249–57, all of which call for vengeance. That she prays while they sing the Hymn to Zeus (160–84) is later revealed as deeply ironic (cf. 973–4 and 1384–87); most characters in this play pray to Zeus but with more openly expressed intentions. Both the presence of the avenger and the actual performance of ritual provide significant enrichment. Although

no one has proved that Clytemnestra is present during the parodos, there seems to be no compelling parallel in Aeschylean drama that would bar her from the stage at this point. Fraenkel (II 51) states the major issue bothering all critics when he notes that she should answer the chorus's questions (83–87); but no one objects to Orestes' silence at the beginning of the *Ch.* when he is being explicitly invoked, or to Clytemnestra's addressing the mute Furies at the beginning of the *Eum.* These are not strictly parallel situations, but in each case the audience accepts the silence of a mute character who provides dramatic enrichment by being in the background.

It should be noted that Atossa, Prometheus, Clytemnestra, Orestes, and the Furies are not examples of the famed Aeschylean "silent character"; for a full discussion of this device see Taplin, "Aeschylean Silences," 57–97.

20. Probably such a cue was given just before line 34 or 35, causing the watchman to turn from the extended metaphor of dice-throwing to summary statements; *d'oun* indicates a break from previous thoughts and movement to a new topic; see Denniston, *Greek Particles* 461f. As Fraenkel notes, there is even a change in the length and structure of the watchman's sentences at this point. "Down to 35 there is a broad and even flow of sentences, some of them built into periods and expanded by subordinate clauses; in the last four lines the ear is arrested by brief *kommata*, fired off as it were in suppressed passion." (II, p. 25).

21. Critics and translators have only too willingly dictated action into the pause that they create between the speech of the watchman and the entrance song of the chorus; see especially A. W. Verrall, *The Agamemnon of Aeschylus* (London 1889) liii: "We may conjecture that the rousing of the palace, the sending out of messengers, the kindling of fires upon the altar or altars before the entrance, and the rejoicing of the household, was typically represented in action with music . . ."; also Wilamowitz, *Aischylos Interpretationen* (Berlin 1944) 163; G. Murray, *Aeschylus: The Creator of Tragedy* (Oxford 1940) 209; and A. Y. Campbell, *The Agamemnon of Aeschylus* (London 1940) *ad loc.* Yet the assumption that there should be a pause between speech and choral song must be made to outweigh two obvious occurrences of continuous staging. At *Ch.* 10 and *PV* 114–18 the entrance (presence) of the chorus occurs during the speech of an actor and is noted. The consequent lack of time to present actual sacrifices (88–96) or to announce and celebrate the joyful news (26–30ff.) is also common in drama and can be handled by the audience's imagination with the same ease they demonstrate when Agamemnon's herald and the king himself enter only moments after the lighting of beacons has shown that Troy has fallen; cf. also the rapidity of Atossa's prayers and preparations between *Pers.* 521 and 598, the swiftness of the battle in the *Seven* between lines 719 and 791, and the amazing efficiency with which Greek councils reach decisions in the *Seven* (between lines 791 and 1011) and in the *Suppliants* (between 523 and 600).

22. On the interchange of happiness and unhappiness in the watchman's speech and the later efforts of the chorus and the herald to conceal the truth, see R. P. Winnington-Ingram, "Aeschylus, *Agamemnon* 1343–71," *CQ* 4 (1954) 26 n. 4.

23. Fraenkel (on lines 40–103) comments on the traditional quality of the parodos and thus indirectly on the audience's expectation of the entrance when they hear the anapaests: "This form of the parodos in which anapaests precede song in lyric meters, seems to be the oldest; it probably goes back to the period before the invention of the prologue. . . ." For a discussion of the normal function of anapaests to introduce choral songs see Brown, "Analysis of Tragic Meter" 51–59.

24. The parodos of the *Pers.* and that of the *Ag.* are identical in length (64 lines); the next longest anapaestic parodos occurs in the *Supp.* (39 lines). Otherwise unified anapaestic passages run from 3 to 26 lines. In contrast, the panicked women in the *Seven* enter tumultuously to short anapaestic dochmiacs in less than half the lines of the Persian and Argive elders. See the study of different entrances by Melchinger, *Theater der Tragödie* 66–72. He offers good arguments to reject a purely formalized entrance song for all three tragedians in favor of a more dramatic effect.

25. There are two short dactylic strophic pairs in the Furies' Binding Song at *Eum.* 349–53 = 360–66 and 368–71 = 377–80. Cf. *Pers.* 853–906, with heroic overtones and a thematic association developed within its own play; see chap. 4, pp. 155–56.

26. Headlam and Thomson on 104–06: "The style, especially in the first part (104–59), is oracular, as befits a prophet, and in keeping with his interpretation of the omen . . ."; and Wilamowitz, *Interpretationen* 166 n. 2 describes the passage as filled with the periphrasis common to oracles.

27. Cf. Schneidewin-Hense on line 115f.

28. For a general discussion of Aeschylus' use of the past in preluding and forecasting future events see J. de Romilly, "L'évocation du passé dans l'*Agamemnon* d'Eschyle," *REG* 80 (1967) 93–99.

29. Kranz *Stasimon* 22, states that the dactylic meter, especially the hexameter, is often used in tragic choruses to stir reminiscences of epic poetry. G. Thomson, *Greek Lyric Metre* (Cambridge 1929) 102–04 finds precise metrical precedent in Stesichorus' narratives *The Sack of Troy* and *Oresteia*, which he feels show the "sweep and fluency of the epic hexameter."

30. Dale's argument here is cogent (*LMGD* 16 and 110); not every cretic or bacchiac is a form of syncopated iambic, but in the vast majority of cases in the *Oresteia* they are used in an iambic context. She argues that the iambic and trochaic are similar in origin and in usage:

> But even in the straight-forward stichic species of iambic and trochaic there is no such fundamental difference of origin and modification as that which separates dactyls and anapaests, and here, if anywhere, the ancient commentators were justified in their idea of an infinite series in *epiploke* . . . ∪−x−∪−x−∪ . . . as a sort of matrix from which you could hack out iambic or trochaic segments according to whether you began with an *anceps* or following long and ended with *anceps* or preceding long.   (70)

The two meters can be so fully intermingled that they are difficult to analyze (18ff. and 93–96). But even Dale admits differences in character between the two meters, based on the rising versus falling opening, the location of the main segments, and probably from delivery (72ff.). See also her "Stichos and Stanza," *Collected Papers* 173–79.

31. Wilamowitz, *AT* 166 n.2, remarks how neat and clear the syntax becomes in this trochaic section of the parodos. Thus meter joins content, syntax, and probably music and dance pattern to set this small section apart from the dactyls that precede and the iambics that follow. B. H. Fowler has identified juxtapositions of rising and falling meters accompanying a change in subject in "Plot and Prosody in Sophocles' *Antigone*," *C&M* 28 (1967) 163–71.

32. Fraenkel (II, p. 59): "Trochaic stanzas of this type are among the most noticeable elements in the choruses of the *Oresteia*. They may in fact be regarded as one of the links by which the unity of the trilogy is emphasized." Fraenkel, however, never fully explores the implications of this unifying meter or the connection of meter to content and characterization.

33. Wilamowitz, *Interpretationen* 166f., compares the parodos of the *Ag.* with that of the *Pers.*, where the "meaningful general thoughts" are placed separately in a mesode; he notes that these thoughts in the parodos to the *Ag.* are set apart in a section with its own distinctive meter.

34. Fraenkel (II. p. 74): "Such *ephymnia*, refrains, belong to the oldest (and from a religious point of view the most important) elements of liturgical song." He quotes O. Müller commenting on the refrain in the Binding Song in the *Eum.*: ". . . such a repetition of the words which express the especial purpose of the whole action was characteristic of incantations and promises of destiny. . . ."

35. The use of *kyrios* seems to stress the completeness of the entitlement: see, e.g., Arist. *EN* 3.5.8 and *Pol.* 3.16.10; Eur. *Supp.* 1189; Thuc. 4.18 and 5.63.

36. See the analyses of the growth of anxious foreboding in the *Agememnon* as seen here in the refrain line and in the whole play by B. Alexanderson, "Forebodings in the *Agamemnon*," *Eranos* 67 (1969) 1–23, and by P. Schwarz, *De Ephymniorum apud Aeschylum Usu* (Diss. Halle 1897) 11ff. Dale, *LMGD* 27, comments that only at line 159 is the refrain line joined through meter and grammar to the preceding colon. The fullness of its meaning becomes clear only at this point, and this clarity motivates the chorus's strong shift in subject and meter.

37. On the placement of this pair of strophes and the development of the chorus's thought see R. D. Dawe, "The Place of the Hymn to Zeus in Aeschylus' *Agamemnon*," *Eranos* 64 (1966) 1–21, answered by L. Bergson, "The Hymn to Zeus in Aeschylus' *Agamemnon*," *Eranos* 65 (1967) 12–24. Dawe finds the hymn in its present location vague because items in it have no specific antecedents; he therefore places it after line 217, where the idea of Zeus will relieve the contradiction between *themis* and *dyssebia*. Bergson's response is adequate, and I can add only that the traditional location reinforces the pattern of avoiding discomfort that occurs in the two other passages in the parodos. Each time, the chorus turns from a specific topic to general statements (67 and 250). The same breaks in thought and reli-

gious escapes are noted by T. J. Sienkewicz, "Circles, Confusion, and the Chorus of *Agamemnon*," *Eranos* 78 (1980) 133–42.

38. See Headlam-Thomson, on 248–57: "The connexion of thought is obscure, but the obscurity is deliberate . . ." because the elders do not want to face the conclusion that Agamemnon must suffer; "they struggle to suppress it, yet it forces itself out, abruptly and disjointedly, in spite of them." Unlike those who regard the old men as the poet's mouthpiece, Headlam-Thomson give the chorus a strongly individualized character. Indeed, much of the comment on this passage has been based—often indirectly—on the belief that the chorus is the spokesman of the poet rather than a character affected by the events of the play in a natural way; see, e.g., T. J. Rosenmeyer, "Gorgias, Aeschylus, and Apate," *AJP* 76 (1955) 225–60. In such studies the effect is all for the audience and none for the chorus members, who are denied the ability to indulge in theological thinking. Such comment denies the consistent development of the thought of the chorus in this play and undercuts the elders' ability to be real characters when it is necessary at 1346–71 and 1643–48.

For a pointed discussion of the chorus as a thoughtful, participating character in the developing events of the play, see T. Plüss, *Die Tragödie Agamemnon und das Tragische* (Basel 1896) 23–32, and P. M. Smith, *On the Hymn to Zeus in Aeschylus' Agamemnon*, *American Classical Studies* 5 (1980).

39. N. B. Booth has correctly interpreted these lines as portraying Zeus as a stern god whose 'gift' to men is the harsh gift "of bringing him to his senses against his will" in "Zeus Hypsistos Megistos: An Argument for Enclitic *pou* in Aeschylus, *Agamemnon* 182," *CQ* 26 (1976) 220–28 on 227; he is answering an improbable construction of these lines by M. Pope, "Merciful Heavens," *JHS* 94 (1974) 100–13. Similar to Booth is M. Ewans, "Agamemnon at Aulis: A Study in the *Oresteia*," *Ramus* 4 (1975) 17–32, who sees the chorus conscious of the sinister aspect of their theology.

40. See Fraenkel (on line 165) who correctly defines *maten* as "the futile, the deluded, the 'vain,' which expresses itself in the denial of existing values and powers." Then he interprets the lines as follows: "Such a misconception is here called *achthos* because it oppresses a man and whelms him in stupor, and because he must cast it from him if he would reach his aim. If he is to succeed in really freeing himself from his burden, there is only one course to take: to recognize that Zeus is supreme and that there is none other like him." Fraenkel construes these words as the true feelings of the poet and the people of Athens. Such may be the case at the end of the *Eum.*, but acceptance of Zeus will not be so relieving to the characters involved in the first two plays. Artemis opposes Zeus's plan, Orestes will be made an unfortunate victim for accepting this plan, and the Furies will receive the supportive votes of six Athenians for protesting against the bloody reign of Zeus. See further the careful interpretation of these lines by P. Smith, *Hymn to Zeus*.

41. See Scott, "Non-Strophic Elements" 188f.

42. The same device is used at *Supp.* 625–97 and appears later in Euripides' Hymn to Heracles (*Herc.* 348–450); cf. Wilamowitz, *Interpreta-*

tionen 168, and, H. Moritz, "Refrain in Aeschylus: Literary Adaptation of Traditional Form," *CP* 74 (1979) 187–213. A similar technique provides metrical unity in the ode at *Supp.* 526–99, where the first lines of the second, fourth, and fifth strophes are metrically identical and the first line of the third stanzas differs by only one short syllable. As will be noted later (chap. 4, pp. 165–71), the *Supp.* shows very balanced musical forms, in keeping with the determined unity of the chorus.

43. Kraus, *Strophengestaltung* 84ff., discusses the high degree of metrical unity in this stasimon. Fraenkel, (on line 367) points out that the lyric is introduced by a close syntactical and structural balance between strophe and antistrophe; thus the first lyric music the audience hears in this song works to establish an expectation of balance and unity.

44. Wilamowitz, *Interpretationen* 168, suggests that the form of this chorus is modeled on sacred ("hieratische") music. If so, the irony would be all the clearer: the chorus sings religious and hopeful words in a song that is highly ordered and balanced in structure, but the meter tells another story.

45. Line 408 contains the only possible resolution, and this has been based on a false reading, as shown by Fraenkel, *ad loc.* and II, 351. The reading of F provides a corresponsion without parallel in the *Oresteia*.

46. A point made by H. D. F. Kitto, "The Dance in Greek Tragedy," *JHS* 75 (1955) 36–41.

47. H. D. F. Kitto, *Form and Meaning in Drama* (London 1956) 10–13, illustrates the chorus's thought by a proportion: "Paris' crime: his destruction:: Agamemnon's crime:?"

48. For an analysis of the consistency of their argument see Alexanderson, "Forebodings" 7ff., and Arnoldt, *Der Chor im Agamemnon*, 39f. Arnoldt notes that at the end of the stasimon the chorus returns to the same principles that they cited at the beginning.

49. This epode has always caused problems for commentators. In addition to the commentaries see Arnoldt, *Der Chor im Agamemnon* 41ff., where he argues that the epode is really part of the following episode and is separated from the lyric by its predominantly iambic meter as opposed to the glyconic/pherecratean system that closes the elements of the lyric. J. H. Schmidt, *Die Eurhythmie* (Leipzig 1868) 166 points out that two lines in the epode are trimeters "möglicherweise mehr gesprochen als gesungen." But the basic difficulty with this epode concerns consistency in the character of the chorus. Fraenkel, II, p. 248f., states one position clearly: "If they had to function as ordinary characters in the play, the sequence of their changing moods would probably be brought into a consistent line of psychological progress. As a Chorus, however, they are possessed of less spontaneity; their words serve in the main as a reaction to the acts and words of the actors or as a means of leading them on. There is, as it were, a certain looseness in the psychological texture of the Chorus." He has been recently supported by R. D. Dawe, "Inconsistency of Plot and Character in Aeschylus," *PCPhS* 9 (1968) 21–62, and by K. J. Dover, "Some Neglected Aspects of Agamemnon's Dilemma," *JHS* 93 (1973) 58–69. Few critics seem to note the attempt to continue the iambic meter as a close connection

to the previous ode, nor do they comment on the chorus's characteristic pattern of avoiding all hostile judgment on Agamemnon. The former feature indicates the necessary continuity between ode and epode, and the latter shows how completely in character the epode is. For discussions of the consistency in ode and epode see Winnington-Ingram, "*Agamemnon* 1343–71" 23–30; O. L. Smith, "Once Again: The Guilt of Agamemnon," *Eranos* 71 (1973) 1–11; and W. C. Scott, "Lines for Clytemnestra," *TAPA* 108 (1978) 259–69.

50. Page regards such a split of roles as probable in "The Chorus of Alcman's *Partheneion*," *CQ* 31 (1937) 94. The lines are split in a variety of ways by Hermann, Müller, Enger, Keck, Arnoldt, Weil, Wecklein, Mazon, Murray, Smyth, Thomson, and Page (in his 1957 edition with Denniston though not so printed in his 1972 *editio maior*).

51. In addition, I have argued in "Lines for Clytemnestra" that the chorus does not continue speaking through 502; rather, Clytemnestra speaks lines 489–502 as a positive assertion to the befuddled and scoffing members of the chorus.

52. Defined by Denniston-Page as "variations on pherecratean."

53. The scansion pattern of this ode shows a modulation to the rising line of the ionic from the falling trochaic rhythm through the mediating choriambic lines 686–87 = 705–06 and 742–43 = 755–56. In this ode it is important to see that the shift from one meter to another is as smooth and orderly as possible, with neither disjointedness in form or content nor disappointed expectation for the audience . For the importance and frequency of such modulating meters in Greek lyric see J. Irigoin, *Recherches sur les mètres de la lyrique chorale greque: La structure du vers* (Paris 1953); B. Snell, *Griechische Metrik* (Göttingen 1955) 47f.; and Brown, "Analysis of Tragic Meter."

54. The only other occurrences of the ionic in this trilogy are in the second stasimon of the *Ch.*, 807–11 and 827–30.

55. The animal fable is clear in itself, but it presents problems when applied directly to Helen; see Denniston-Page on 744ff. He tries to establish clarity by making the subject there the Erinys, not Helen; but such an interpretation, though possible for readers, would not occur to a listening audience. We should admit that the chorus is attempting to find a parallel but is unable to make it work fully. The same is true when the chorus applies the simile of the young vultures to the situation at Troy; there the disparity is sufficient to cause the elders to turn to faith for comfort (60–67). See also the drawing of inadequate mythical parallels at *Ch.* 585–651 discussed on pp. 95–98.

56. Knox, "Lion in the House" 17–25, identifies numerous themes connected with the lion parable; but although the playwright may want to keep these themes alive in the play through a reminder in the parable, the chorus as character is blind to such full implications, as the Cassandra scene shows.

57. Lines 757–58 stress the elders' feeling that the view developed here is theirs. Such a statement testifies to their pride in thinking matters through

for themselves as they continue to express the optimistic doctrine of punishment for crime under justice, a belief that they have sought to maintain since the animal fable in the parodos (49-59).

58. Words for birth and growth proliferate in the last three stanzas of this stasimon: *tiktei, teknousthai, tokou, tokeusin, genei, gennai, apaida, kallipais, blastanein.*

59. Cf. Arnoldt, *Der Chor im Agamemnon* 48: ". . . der Gedankengang . . . stetig durch das Chorikon fortschreitet und von Anbeginn bis zum Schlusse in bewussterweise einem bestimmten Ziele zustrebt, so dass wer das Letzte dachte und aussprach auch das Erste gedacht und gesprochen haben muss."

60. The most famous similar Aeschylean entrance is that of the unknowing Aegisthus at *Ch.* 838; see also *Pers.* 909, *Seven* 792, and *Supp.* 825, where characters enter on appropriate—even ironically appropriate—words. For a study of other remarks that have a truer meaning than first appears, see J. J. Peradotto, "Cledonomancy in the *Oresteia*," *AJP* 90 (1969) 1-21.

61. This is a common meter to accompany more formal or ceremonial entrances of characters; cf. *Pers.* 150-54 and *Seven* 861-74. Brown, "Analysis of Tragic Meter" 67-71, cites further examples where postlyric anapaests are a customary transition meter between lyric song and spoken lines.

62. I have taken much of value for the discussion of the stasimon from J. de Romilly, *La crainte et l'angoisse dans le théâtre d'Eschyle* (Paris 1958); I feel, however, that her detailed discussion of this passage (pp. 60-80) does not adequately explain the dilemma of the chorus. She describes their fear for Agamemnon but does not discuss the source of their hope that Agamemnon may escape death.

63. For fuller discussion of this stasimon see W. C. Scott, "The Confused Chorus (*Agamemnon* 975-1034)," *Phoenix* 23 (1969) 336-46.

64. Fraenkel (on line 1124) notes the similarity of the images in the two passages.

65. Fraenkel points out (on line 979) that Aeschylus makes the gruesomeness of the secretly heard music especially effective by the words *akeleustos, amisthos,* and *aneu lyras.* This is music "altogether different from the song which is sung at meal-times or on some festal occasion." Commenting on *autodidaktos* at 922, he states: "Here again, then, the awful chant which the heart sings as a *threnos* of the Erinys is set against the background of that festal song which is the delight of all." In both the stasimon and the Cassandra scene Aeschylus makes clear that the music is discomforting and unpleasant.

66. Dale, *LMGD* 110f.

67. Neither Alexanderson, "Forebodings" 19-23, nor Dawe, "Inconsistencies of Plot" 46, feels that the chorus is consistent in ignoring the warnings of Cassandra. But in this context one should bear in mind the truth that there are none so deaf as those who will not hear. If the chorus is a character in this play, the old men should be consistent here with their confused posture in the third stasimon; otherwise they become a spineless

stage property. The depth of their hope and faith as expressed in the previous odes is adequate explanation for their unwillingness to take obvious hints that they should renounce their belief. See the fine analysis of this scene by Winnington-Ingram, "*Agamemnon* 1343–71, esp. 26–29. It is on the grounds of consistent characterization that this issue should be argued; there is no need to depend solely on Apollo's curse as does P. A. L. Greenhalgh, "Cassandra and the Chorus in Aeschylus' *Agamemnon*," *RSC* 17 (1969) 253–58.

68. On normal form of such an amoibaion, in which the chorus leads the actor, see Fraenkel, III, p. 487f. For an analysis of the effect of iambic trimeters interspersed among lyric lines, see Pickard-Cambridge, *DFA* 162ff.

69. Few commentators set this passage in context. It is of central importance to note that the sentence is both conditional and a question. Lines 1331–37 tell of the great good fortune that the gods have given to Agamemnon and explain why it was only natural for him to accept it. Then comes the condition: if he dies, then all are condemned. But the chorus continues its pattern of avoiding negative comments about Agamemnon; the elders' continuing inability to understand Cassandra's simple statements shows that they are not ready to accept the need for Agamemnon's death. Since the existence of the *daimon asines* (harmless divinity) or his opposite is based on a condition, there is no need for either to exist if the supposition is not true. "If criminal X were to be acquitted, then would the law code be working?" implies that X will be condemned and that the speaker is reasonably sure that the law code is working. Similarly, 1338–42 is in fact a positive statement expressing tentative trust in the same benevolent, if harsh, deity that the chorus has described since the Hymn to Zeus.

70. See the discussion of the introductory function of anapaests by Brown, "Analysis of Tragic Meter" 51 ff., and J. Rode, *Untersuchungen zur Form des aischyleischen Chorliedes* (Diss. Tübingen 1965) 45–48.

71. Cf. the discussion by H. D. Broadhead, "Some Passages of the *Agamemnon*," *CQ* 9 (1959) 312–15; G. Wills, "*Agamemnon* 1346–71, 1649–53," *HSCP* 68 (1963) 255–62; and Peradotto, "Cledonomancy," esp. 14–17. Winnington-Ingram, "*Agamemnon* 1343–71," goes too far in finding a structured debate in the lines of the chorus, but he does show that their evasiveness here arises from previous characterization.

72. It may be significant that only at this point does the scholium preserved in Triclinius' commentary on *Ag.* 1343 describe the members of the chorus as *hypokritai*; generally the word is used only of individual actors. Cf. the similar challenge to the function of the tragic chorus at Soph. *O. T.* 863–910, a passage well discussed by U. Hölscher, "Wie soll ich noch tanzen?" in *Sprachen der Lyrik. Festschrift für Hugo Freidrich zum 70. Geburtstag* (Frankfurt 1975) 375–93.

73. For a discussion of Clytemnestra's growing insight into her act, see E. R. Dodds, "Morals and Politics in the *Oresteia*," *PCPhS* 186 (1960) 19–31, republished in *The Ancient Concept of Progress* (Oxford 1973) 45–63, esp. 60f.

74. Notice the imperatives in lines 1462 and 1464, as well as her compliment to the chorus on correcting themselves, 1475–77.

75. Clytemnestra replies in five separate stanzas of anapaests, the first two of which are similar in form (1462–67 and 1475–80), each with five lines in the same pattern: dimeter, monometer, three dimeters, paroemiac; see W. Christ, *Metrik* (Leipzig, 1879) 263. At 1497–1504, 1521–29, 1551–59, and 1567–76 the parallelism ceases, the stanzas being respectively eight, eleven, nine, and ten lines (1521–29 is impossible to count precisely because there is a lacuna at 1522–23). Other attempts at quasi-strophic balance, at *Ch.* 1006–20 and *Eum.* 948–95, are discussed in their place later in the chapter. A. Peretti, *Epirrema e tragedia* (Florence 1939) argues for the approximate balance in anapaestic epirrhematic stanzas both as a traditional form and as one used often by Aeschylus. This claim is questionable, given both the lack of evidence and the imprecise balance in the customary colometry of these sections. Yet in a scene between two speakers in which there is indication of an attempt to organize speeches in corresponding sections, his analysis does point to the use of form to enhance Clytemnestra's inability to achieve order in form as well as thought. For the device of quasi-strophic anapaests, cf. *Seven* 879–80 = 886–87 and Eur. *And.* 515–22 = 537–44.

76. C. J. Herington has pointed out to me the clear coincidence of word-end and metrical unit in *Ag.* 1485–87 and—only slightly less striking—1509–11. This is carefully marked iambic meter.

77. On the structure of this scene, see Kranz, *Stasimon* 91 ff. Fraenkel in his comment on line 1560 regards these lines as an expression of confusion because the old men are "faced with an insoluble dilemma," but the sense of confusion does not necessarily spread this far from the third stasimon (975–1033). Since that song, much has happened to give them certainty. Here they retain their basic belief in a god who exacts punishment for crime (*thesmion gar*), and they have seen Agamemnon killed. Even though the events of the play have made their belief in a god who cares for men untenable, they can see clearly the justification for another act of blood. Clytemnestra, who also can see this conclusion, attempts to strike her bargain with the *daimon*. On both sides there is more clarity than confusion—although neither is happy with its new understanding.

78. The parallels to the second stasimon are: Eris, 698 and 1460; *haimatoessa, haima* 698, 716, and 1460; Helen as a flower and flower-giver, 743 and 1459; Helen as destroyer of Troy, 699–716 and 1456.

79. Fraenkel (III, pp. 661 f.) notes that the broken pattern of choral response in this scene is surprising, especially in view of metrical and verbal similarities between the ephymnia: "It is true that the parallelism between the ephymnia of I (1455 ff.) and III (1537 ff.) and those of II (1489 ff. = 1513 ff.) is marked not only by the uncommon metrical form, i.e. an anapaestic period followed by purely lyrical lines, but also by the similarity of the opening exclamations: "ἰὼ παράνους Ἑλένα/ἰὼ ἰὼ βασιλεῦ/ἰὼ ἰὼ γᾶ γᾶ."

80. The closest parallels to such a scene in which different points of view are presented in a balanced exchange are *Seven* 202–30, *Supp.* 348–417 and 734–63, and *Ag.* 1072–1177.

81. See Scott, "Non-Strophic Elements" 185–87, for a full discussion of this passage, with bibliography.

82. There has been some dispute on what the proper ending for this play should be. A. Kirchhoff, "Über den Schluss von Aischylos *Agamemnon*," *Sitzungsberichte der Akademie der Wissenschaften, Berlin* (1894) 1037–53, postulates that the concluding choral lines have been lost but also argues that the ending of the play should be suitable to the situation (esp. in the *PV*). This line of argument has been developed by T. Plüss, *Die Tragödie Agamemnon* 21f., and by Wilamowitz, "Excurse zum *Oedipus* des Sophokles," *Hermes* 34 (1899) 67f. and *Interpretationen* 177; both scholars provide refutation of Kirchhoff and define the effect that Aeschylus was trying to create at the end of the *Ag*. See also Fraenkel III, pp. 803ff.

83. Whatever the precise words of Orestes at the beginning of the play were, he appears as a grieving mourner sneaking to his father's tomb. His speech provides an interesting parallel to the watchman's. Both, seeing the chorus begin to enter, speak as it comes on stage, thus joining the prologue closely to the parodos with no room for a break. Orestes may come with a purpose and Apollo's blessing, but his behavior on stage should introduce a feeling of fear and suspicion reminiscent of the watchman's speech and here carried over into the chorus's words.

84. Kraus, *Strophengestaltung* 97, introduces an ithyphallic or a dochmiac because the long and unrelieved section of iambics seems not to fit in next to the smaller sections: ". . . neben den übrigen kurzen und klaren Gliedern erscheint jene Langreihe an ihrer Stelle wenig glaublich." On the contrary, the dullness of meter in this chorus and in this whole play seems not only conceivable but thematically appropriate.

85. The more standard stage direction of commentators that the women and Electra do not enter until line 22 makes Orestes' speech odd. If they were entering during the parodos, he could see them in the distance and finish his speech before they enter. But these ladies come from the palace— that is, out through the door in the scene building. Either Orestes and the audience together see them or they do not. Since Orestes not only uses the verb *leusso* but also describes the color of their garments, identifies the jars in which they carry their libations, and recognizes Electra, we may safely assume that this is not the precursor of the comic device of the creaking door. A scene for contrast is Sophocles, *OT* 1294–96, where the messenger describes the opening of the doors before the blinded Oedipus enters. I believe the chorus enters from the palace because it is there, visible to all, and because the women say that they are sent from it, but a number of critics make them enter from the side—usually to avert having the tomb so unrealistically close to the palace; see Taplin, *Stagecraft* 336, with the bibliography cited there. But this is a needless problem and has been explained away by Bodensteiner, "Szenische Fragen": "Während die Schauspieler am Orte bleiben, kann der Ort nicht wechseln. Aber kann er nicht wechseln, während die Schauspieler selbst unterwegs sind?" (658); and A. M. Dale, "Interior Scenes and Illusion," *Collected Papers* 267, feels uncomfortable about assenting to a side entrance.

86. N. B. Booth, "Aeschylus, *Choephori*, 61–65," *CQ* 7 (1957) 143–45, and "The Run of the Sense in Aeschylus' *Choephori* 22–83," *CP* 54 (1959) 111–13, argues that the chorus is despairing throughout this ode. But this chorus characteristically shows no such despair when it instructs Electra, and it continually encourages the speakers in the kommos. Yet Booth sees the sequence of light-twilight-night as parallel to immediate-delayed-never in terms of the persecution of a sinner and interprets 65 to mean that some men escape punishment completely (*akrantos*). His point seems sound, and we can probably remove any contradiction by realizing that the women can be optimistic and eager in pursuit of vengeance even though they are unhappy about the long years of delay. This chorus is willing to aid swift justice (61–62) simply on the basis of a fear that Clytemnestra and Aegisthus will escape punishment indefinitely (63–74) or forever (65). The women's unquestioning passion for vengeance stands in contrast to the certainty of the cosmic justice desired by the chorus in the *Ag*.

87. See Scott, "Non-Strophic Elements" 191.

88. There is a parallel in rising emotions in this scene. Electra, initially questioning, must be coached but then prays forcefully for revenge; the chorus speaks in iambics but then responds to her prayer in this emotional lament largely in dochmiacs.

89. S. Srebrny, *Wort und Gedanke bei Aischylos* (Breslau 1964) 90–99, shows how this scene builds from line 106. Neither Electra nor the chorus wants to say Orestes' name, but both lead toward it so clearly that he is the obvious answer to her prayer at 142–44. The choral lyric then parallels this prayer at a higher emotional level: lines 152–58 are a prayer for aid in answer to the libations, and 159–63 a prayer for an avenger. Thus the scene moves always in general terms, but the specific solution is persistently clear to all and moreover is concretely visible to the audience. As Electra and the chorus exchange lines, they become increasingly bold and outspoken. It is in this growth of spirit that the force of the dead seems to come alive prior to this lyric. Cf. also Weil (1860) on 147ff.

90. Rode, "Das Chorlied" in Jens, *Bauformen* 90–103.

91. So designated by Dale, *LMGD* 106.

92. Wilamowitz, *Interpretationen* 209.

93. There is a similar use of framing anapaests in the parodos to the *Pers*. Note also the return to earlier meters: 467–68 = 318, 320, 322, 353, 383, and 387–90; 469–70 = 331 and 384 are related to the Aeolic meters at 317, 321, and 325–26.

94. See *Ag*. 1462–67 and 1475–80, *Eum*. 968–75 and 988–95, and the discussions on pp. 68–73 and 132–33.

95. Schütz was the first to move these lines to a position following 455; he was followed by Weil and Pohlenz, *Die Griechische Tragödie* 2 vols. (Leipzig and Berlin 1930) II, 36–38 and strongly defended by Wilamowitz, *Interpretationen* 205ff., and in his commentary on the *Choephoroi*, *Aischylos Orestie* (Berlin 1896); and by A. Lesky, "Der Kommos der *Choephoren*." I follow Schadewaldt, "Der Kommos in Aischylos *Choephoren*," who argues for retaining these lines in their manuscript position and has been sup-

ported by, among others, Smyth, Murray, Mazon, and Page. Lebeck, *The Oresteia* 110-30, gives a sensitive reading concluding that the kommos is a "lyrical statement of the forces which lead to decision, a study of dilemma and choice" (114) by a committed Orestes. See the evaluation of previous interpretations of the kommos in D. J. Conacher, "Interaction between Chorus and Characters in the *Oresteia*," *AJP* 95 (1974) 330-39.

96. It is weakening to Lesky's interpretation that Electra must be intellectually as well as emotionally strong during the kommos to encourage a wavering Orestes. She is portrayed as paralyzed and indecisive during the first part of the play when she asks for advice on how to pray (84-105), seems unwilling to mention Orestes' name (164-78), and places all her hope in Orestes (235-45).

97. Aeschylean characters make their decisions quickly without openly debating issues onstage. Eteocles (*Seven* 654-56) has three lines of frustrated rage before he states his determined decision, and then defends it resolutely against the chorus. The Erinyes rage when they lose their case but change their minds quickly at *Eum.* 892-902 in a stichomythia that focuses on contractual arrangements rather than on the greater issues of respect for the old law, cooperation of new gods with old, or a new relationship between gods and mortals; those issues have already been resolved in Athena's persuasive speeches (esp. 804-07, 832-36, 854-57, 867-9, 890-91). Pelasgus (*Supp.* 323-489) also provides a poor parallel to Orestes. Up to 417 he offers reasons why he should not be involved in the issue, and in his speech at 438-54 he acknowledges that pain may be involved in his decision but does not speak words of personal emotion. At 466 he finally admits that he feels anguish, and even the chorus seems to realize in 467 that only here have they made Pelasgus' personal dilemma clear to him. But then in thirteen lines, with little weighing of costs and alternatives, the problem is stated, quickly decided, and the decision executed. There is little personal involvement to compare with the emotional questioning or outcries at *Ch.* 408-09, 418-19, and 429-30; nor any indication of physical response to the decision as at *Ch.* 410-14. Pelasgus is remarkably self-contained and rational in this whole debate, and his process of decision is not really like the openly portrayed suffering and despair seen by Lesky in Orestes (see also chap. 4, pp. 167-69). And, of course, Agamemnon's decision at Aulis is reported indirectly but with little overt emotion in the balancing of issues. Indeed, the expression "may it turn out well," used by both Pelasgus and Agamemnon, shows a desire to shift the burden of decision from one's own shoulders by placing faith in external powers (*Supp.* 454 and *Ag.* 217); see Athena's dilemma at *Eum.* 470-88. Thus, in Aeschylean drama there is no parallel to Lesky's view of Orestes in the kommos.

98. Wilamowitz, *Orestie*, tries to minimize this problem by stating that the choral songs were added independently after the composition of the dialogue. Even if we could ever know such a thing, Aeschylus does not present other characters who segment their decisions into sequential presentations. More useful are the comments on the combinations and integration of older forms into new unities in the *Oresteia* by W. Schadewaldt,

"Ursprung und frühe Entwicklung der attischen Tragödie," in *Wege zu Aischylos I* (Darmstadt 1974) 104–47; and Rode, *Untersuchungen* 185–91.

99. Schadewaldt, "Der Kommos in Aischylos *Choephoren*" 336–38, and the reconstructions and comments by Weil, Wecklein, Tucker, Verrall, and others. Wilamowitz, *Orestie* 199 on the other hand, considers the text too corrupt to interpret and continues to see choral dismay at Orestes' despair. Lesky, "Der Kommos der *Choephoren*" 82 interprets 415–17 as the first glimmer of hope for a future decision.

100. So Blass and Tucker. Verrall feels that she only wants to sustain their spirits. Both positions are suited to a view of a weaker Electra and are complementary to my interpretation.

101. This line should be seen as a welcoming of death once he has committed the murder; cf. Eur. *Electra* 281 and Soph. *Ajax* 391. For a perceptive discussion of the motives of both Electra and Orestes see J. de Romilly, "La haine dans l'*Orestie*," *Dioniso* 48 (1977) 33–53.

102. Other Aeschylean passages that have such split roles and are cited by Page, "The Chorus of Alcman's Partheneion" 94–99, show disunity of thought among chorus members; cf. *Seven* 78–107 and 1066–78, *Supp.* 1052–61, *Eum.* 143–77 and 254–75. The examples from Sophocles and Euripides have other uses such as lament, excitement, and characterization but do not seem to be used to show an internal disunity. That there were occurrences of individual singers in otherwise unified forms is stated (though long after the fifth century) at Athenaeus *Deip.* 694a–c. The reference here is to a totally different genre of singing, but at least there is this ancient indication that the splitting of songs implied increased disorder.

103. Only at 500–2 does Electra make her final appeal; the members of the chorus conclude the invocation by 510–13 in which they turn to action and are seconded by Orestes in 514–17.

104. Obviously the markings in themselves do not possess great authority, but in this case they are supported by dramatic considerations that some scholars have judged determining. This section is split between the chorus and Orestes/Electra by Hartung, Schoelefield, Peile, Blass, and Tucker; between semichoruses by Bamberger, Hermann, and Paley; between all and the coryphaeus alone by Kirchhoff, Wecklein, and Verrall. Dindorff, Blomfeld, Wellauer, Weil, Sidgwick, Wilamowitz *AT*, Mazon, Smyth, Thomson, Page, and Lloyd-Jones assign the section to the unified chorus.

105. Wilamowitz *AT*; Lesky, "Der Kommos der *Choephoren*" 103; and Mazon, suggest that after the kommos Orestes and Electra mount upon the tomb and begin to pound it.

106. Thomson, *Greek Lyric Metre* 123f., shows how these themes are balanced in the corresponding stanzas of Orestes and Electra.

107. For studies of similar choral misapplications of mythical precedent, see Murray, *Motif of Io*, esp. 46–76; and K. Neuhausen, "Tereus und die Danaiden bei Aeschylus," *Hermes* 91 (1969) 167–86. E. B. Holtsmark, "On *Choephoroi* 585–651," *CW* 59 (1966) 215–16 and 251, agrees on the chorus's intent in citing the three ethical exempla. Among recent studies

A. Lebeck, "The First Stasimon of Aeschylus' *Choephoroi*: Myth and Mirror Image," *CP* 62 (1967) 182–85, sees a reference to all the murders of the house in this centrally placed ode. In a general poetic sense, one must agree; however, given that the audience will be far more aware of the immediate direction of the chorus's words, the closing reference to the Erinys that brings the son back to the house calls for direct application of these mythical paradigms to the situation in the play. T. C. W. Stinton, "The First Stasimon of Aeschylus' *Choephoroi*," *CQ* 29 (1979) 252–62, is the most recent to recommend reversing the third strophe and antistrophe to make all the mythical examples point only to the need for retribution; but this produces a precision in parallels not present in the thoughts of the chorus, who are seeking parallels for an act of justice (see 639–51).

108. Of the standard sources for the story of Althaea only Apollodorus 1.8.1 and Diodorus 4.34 report that she hangs herself in remorse for killing her child; see Ovid, *Met.* 8.531–32. Otherwise she fades from the myth with no vengeance being sought against her.

109. Apollodorus 3.15.18 reports that Minos tied her to his ship and drowned her. Vengeance could come only from her own family; Minos was punishing her as a traitorous woman even though she aided him. Alternatively she is turned into a ciris.

110. Only Apollonius Rhodius 1.609ff. shows the Lemnians after the crime. There is no overt act of vengeance, but they are punished by sexual longing and the fear of dying out totally.

111. W. Headlam, "Upon Aeschylus," *CR* 14 (1900) 196f. (later taken up by Thomson in his commentary on lines 623–38), argues that strophe g contains an objection by a second voice, which is then corrected. But Page, "The Chorus of Alcman's *Partheneion*" 95, correctly denies such a splitting of the chorus in this spot. Headlam himself acknowledges that the three mythological examples are precedents only for the commission of crimes by misguided women.

112. Taplin, *Stagecraft* 351f., describes this movement well; see also the general comments on the second part of the *Ch.* by Schadewaldt, "Ursprung und frühe Entwicklung" 136ff.

113. The clearest example of such disjunction is Eur. *Alcestis* 741–45, where there is a similar replacement of lyric by anapaests. The stage is deserted even by the chorus, and a new phase of action begins. Other choral anapaestic stanzas (Soph. *Ajax* 1163–67; Eur. *Medea* 357–63, 759–65, and *Herakleidae* 288–96) are called markers by Brown, "Analysis of Tragic Meter" 49ff., but these do not occur while the stage is empty even though they do divide the scene into movements.

114. Wilamowitz would complicate this simple intent; at *Orestie* 227f. he states that the chorus realizes how much of a crime is involved in their reference to Perseus; they see that the precedent of pursuit by the Gorgons may lead to vengeance here—and yet they continue to urge Orestes to the deed. Still they forget their fears quickly at 855–68 and do not allude to possible punishment until 931–34. Rather the chorus here is using a technique from the preceding stasimon, where they used mythological exam-

ples that were only partially apt and offered little justification if the whole myth was applied. It is for the audience to appreciate the short-sightedness of the chorus; there are no signs in this part of the play that the chorus understands the cost following on the murder.

115. See pp. 51–56.

116. 825 = 836 could be scanned as 2 cr + ia; similarly, 826 = 837 could be cr + ia (so Schroeder but not Untersteiner). Elsewhere I have tried to see the lecythion wherever possible because it is the meter that is least suited to my interpretation of the musical design of the trilogy and thus constitutes negative evidence. Even if this scansion is not accepted, the repeated lecythion from the first strophe is broken up by the intrusion of iambs in the third strophe so that there is still a turn away from lecythion to iambic. At issue is only the forcefulness of that turn.

117. See Scott, "Non-Strophic Elements" 191f.

118. The suspense created by this short anapaestic song is well described by Rode, *Untersuchungen* 152f. Brown, "Analysis of Tragic Meter," 53f., notes the similarity to the anapests at the moment of Agamemnon's death cries at *Ag.* 1331ff.

119. Dale, *LMGD* 110f.

120. The dochmiac will also be found in the more bloodthirsty songs of the Erinyes when they are pursuing Orestes at *Eum.* 143–77 and 254–75 and when they are threatening murderous vengeance upon Athens at 778–92 = 808–22 and 837–46 = 870–80. In each case the dochmiac should make the audience think that yet another act of violence is about to be accomplished in the name of (a flawed) justice.

121. See Scott, "Non-Strophic Elements" 192–94.

122. For discussions of similarities in the stage arrangements in the *Ag.* and the *Cho.* see G. Murray, *Aeschylus* 180; A. Lesky, "Die *Orestie* des Aischylos," in his *Gesammelte Schriften* (Bern 1966) 103–05; and Taplin, *Stagecraft* 342f and 356–61.

123. See Dale, *LMGD* 115f.

124. Aeschylus joins these two seemingly opposed meters at several other places (*Pers.* 1072–77; *Seven* in the parodos and often thereafter; *Supp.* 348 = 59, 370 = 81, 656–66 = 667–77, 738 = 45; *Ag.* in the Cassandra scene and in the lyrics 1407–61; *Ch.* 152–63, 935 = 71; *Eum.* 780–92) but never at such length and with the persistent alternation of these two entering songs.

125. Two other victims of the harsh world of the *Oresteia* are also women who are compelled to acknowledge rugged forces in control of a universe that they hoped was beneficient and permanent: Iphigenia, portrayed as the innocent maiden who sang at her father's banquet, and Cassandra, whose mind reels as she foresees the slaughter that her patron and would-be lover has planned for her (*Ag.* 243–47 and 1072–92). One might also add Electra, who was locked up during her father's funeral (*Ch.* 444–49).

126. Diodorus 17.92 uses *mugmos* to describe doglike sounds; thus there is a possible relationship between these sounds and the characterization of the chorus as hunting dogs.

127. It is disputed when this chorus appears and how it makes its entrance. Müller, Blass, Mazon, Young, and Lloyd-Jones have them made visible with Apollo and Orestes at line 64; Hermann brings them on at line 94; Bodensteiner, "Szenische Fragen" 663 f., Verrall, and Rose, among others, have them enter at 140. But the entrance at 94 is unfeasible; there is no real way to have them enter as they are being told that they are asleep unless they ride the eccyclema—but then they would have been visible earlier when the doors were open. At 64 they would enter along with the whole tableau scene from the interior of the temple, and this solution tends to have a fatal attraction to those who believe in the early existence of the eccyclema; but there are problems with the number of Erinyes and the size and maneuverability of this device, if it even existed at this early time (Bodensteiner, "Szenische Fragen" 663 f.). Taplin, *Stagecraft* 369 f., argues vigorously for a late entrance of the Erinyes at 140 on the basis of two considerations: the chorus normally enters to its music and not before it, and the late entrance creates suspense and is effective theater. In regard to the first point Taplin himself admits that a very good reason would allow a chorus to enter before its music began (371); and, indeed, in this case there is such a reason, for this scene embodies the full breakdown of the form of the chorus, which is appropriately an element in this series of "summary" scenes at the beginning of the *Eum.* On his second point, I am sure that he has described the effect desired in bringing the Furies onstage, but there are other ways to achieve this effect. I am surprised that he does not consider having them there from the beginning in what he calls at several other places in his book a "cancelled entry." The Erinyes, Orestes, and Apollo would enter from the stage building and remain on the stage as a kind of tableau before the play begins. The priestess enters through one of the parodoi but does not notice the characters because they are "in" the temple and she is still outside. After line 33 she turns and goes toward the stage building. As she reaches the steps, she sees the scene and recoils and then, returning to the orchestra, delivers lines 34–64 (thus solving Taplin's problem with her midscene entrance and exit).

The priestess's *ek domon* (35) could refer to her movement back away from the stage; her description of the tableau would call attention to and introduce the characters. Such staging would also arouse the desired suspense, for the Erinyes would appear only as huddled, amorphous lumps if they covered their masks so that they could shock the audience when they revealed them later and came closer to them by entering the orchestra. The convention of having scenes properly interior on the stage while the orchestra represents the outside is precedented at *Ag.* 1372–98 ff. (cf. 1379). And there are scenes in which characters or chorus wait without words until an entering speaker notices them; see the herald who notices the chorus at *Ag.* 538, Agamemnon ignoring Clytemnestra at *Ag.* 810, and Aegisthus not noticing the chorus at *Ag.* 1577–1611. See the discussion of the full employment of this device by D. Bain, *Actors and Audience* (Oxford 1977). The staging that I have suggested for the *Eum.* would be unique because it combines these two conventions; yet Greek drama continually combines and enriches standard conventions and devices.

Taplin's design of a late entrance is also possible, but there are problems because of the close relationship between Clytemnestra and the Erinyes. She continually addresses them as though they were present (e.g., 95, 96, 98) and even shows them her wounds (103). I feel that they must have been present for this scene, and the canceled entry is the only possible way of bringing them on before Clytemnestra appears.

128. There is strong disagreement among editors on the singers of these lines. I have given Murray's markings on the scansion chart. Wellauer, Bamberger, Hermann, Müller, Sidgwick, de Falco, and Young would split at least part of this song among separate voices. Rossbach, Kirchoff, Westphal, and Wecklein give sections of the song to semichoruses. Schütz, Paley, Weil, Wilamowitz, and Page retain a united chorus—although Page, "The Chorus of Alcman's *Partheneion*" 94, earlier considered some sort of split almost certain.

129. ". . . quick and direct, quite likely at a run" (Taplin, *Stagecraft* 375).

130. C. J. Herington, "The Influence of Old Comedy on Aeschylus' Later Trilogies," *TAPA* 94 (1963) 113–23, comments on the unique nature, appearance, and function of the chorus in the *Eum.*; this tragedy alone of the surviving plays is constructed "around the raging opposition of the chorus to all the actors, followed by its abrupt conversion to an equally intense benevolence" (116f.).

131. Page, "The Chorus of Alcman's *Partheneion*" 95, calls this a certain split. The parallel usually offered is *Ajax* 866ff.; but there the commands of Tecmessa at 803–12 and the obvious responsiveness of one group to another suggests semichoruses. The scene in the *Ajax* is not parallel to that in the *Eum.* in having symmetrical entrances from opposite directions; the image of hunting dogs suggests more random movement than this. Also the speeches of the Erinyes do not indicate a conversation, with one group answering only one other group.

132. B. Todt, "Beiträge zur Kritik der *Eumeniden* des Aischylos," *Philologus* 44 (1885) 35ff., noted that the lecythion closes not only ephymnium a but also each strophe. The effect is to give more prominence to that meter, which will emerge more forcefully in the next ode, and to dilute the cumulative effect of the iambics.

133. See Scott, "Non-Strophic Elements" 189–91.

134. Cf. Wilamowitz, *Interpretationen* 181; Kranz, *Stasimon* 172; K. Reinhardt, *Aischylos als Regisseur und Theologe* (Bern 1949) 154–59; H. Lloyd-Jones, *The Justice of Zeus* (Berkeley and Los Angeles 1971) 92; and Lebeck, *The Oresteia* 160. Dawe, "Inconsistency of Plot" 58f., does not view this ode as opening toward a broader view of the Erinyes and their function. He considers the change from hostility to friendliness too abrupt, but an audience both hearing music and seeing dance patterns that relate to earlier thematic meters would not be so surprised.

135. For a discussion of the early history and function of the Erinyes see B. C. Dietrich, "Demeter, Erinys, Artemis," *Hermes* 90 (1962) 129–48.

136. Both K. J. Dover, "The Political Aspect of Aeschylus' *Eumenides*," *JHS* 77 (1957) 230–37, and Taplin, *Stagecraft* 391f., interpret this ode as

beginning with a reference to the specific case of Orestes and the court established to handle it, and then developing into a broader concern as it encompasses the more general cause of justice.

137. See Dale, *LMGD* 106.

138. Ibid.

139. Taplin, *Stagecraft* 410–14, limits the cast of characters to the Eumenides, Athena, the jurors as escorts, and two sacrificial victims with attendants; cf. G. Hermann, in "De Re Scenica," at the end of his *Adnotationes* (Berlin 1859) 657f. But Taplin rejects the women and children with little explanation of the precise list given in line 1027. Until more proof is offered, I would include them as a separate escort. See C. W. Macleod, "Clothing in the *Oresteia*," *Maia* 27 (1975) 201–03. But this is all; Taplin rightly protests that Aeschylean criticism has gone to extremes in enrolling extras for this final scene.

140. See above, n. 120.

141. Noticed by Murray, *Aeschylus* 210; Thomson, *Greek Lyric Metre* 131, recognizes the return of a meter familiar from the preceding two plays but does not trace it back to the Hymn to Zeus and its initial associations in the trilogy, nor does he remark on its continued use at the end of the *Eum.*, when the Erinyes are reconciled to a new life in Athens. In fact Thomson seems to feel that music does not unite the greater themes of the play but rather strives for a much more limited effect in terms of small nuances and suggestions in recalling previous odes and motifs. For example, although there is no meter for the Justice of Zeus in Thomson's scheme, he allows that the fourth paeonic has an overtone of bloodshed and that it occurs in several odes (pp. 113, 117f., and 130f.).

142. Both P. C. Wilson, "Notes on *Eumenides* 881–91," *CP* 42 (1947) 122–23, and Peradotto, "Cledonomancy," define the new force of persuasion brought by Athena.

143. See pp. 68–73 and 89–90 and n. 75. Peretti, *Epirrema e tragedia* 193–97, provides a good analysis of the structuring of this whole scene.

144. Such anapaestic formal exit passages occur commonly in the plays of Sophocles and Euripides and also in endings to the *Seven* (if genuine) and the *Ch.*

CHAPTER 3

1. See pp. 1–5.

2. See pp. 10–21.

3. These two dramatic themes of the *Oresteia* have been discussed often in recent years, most carefully by Kitto, *Form and Meaning* 1–86; Dodds, "Morals and Politics"; Lloyd-Jones, *The Justice of Zeus* 79–103; and Gagarin, *Aeschylean Drama* (Berkeley 1976) 57–118. Each critic has his own view of the relation between justice and necessary punishment, especially in regard to their mutual development and final incorporation into the new system at the end of the *Eum.* These opinions usually depend on an assessment of a "developing" versus a "static" Zeus.

4. See pp. 58–68 and Scott, "The Confused Chorus."

5. Confusion is seldom attributed to the choruses of the *Oresteia*. Generally critics have assumed that each chorus holds clear and decided views and have explained any reticence in terms of external features. Fraenkel, for example, explains the epode at *Ag.* 475–87 thus: "As a Chorus . . . they are possessed of less spontaneity; their words serve in the main as a reaction to the acts and words of the actors or as a means of leading them on. There is, as it were, a certain looseness in the psychological texture of the Chorus" (II, pp. 248f.). Contrary to such views see Dover, " Neglected Aspects of Agamemnon's Dilemma," and the careful study of implied meaning in Aeschylean drama by Srebrny, *Wort und Gedanke*. Those who acknowledge the chorus's inability to understand and to express a clear view of the situation are Peradotto, in his discussion of the despair and inaction of the chorus in the *Ag.* (here attributed to their desire to speak only good wishes for Agamemnon—not to confusion) in "Cledonomancy," and Lebeck, *The Oresteia* 32. There are particularly good discussions by Kitto, *Form and Meaning* 24ff. and 32ff., and O. L. Smith, "Once Again: The Guilt." See also Scott, "The Confused Chorus."

6. This new understanding has been discussed often in the same general terms but with a wide variety of emphases. The most extensive and helpful discussions on political and social themes are those by Thomson, *Aeschylus and Athens*, and Gagarin, *Aeschylean Drama*; on new alignment among men and gods, those by Reinhardt, *Aischylos als Regisseur*, and Kitto, *Form and Meaning*; on achievement of civilization, those by Owen, *The Harmony of Aeschylus*, and Golden, *In Praise of Prometheus*. Kuhns, *House, City, and Judge*, presents the resolution of the widest range of issues but on little real evidence from the text.

7. Exhaustive catalogues of additional themes and motifs in the *Oresteia* are offered by Kuhns, *House, City, and Judge*, and by E. Petrounias, *Funktion und Thematik der Bilder bei Aischylos* (Göttingen 1976) 127–316.

8. This interpretative paraphrase is based on *Ag.* 67–8, 160–66, and 250–55.

9. See discussions of the chorus as a character within the play rather than as an external commentator by Plüss, *Die Tragödie Agamemnon* 23–31; Winnington-Ingram, *"Agamemnon* 1343–71" 23–30; Rosenmeyer, "Gorgias, Aeschylus, and Apate"; J. J. Peradotto, "The Omen of the Eagles and the Ethos of Agamemnon," *Phoenix* 23 (1969) 249ff.; Dover, "Neglected Aspects of Agamemnon's Dilemma"; O. L. Smith, "Once Again: The Guilt"; and P. M. Smith, *On the Hymn to Zeus*.

10. Page's text (Oxford 1972) with *pou* as enclitic supports the interpretation that the chorus is puzzled by the presence of pain in a world ruled by Zeus although they can gain momentary calm by entrusting their future to that high god; this reading is well argued by N. B. Booth, "Zeus Hypsistos Megistos," against Pope, "Merciful Heavens."

11. There is a dispute whether Cassandra is to be seen as a wrongdoer who deserves just punishment or as a victim of a vindictive Apollo. I incline toward the latter for three reasons: she regards her continued ill treatment as outrageous (see 1082 and 1275–76); her defilement of her priestly

attire is such an extreme act that she must be justified in order to continue to deserve the chorus's pity; and her punishment is excessive in the same way that Troy's extinction is too great a price for the crime—thus she becomes another case of the god's warped pursuit of justice in the play. Recent discussions are: R. P. Winnington-Ingram, "The Role of Apollo in the *Oresteia*," *CR* 47 (1933) 97–104; Reinhardt, *Aischylos als Regisseur* 102ff.; H. L. Jansen, "Die Kassandragestalt im Aischylos' *Agamemnon*," *Temenos* 5 (1969) 107–19; D. M. Leahy, "The Role of Cassandra in the *Oresteia* of Aeschylus," *BRL* 52 (1969) 144–77; J. Fontenrose, "Gods and Men in the *Oresteia*," *TAPA* 102 (1971) 71–109, esp. 107–09.

12. Alexanderson, "Forebodings," points out the uniqueness of Cassandra's clear vision among the other characters in the *Ag.*, who continually offer varied and ambiguous hints about future developments.

13. This identification is also implied by the phrasing of *Ag.* 1431–33. Cf. discussions by N. G. L. Hammond, "Personal Freedom and its Limitations in the *Oresteia*," *JHS* 85 (1965) 44f.; and by A. F. Garvie, "The Opening of the *Choephoroi*," *BICS* 17 (1970) 80.

14. The mss. transmit *Haidou*, but this is probably a gloss. Zeus is thought to be a chthonic divinity by other unfortunate Aeschylean characters who yearn for a Zeus who controls the whole universe: Orestes, *Ch.* 382; the suppliant maidens, *Supp.* 158 and 231; but the Erinyes state the truth at *Eum.* 273. This title is known for Zeus earlier at *Iliad* 9.457 and Hesiod, *Erga* 465.

15. Such self-deception is common among Aeschylean characters; the Persian counselors learn how insecure Persian aspirations are even though they thought them to come from god (*Pers.* 101); Eteocles acts as though he is free of Oedipus' curse up to line 653; the suppliant women feel that Zeus will protect Argos, although the Argives are forced to surrender them in the second play; Agamemnon thinks that he is pursuing justice in decimating Troy. Like Clytemnestra, all these characters learn how confused or deluded they are—but only after it is too late.

16. Reinhardt, *Aischylos als Regisseur*, 108–10, is especially acute in his discussion of Aegisthus' role in the design of the last scene.

17. These lines are seriously corrupt. I have used Fraenkel's readings although he is not confident of his text; see his detailed discussion, pp. 792–96.

18. This deception is well analyzed as a motif of the trilogy by Zeitlin, "The Motif of the Corrupted Sacrifice."

19. Against the arguments by Lesky, "Der Kommos der *Choephoren*," which require the shift of lines 434–38 to achieve a symmetry that may not be present by design, I prefer the interpretation of the kommos by Schadewaldt, "Der Kommos in Aischylos' *Choephoren*," which finds meaning in the delivered text and keeps the role of Apollo as a causative force in its proper perspective. See also the recent discussion by de Romilly, "La haine dans l'*Orestie*," concerning the proper determination of Orestes' motives.

20. The most helpful discussions in the vast bibliography on this subject are: W. Nestle, *Griechische Religiosität von Homer bis Pindar und Aischylos* (Berlin 1930) 117–33; F. Solmsen, *Hesiod and Aeschylus* (Ithaca, N.Y. 1949)

178–224; A. Lesky, *Die Tragische Dichtung der Hellen* (Göttingen 1956) 50–98; Kitto, *Form and Meaning*, 1–86; H. Lloyd-Jones, "Zeus in Aeschylus," *JHS* 76 (1956) 55–67, and *The Justice of Zeus*, 79–103; Golden, *In Praise of Prometheus*, 100–26; T. B. L. Webster, in *Fifty Years (and Twelve) of Classical Scholarship* (New York 1968) 104–06; Peradotto, "Omen of the Eagles"; G. M. A. Grube, "Zeus in Aeschylus," *AJP* 91 (1970) 43–51; Fontenrose, "Gods and Men"; and Gagarin, *Aeschylean Drama*, 119–38.

21. D. J. Connacher, *Aeschylus' Prometheus Bound: A Literary Commentary* (Toronto 1980) 120–37, argues strongly for a similar political solution in the *PV.*

22. On this and the following points see the useful discussions by Thomson, *Aeschylus and Athens*; Reinhardt, *Aischylos als Regisseur*, 140–62; Kitto, *Form and Meaning* 81–86; Kuhns, *House, City, and Judge*; and P. G. Schmidt, "Das Humane bei Aeschylos," in *Die Gesellschaftliche Bedeutung des antiken Dramas für seine und für unsere Zeit* (ed. W. Hofmann and H. Kuch (Berlin 1973).

23. Peradotto, "Cledonomancy," especially his final note:

> Discourse is, of course, an indispensable element of the whole concept of communal life and especially of the polis. For an Athenian, the opposite of *anarchia* was *peitharchia* (*Antigone* 676), obedience to the laws based, as the word implies, upon persuasive speech rather than fear of brute compulsion. In Thucydides' classic description of *stasis* at Corcyra, the internal disintegration of the *polis* is accompanied by the decomposition of traditional verbal meanings (III, 82, 4). One of Aristotle's proofs that man is by nature a *politikon zoon* is that he alone among animals possesses speech, the natural purpose of which is to communicate that for which the *polis*-partnership is formed—the advantageous and the harmful, and therefore the right and the wrong (*Pol.* 1253a8–19).

24. Dover, "Political Aspect of *Eumenides*," and Schmidt, "Das Humane bei Aeschylos."

25. Such relevance is general and not tied to specific events in Athens. Attempts to see Aeschylus' plays as vehicles for political advice to the Athenians are interesting but questionable. They are usually based on small elements in the text that are not essential to the dramatic theme—such as the good feelings of Argos (*Eum.* 754–77) or cautions against staining the laws by the admission of evil influences (*Eum.* 690–703)—or on an interpretation of the major event, the establishment of the Areopagus. But tragedy, unlike blatantly political or guerrilla theater, usually seeks a more general education of the audience in the hope that the consequently wiser citizens will decide all issues well. The problem for commentators is to discriminate between overt political propagandizing or preaching by Aeschylus on contemporary issues and the use of contemporary objects and procedures as aids in communicating his basic themes (which did have lasting application even in contemporary Athens). The best discussions of this point are Dover, "Political Aspect of *Eumenides*" 230–37; Dodds, "Morals

and Politics"; and A. J. Podlecki, *The Political Background of Aeschylean Tragedy* (Ann Arbor 1966).

26. This world of opposites in conflict is well defined by C. J. Herington, "Aeschylus in Sicily," *JHS* 87 (1967) 74–85. De Romilly, *La crainte et l'angoisse*, describes the reactions of mortals confronting such a world.

CHAPTER 4

1. Such cries are expected in laments (cf. end of *Pers.*, *Seven* 875 = 881, and 966–1004), but they are so completely worked into the strophic structure of the odes in the *Pers.* that they are repeated as markers in these songs and may be used to complement the oriental words and costumes of the chorus.

2. Cf. H. D. Broadhead, *The Persae of Aeschylus* (Cambridge 1960) 310–17; and M. Alexiou, *The Ritual Lament in Greek Tradition* (Cambridge 1974) 131–60.

3. J. A. Haldane, "Barbaric Cries (Aesch. *Pers.* 633–639)," *CQ* 22 (1972) 42–50, comments on the accumulated epithets and onomatopoeic sounds; one should add also the repetitions *phil–* in 648, *Aidoneus* in 650, *Theomestor* in 655, *balen* in 658, *despot–* 666, and *naes anaes, anaes* in 680.

4. See the discussion by Alexiou (*Ritual Lament*, esp. 131ff.) of the traditional ritual forms that appear here and in other plays. In the exodos see lines 955 = 966, 1004 = 1010, 1040 = 1048, 1043 = 1051, 1055 = 1061, 1057 = 1064.

5. Examples include the lament of Cassandra, the invocation by the chorus at *Ch.* 152–63, the lament and invocation sections of the kommos in the *Ch.*, and the Binding Song in the *Eum.* For additional examples of such elements, see pp. 16–19.

6. R. Hölzle, *Zum Aufbau der lyrischen Partien des Aischylus* (Diss. Freiburg im Breisgau 1934), shows how during his career Aeschylus is increasingly successful in mixing pure song forms with elements of the dramatic situation. The songs of the *Persians* most clearly reveal this basic form. This point has been more recently demonstrated in the detailed study by Rode, *Untersuchungen.*

7. Haldane, "Musical Themes and Imagery," 35f., notes the opposition between the paean and the *ololyge* versus the lament.

8. J. T. Kakridis, "Licht und Finsternis in dem Botenbericht der *Perser* des Aischylos," *GB* 4 (1975) 145–54.

9. At 605 Atossa says she hears a *kelados ou paionios.* As Haldane "Musical Themes and Imagery," 35 and n. 19 correctly observes, this is a reference to the paean call when applied to a shout.

10. See the metrical scheme in appendix II in Broadhead, *Persae*, and the careful analysis of the parodos by Korzeniewski, *Griechische Metrik* 172–82.

11. What ethos the Greeks attached to various meters is still unclear, but this section of ionics has been interpreted as eastern in tone. See the discussions with examples by Thomson, *Greek Lyric Metre* 54–7, and Dale, *LMGD* 120ff. and 124.

12. There are some heavily Ionic passages such as 650 = 55, 694–96 = 700–02, and 950–52 = 968–65; but in other cases it is difficult to separate

ionics from choriambics, especially at 647–48 = 653–54 and 657–63 = 664–71—although Broadhead, *Persae* 292, argues effectively for taking 657–71 as basically choriambic.

13. Cf. Aristophanes, *Frogs* 1028–29, where Dionysus recalls only the clapping and sounds of the chorus in this scene.

14. For the most recent study on the placement of this stanza see W. C. Scott, "The Mesode at *Persae* 93–100," *GRBS* (1968) 259–66.

15. Cf. *Ag.* 355–60 and 1115–17; *Ch.* 980–89; *Eum.* 147; and above, pp. 41–43.

16. There have been several attempts to make these verses correspond, but all involve an unacceptably large number of alterations to the text. Broadhead, *Persae*, is only the latest editor to find strophic corresponsion in this mesode. But to do so he must not only reject 96b but also invert the order of the final line. These represent a great many changes based on three questions whose answers are not as easy as Broadhead would like: (1) how did *poti–* or *para–* disappear from the word *sainousa*? (2) why is there an unusual midstanza anaclastic line at 95b? (3) why does the stanza not close with an anaclast as do the preceding stanzas? The first question admits of too many possible explanations to be decisive, although few would find fault with Seidler's ingenuity; in this same song there is confusion about another prefix in line 136. Certainly such corruption would be far less than the later inversion of word order in Broadhead's text, which is similarly unexplained on paleographic grounds. In addition, Groeneboom makes a good point when he asks what reference *to proton* in a gloss has to the conjectured text. The second question simply ignores those passages where Aeschylus breaks up runs of the same unvaried meter with lines that are either recognized alternatives or related to previous meters. The closest parallels for alternatives are: *Pers.* 78–85 = 992 = 1000; *Supp.* 154–60 = 168–74; *Ag.* 144, 690–95 = 707–12, and 744–47 = 757–60; and *Eum.* 919; parallels for lines related to previous meters are *Ag.* 165, 197, 225–27 = 235 = 37, 241–42 = 251–52, 723–24 = 733–34, 977, and 1015. In regard to the third suspected irregularity about the meter of his line 114, Broadhead quotes Page in a footnote on p. 256: "There is nothing intrinsically unlikely in it." None of these suspicions is substantial enough to warrant large changes in the text in the hope of restoring strophic construction to these lines.

17. Editors place Darius' entrance after 680, thus permitting him to interrupt the chorus's song. Such interruption would be impossible if Darius rises during the song, and there are at least two scenes in which Aeschylean characters can be argued to appear during a choral lyric, although neither example is without severe problems. One is the entrance of the funeral procession with the bodies of Eteocles and Polyneices at *Seven* 848–60; Taplin, *Stagecraft* 169ff., cogently argues for adapting the text to make 848–53 an astrophic entrance announcement leading to a brief prelude (854–60) prior to the continuing lyric of the chorus at 875ff. In this structure the bodies are presented in the same way that characters are usually brought on, with a separate nonstrophic choral announcement after the strophic song is finished. The second example is Clytemnestra's possible

entrance during the parodos of the *Ag.*; yet even in this case she would not enter during strophic lyric but rather during anapaests (83), an entrance that has only imprecise parallels at *Pers.* 150–54 and *Ag.* 783–809. It seems that there is no clear case for the entrance of a character during a choral ode. Thus I assume that Darius must be seen to enter at the end of this ode, at which point the chorus falls silent in awe before the old king.

18. See the discussion by B. Alexanderson, "Darius in the *Persians*," *Eranos* 65 (1967) 1–11, which shows in more precise terms that Aeschylus introduced Darius onstage as a figure designed to enhance the basic themes of the drama despite the problems of motivating his appearance and of writing a believable speech for a character who possesses special knowledge. The contrast between Darius and Xerxes is best discussed by Broadhead, *Persae* xxviii–xxix; E. B. Holtsmark, "Ring Composition and the *Persae* of Aeschylus," *SO* 45 (1970) 5–23; Taplin, *Stagecraft* 125f.; and W. G. Thalmann, "Xerxes' Rags: Some Problems in Aeschylus' *Persians*," *AJP* 101 (1980) 260–82.

19. See the discussion of "mirror scenes" by O. Taplin, "Significant Actions in Sophocles' *Philoctetes*," *GRBS* 12 (1971) 25–44; idem, *Stagecraft* 99–103 and 356–59, and elsewhere with discussions of pertinent passages; and in his *Greek Tragedy in Action* 122–139. The term, though current in dramatic criticism, is not precise, because the parallel is not always a mirror image but rather a strong suggestion of a previous scene with strong differences and contrasts, as in these two scenes from the *Persians*.

20. Broadhead catches the whole effect of the ending in meter and form in *Persae* 315f., and Taplin describes its point well: "This procession . . . is not grand or honorific. Rather, Xerxes' total involvement in the procession . . . shows him as a shattered man, sharing the humiliation and despair of his citizens. He has none of the authority and aloofness of his parents. The procession also suggests . . . the final exhaustion of the lamention" (*Stagecraft* 128). See also the discussion of the basic theme of the *Persians* by S. M. Adams, "Salamis Symphony," in *Studies in Honor of Gilbert Murray* (Toronto 1952) 46–54.

21. It remains uncertain whether these lamenting lines are to be given to semichoruses or to the two sisters. Page (Oxford 1972) admits that there is nothing in these lines that must of necessity be assigned to the sisters, but the whole issue is involved with suspicions that beginning at 861 the play is seriously corrupted (on this matter see below, n. 37 and 40). Most editors accept the genuineness of the lament at 875–960, but I can find no convincing evidence for line assignment within the words themselves. Therefore, the assumption of the presence or absence of the sisters determines the line of argument. If they are there, critics are uncomfortable about having the sisters present but remaining silent (cf. Taplin, *Stagecraft* 179f., and most forcefully in "Aeschylean Silences" 84–89). But such critics seldom take into account the gain in dramatic meaning from the presence of characters in the background even though they are not specifically mentioned as being silent. I would place both Eteocles and Orestes visibly onstage and yet significantly silent during the parodoi of the *Seven* (see below, n. 24) and the *Ch.*; and critics have long noted the effectiveness of Atossa's silent

presence at *Pers.* 246–90 even though it is not specifically mentioned by other characters. I would therefore conclude that the assignment of lines in this ode is a *non liquet*, but would prefer to give the lines to the chorus. If the sisters are not there, the chorus necessarily has the lines; if they are there, they are left free to perform actions appropriate to a lament and thus to establish the affection for the brothers that will be used as motivation for the division of roles at the end of the play.

22. See Haldane, "Musical Themes and Imagery" 36f., for a sensitive discussion of the metaphorical use of musical terms.

23. One small additional passage: at 961–65 Antigone and Ismene sing a small lyric that has all the marks of a traditional lament; cf. Alexiou, *Ritual Lament* 150f.

24. Because the contrast is so basic to the first part of the play, I would prefer to have Eteocles remain onstage during the parodos; cf. F. W. Dignan, *The Idle Actor in Aeschylus* (Diss. Chicago 1905) 20. This scheme is rejected by R. J. Stephenson, *Some Aspects of the Dramatic Art of Aeschylus* (Diss. Stanford 1913) 10, and by Taplin, *Stagecraft* 139–41. Stephenson feels that Eteocles would reprimand the women sooner if he were present, but this is to import reactions from real life into the controlled world of the theater: on such grounds Atossa's questions (*Pers.* 230–43), her restraint during the messenger's long speeches (302), and many other Aeschylean scenes are objectionable. Taplin *Stagecraft* offers a more reasonable explanation for Eteocles' exit: he must be in action and appear the commander. Here one must choose between two desirable effects: the actual efficiency of the commander versus his presence onstage to offer visual contrast to the words of the chorus. Contrary to Taplin's "Aeschylean Silences," a character can remain significant and still be in the background; see J. T. Allen, "The Idle Actor in Aeschylus," *CQ* 1 (1907) 268–72 (although he is dubious about Eteocles' presence during the parodos), and Scott, "Lines for Clytemnestra," esp. nn. 17 and 18.

25. Probably A. Lesky, "Decision and Responsibility in the Tragedy of Aeschylus," *JHS* 86 (1966) 78–85, and "Eteokles in den *Sieben gegen Theben*," *WS* 74 (1961) 5–17, is on the firmest ground when he says that Eteocles' actions in assigning men are the combined result of the curse and his own free choice. The most helpful discussions in balancing the forces at work on Eteocles are: F. Solmsen, "The Erinys in Aischylos' *Septem*," *TAPA* 68 (1937) 197–211; H. Patzer, "Die dramatische Handlung der *Sieben gegen Theben*," *HSCP* 63 (1958) 97–119; E. Wolff, "Die Entscheidung des Eteokles in den *Sieben gegen Theben*," *HSCP* 63 (1958) 89–95; B. Otis, "The Unity of the *Seven against Thebes*," *GRBS* 3 (1960) 145–74; K. von Fritz, "Die Gestalt des Eteokles in Aeschylus' *Sieben gegen Theben*," in *Antike und Moderne Tragödie* (Berlin 1962) 193–226; H. Erbse, "Interpretationsprobleme in den *Septem* des Aischylus," *Hermes* 92 (1964) 1–22; H. D. Cameron, *Studies on the* Seven against Thebes (The Hague 1971); A. P. Burnett, "Curse and Dream in Aeschylus' *Septem*," *GRBS* 14 (1973) 343–68; R. P. Winnington-Ingram, *"Septem contra Thebas,"* YCS 25 (1977) 1–45; and W. G. Thalmann, *Dramatic Art in Aeschylus's* Seven against Thebes (New Haven and London 1978), especially 146–49.

26. It is probable that Aeschylus was the first playwright to use the dochmiac. It appears at *Pers.* 268 and in the exodos to that play. It is next used with great effectiveness in characterizing the frantic women in the *Seven*. On the first use of the dochmiac in drama see Snell, *Griechische Metrik* 52; Dale, *LMGD* 104; and Webster, "Tradition in Greek Dramatic Lyric." For the presentation of the emotional women through the astrophic iambodochmiacs with probable divided individual parts among the members of the chorus, see A. W. Verrall, *The* Seven against Thebes *of Aeschylus* (London 1887) 130f.; Wilamowitz, *Interpretationen* 69–73; and Rode, *Untersuchungen* 34–39.

27. Wecklein's *Appendix* reveals the varieties of line assignment up to his time, and there is no unanimity even among recent editors. A division of 78–107 among individual speakers is favored by Hermann, Paley, Verrall, Murray, Dawson; also see F. Bücheler, "De *Septem* Aeschylea," *RhM* 32 (1877) 312f. C. Robert, "Die Parodos des aischyleischen *Septem*," *Hermes* 57 (1922) 161–70, assigns these lines to semichoruses. According to Wilamowitz *Interpretationen* 69ff. [see "Parerga." *Hermes* 14 (1879) 174f.], and J. Mesk, "Die Parodos der *Sieben gegen Theben*," *Philologus* 89 (1934) 454–59, the chorus sings these lines together.

28. Cf. Verrall, *Seven against Thebes* 130f.; Wilamowitz, *Interpretationen* 69–73; and S. Bernardete, "Two Notes on Aeschylus' *Septem* I," *WS* 80 (1967) 22–30, who compares the more settled and reflective quality of the first stasimon with the animated words of the parodos.

29. For a parallel movement from disorder to order see the discussion of Clytemnestra's words versus her meters in relation to the chorus's responses at the end of the *Ag.*, pp. 68–73.

30. Noted by T. G. Rosenmeyer, "*The Seven against Thebes*: The Tragedy of War," *Arion* 1 (1962) 48–78. Also K. Wilkens, *Die Interdependenz zwischen Tragödienstruktur und Theologie* (Munich 1974) 24–113, argues for a careful proportioning of the paired speeches of Eteocles and the scout, which is broken by the emotional speech of Eteocles.

31. The disorder evident in the nonstrophic opening to the parodos continues in the interjections of the women in the second strophic pair and in their repeated short petitions for the gods' help.

32. W. Schadewaldt, "Die Wappnung des Eteokles," in *Eranion. Festschrift für H. Hommel* (Tübingen 1961) 105–16. Some of this repeated structure is noted in a fine article by A. L. Brown, "Eteocles and the Chorus in the *Seven against Thebes*," *Phoenix* 31 (1977) 300–17, in which he argues that similar form shows the attitudes of the characters, which remain constant in different situations; this structural balance is also noted by Thalmann, *Dramatic Art in Aeschylus's Seven* 93f.

33. Taplin, *Stagecraft* 167, notes this pattern, but does not consider the larger scene, including the parodos and the reversal in musical structure that comes at the end of the play. In addition, cf. A. J. Podlecki, "The Character of Eteocles in Aeschylus' *Seven against Thebes*," *TAPA* 95 (1964) 283–99, esp. 289–95.

34. H. Engelmann, "Der Schiedsrichter aus der Fremde," *RhM* 110 (1967) 97–102, discusses how the ode at 720–91 shows the chorus's process

of riddle-solving that brings the women to clear understanding of their world. Such an understanding comes to Eteocles at 654ff.; see above n. 25.

35. T. B. L. Webster, "Preparation and Motivation in Greek Tragedy," *CR* 47 (1933) 117–23, notes that weak preparation for a character's entrance is a sign of strong and explicit motivation—in this case strong motivation from the Erinys, a force offstage and outside the sphere of the onstage characters' desires.

36. It is at the words *tad' autodela* (847) that the procession with the corpses becomes visible to the spectators. Taplin, *Stagecraft*, wants to postpone their appearance until 861 on the basis of orderly parallels elsewhere; but the whole point to this odd lyric is that the appearance of the corpses breaks into an orderly form, upsetting the musical structure expected by the audience.

37. Confusion reigns among critics at this point. Countless scholars have censured lines 861–74 (in addition to the whole ending of the play) in protest against the introduction of the sisters; for the two most recent attacks, see E. Fraenkel, "Zum Schluss der *Sieben gegen Theben*," *MH* 21 (1964) 58–64, and Taplin, *Stagecraft* 176–91. Yet the point made by H. Lloyd-Jones, "The End of the *Seven against Thebes*," *CQ* 9 (1959) 80–115, remains untouched; no one has yet proved that this scene is not by Aeschylus. See further on the end of the play below, n. 40.

38. See the discussions on pp. 50–51 and 112–18.

39. The ending of the *Seven* does not contain forms unusual for an Aeschylean drama. The anapaests are customary for a final exodos, but in addition the songs at the end of the *Pers.* and the *Supp.* are split among two separate parts. Moreover, it is not necessary for the chorus to end a drama on a fully organized and harmonious note if the intent of the playwright is to portray continuing disorder; cf. the ending of the *Pers.*, where music is replaced by cries of lamentation, and the ending of the *Ag.*, where there is no final music. In both cases the audience should be left with the feeling that the future is not a happy one.

40. For recent discussions by critics who see a purposeful ending of a calculated disorder rather than seeking an organized resolution to every trilogy, see Otis, "Unity of the *Seven*"; Golden, *In Praise of Prometheus* 42–61; and Bernardette, "Two Notes on *Septem*."

I have passed over the numerous flaws in the final segment of the *Seven* found by critics, the most recent of whom are E. Fraenkel, "Zum Schluss der *Sieben*"; R. D. Dawe, "The End of the *Seven against Thebes*," *CQ* 17 (1967) 16–28; and Taplin, *Stagecraft* 169–191. I have ignored their strong argumentation in order to show the reversed musical pattern, a form that almost necessarily presupposes the authenticity of the ending as it stands unless one assumes a musically acute forger. Given Aeschylus' skill in handling the modulation from song to speech and vice versa in organizing his scenes and the other playwrights' more direct management of musical forms, there does appear to be an Aeschylean concept at the basis of the design of this scene. I cannot argue away the inconsistencies or oddities of language and thought so clearly delineated by the scene's critics, but several of them may be related to the playwright's desire to blunt the sense of order and completion at the end of the play. The strange form of 861–74, for example, marks the reversal of the previous pattern by having the chorus make a formal introduction to the characters who are involved in the lament as well as introducing their own song. It should also be noted that even in his most polished work Aeschylus does not always carefully coordinate all details. He seems to have been far more interested in the effectiveness of the whole drama; see Dawe, "Inconsistency of Plot," who acknowledges Aeschylean inconsistencies but feels that they can be explained in terms of the required consistency of the total play.

I started this study firmly believing that the ending of the *Seven* was spurious; having discovered the formative role of musical design in my analysis of the *Oresteia*, I now tentatively accept the ending of the *Seven* as genuine but continue to seek explanations for the remaining inconsistencies, the two greatest being the coordinated understanding of 827–28f., 840–41, and 902–03 (the relation between the continuing problems of the city and the death of Eteocles), and the implications of 727–33, 785–91, 818–19, 914(?), and 1002–04 that Oedipus prophesied a burial for the brothers that the ending does not fulfill. At the moment I accept the conclusion of Lloyd-Jones, "The End of the *Seven*," that despite odd and clumsy features the final scene has not yet been proved spurious.

41. The closest study of stylistic and structural features in the *Suppliants* is A. F. Garvie, *Aeschylus' Supplices* (Cambridge 1969) 29–140. Cf. also A. Lesky, "Die Datierung der Hiketides und der Tragiker Mesatos," *Hermes* 82 (1954) 1–13; R. D. Murray, *The Motif of Io in Aeschylus' Suppliants* (Princeton 1958) 88–97; C. J. Herington, "Aeschylus: The Last Phase," *Arion* 4 (1965) 387–403; and idem, "Aeschylus in Sicily," *JHS* 87 (1967) 74–85.

42. Haldane, "Musical Themes and Imagery" finds references to music only at 115f. and 625–709.

43. Hölzle, *Zum Aufbau der lyrischen Partien*, shows that the songs/prayers of the suppliants are the situation rather than the accompaniment to the characters' situation.

44. R. P. Winnington-Ingram, "The Danaid Trilogy of Aeschylus," *JHS* 81 (1961) 141–52; and Garvie, *Aeschylus Supplices* 163–233.

45. Thus belying their words *ielemoi* and *gooi* (115–16) as true descriptions of their stage action. They are harassed but not frantic; they can present their sorrow effectively but are quite purposeful and even calculating in seeking their own safety.

46. I can find only Rode, *Untersuchungen*, who opposes the repetition of the final ephymnion.

47. For parallel use of nonstrophic form see *Pers.* 94–100 and 1066–77, *Ag.* 140–59, *Cho.* 75–83, and *Eum.* 307–96; the latter three are discussed in Scott, "Non-Strophic Elements."

48. Murray, *Motif of Io*, and T. Gantz, "Love and Death in the *Suppliants* of Aeschylus," *Phoenix* 32 (1978) 279–87, who extends such irony even to the unwitting puns, double meanings, and innuendos in the maidens' speeches.

49. I am persuaded by the latest study, M. McCall, "The Secondary

Choruses in Aeschylus' *Supplices*," *CSCA* 9 (1976) 117–31. He argues effectively that only the Danaids sing, splitting the strophic stanzas at 1052–61 into semichoruses; he supports the previous study by C. van der Graaf, "Les suivantes dans le choeur final des *Suppliants* d'Eschyle," *Mnemosyne* 10 (1942) 281–85. However, H. Lloyd-Jones, "The *Supplices* of Aeschylus: The New Date and Old Problem," *AC* 33 (1964) 356–74, argues for a role for the handmaidens; and H. Friis Johansen, "Progymnasmata," *C&M* 27 (1966) 61 ff., would give the opposing lines to a secondary chorus of Argives (see also the review of Garvie by Whittle *CR* 20 (1970) 298 f.).

50. On the careful structuring of this scene see Peretti, *Epirrema e tragedia* 107–18.

51. Lesky, "Decision and Responsibility," and A. Rivier, "Remarques sur le "nécessaire" et la "nécessité" chez Eschyle," *REG* 81 (1968) 5–39.

52. Although characters do interrupt one another even in the midst of sentences in speech, it is unprecedented in Aeschylean drama for a chorus to be interrupted in midline; it always finishes its grammar, and then the stage action shows that an interruption has taken place. Such interruptions of choral form are clearest when an antistrophe is suppressed by a character who interrupts the chorus before it has the chance to complete its full form; examples are discussed in Scott, "Non-Strophic Elements" 184 ff.

53. Haldane, "Musical Themes and Imagery" 34.

54. For general discussion of conflicting views on this play see the recent full-length studies by C. J. Herington, *The Author of the Prometheus Bound* (Austin and London 1970), and M. Griffith, *The Authenticity of the Prometheus Bound* (Cambridge 1979); also Taplin, *Stagecraft* 460–69. The bibliographies in each study list previous discussions of the problems.

55. In fact, doubts about the authenticity of the *PV* began with problems concerning metrical pecularities in choral songs as well as in trimeters, cited by R. Westphal, *Prolegomena zu Aischylos Tragödien* (Leipzig 1869).

56. A subject discussed fully by Rode, *Untersuchungen* 174–81.

57. Haldane, "Musical Themes and Imagery" 34 f., provides a full survey of musical words in the *PV*, but this list is short.

58. Griffith, *Authenticity* 19–67, carefully analyses the lyric lines, concluding: "They reveal, both in many points of detail, and in the overall choice and treatment of the basic metres, differences from Aeschylus' normal style which far exceeded the individual and minor oddities of each of his extant plays."

59. Griffith, *Authenticity* 25–33, comments extensively on problems in determining the colometry of 128–35 = 144–51 and 397–414. In determining this percentage I have counted them as Page does, as essentially choriambic rather than ionic. But Griffith is correct in noting that all three tragedians write similar passages in which there is an ambiguity between choriambic-iambic and anaclastic ionic. In addition, 545–60 are so uncertain in form that they have been counted as outside the group of basic meters in the play.

60. See 109–11.

61. See Griffith, *Authenticity* 108–10, for a listing of the peculiar features

of this monody. Wilamowitz, *Interpretationen* 158f., rationalizes these features by finding parallels in the works of Sophocles and Euripides, but such comparisons do not fully explain the odd features. S. V. Tracy, *"Prometheus Bound* 114–117," *HSCP* 75 (1971) 59–62, even suggests that the audience anticipates the entrance of the eagle at the odd lines 114–17. This fanciful claim is effectively refuted by B. E. Donovan, *"Prometheus Bound* 114–117 Reconsidered," *HSCP* 77 (1973) 125–29.

62. G. Murray, *Aeschylus* 45, believes that the shifting of meters in successive sections is "meant to convey the effect of a series of long solitary periods of waiting."

63. Although Wilamowitz, *Interpretationen* 158ff., tries to find sufficient parallels, even Herington (*Author of Prometheus Bound*), a strong proponent of Aeschylean authorship, admits this monody to be unique. This song also presents several staging problems; see Griffith, *Authenticity* 143–46, and Taplin, *Stagecraft* 252–60.

64. Anapaestic lines spoken by a character between strophic choral stanzas appear in the parodoi to the *Ajax* and the *Philoctetes*; slightly modified versions of the same form occur in the opening songs of the *Antigone* and the *Oedipus at Colonus*. Cf. also the parodoi to the *Alcestis*, the *Medea*, and the *Rhesus*.

65. Kranz, *Stasimon* 226–28, attacks the authenticity of this inconsequential song.

66. Confusion reigns about the structuring of the final lines of 397–435. Most editors print them as one epode, but some (including Schütz, Hermann, Schmidt, Paley, Wecklein, and Bassi) have made several emendations in order to make a strophic structure; Morell and Smyth print two separate epodes.

67. See parallels in Scott, "Non-Strophic Elements" 184ff.

68. The most recent comments on this "silence" are by Taplin, "Aeschylean Silences" 83f. and *Stagecraft* 263–65, and Griffith, *Authenticity* 116–18.

69. Cf. Wilamowitz, *Interpretationen* 122–23; Pohlenz, *Die Griechische Tragödie* 64; G. Méautis, *Eschyle et la trilogie* (Paris 1936) 87–89; and H. D. F. Kitto, *Greek Tragedy*, 2d ed. (London 1950) 112.

70. Well discussed by Griffith, *Authenticity* 128–30 and 135f.; cf. also Rode, *Untersuchungen.*

71. O. Hiltbrunner, *Wiederholungs- und Motivtechnik bei Aischylos* (Strasbourg 1946) 75–77, reaches the same conclusion in regard to repetitions of motifs.

SELECT BIBLIOGRAPHY

Editions and translations: For a list of editions and translations published prior to 1974 and cited by the editor's or translator's name in this study see A. Wartelle, *Bibliographie historique et critique d'Eschyle* (Paris 1978).

Books and Articles: The following books and articles have been of continuous help in my work on the performance of the choral lyrics of Aeschylean drama.

Die Bauformen der griechischen Tragödie, heraug. v. W. Jens (Munich, 1971).

Bodensteiner, E. "Szenische Fragen über den Ort des Auftretens und Abgehens von Schauspielern und Chor im griechischen Drama." *Jahrbücher für classiche Philologie*, Suppbd. 19 (1893).

Brown, S. A. "A Contextual Analysis of Tragic Meter: The Anapaest" in *Ancient and Modern*: Essays in Honor of Gerald F. Else (Ann Arbor, 1977) 45–77.

Dale, A. M. *Collected Papers*. (Cambridge, 1969).

————. *The Lyric Metres of Greek Drama*. 2d ed. Cambridge, 1968.

Else, G. F. *The Origin and Early Form of Greek Tragedy*. Martin Classical Lecture 20. Cambridge, 1965.

Flickinger, R. C. *The Greek Theater and Its Drama*. 4th ed. Chicago, 1936.

Gantz, T. "The Chorus of Aischylos' *Agamemnon*." *Harvard Studies in Classical Philology* 87 (1983) 65–86.

Haldane, J. A. "Musical Themes and Imagery in Aeschylus." *JHS* 85 (1965) 33–41.

Helmreich, F. *Der Chor im Drama des Äschylus*. Kempten, 1915.

Hermann, G. *Aeschyli Tragoediae*. 2d ed. Berlin, 1859.

Hölzle, R. *Zum Aufbau der lyrischen Partien des Aischylos*. Diss. Freiburg, 1934.

Kitto, H. D. F. *Form and Meaning in Drama*. London, 1956.

————. *Greek Tragedy*. 2d ed. London, 1950.

Kranz, W. *Stasimon: Untersuchungen zu Form und Gestalt der griechischen Tragödie*. Berlin, 1933.

Kraus, W. *Strophengestaltung in der griechischen Tragödie, I. Aischylos und Sophokles. Sitzungsberichte der Akademie der Wissenschaften, Wien* 231 (1957).

Lebeck, A. *The Oresteia: A Study in Language and Structure*. Cambridge, Mass., 1971.

Maas, P. *Greek Metre*. Translated by H. Lloyd-Jones. Oxford, 1962.

Müller, K. O. *Aeschylos Eumeniden*. Göttingen, 1833.

Peretti, A. *Epirrema e tragedia*. Florence, 1939.

Pickard-Cambridge, A. W. *Dithyramb, Tragedy, and Comedy.* 2d ed., rev. T. B. L. Webster. Oxford, 1962.

————. *The Dramatic Festivals of Athens.* 2d ed., rev. J. Gould and D. M. Lewis. Oxford, 1968.

Podlecki, A. J. "The Aeschylean Chorus as Dramatic Persona." In *Studi Classici in Onore di Quintino Cataudella,* 187–204. Catania, 1972.

Reinhardt, K. *Aischylos als Regisseur und Theologe.* Bern, 1949.

Rode, J. *Untersuchungen zur Form des aischyleischen Chorliedes.* Diss. Tübingen, 1965.

Rosenmeyer, T. G. *The Art of Aeschylus* (Berkeley, 1982).

Snell, B. *Aischylos und das Handeln im Drama. Philologus,* Suppbd. 20, hft. 1 (1928).

Taplin, O. *The Stagecraft of Aeschylus: The Dramatic Use of Exits and Entrances in Greek Tragedy.* Oxford, 1977.

Thomson, G. *Greek Lyric Metre.* Cambridge, 1929.

Webster, T. B. L. *The Greek Chorus.* London, 1970.

Wilamowitz-Moellendorff, U. von. *Aeschylos Orestie.* Vol. 2. Berlin, 1896.

————. *Aischylos. Interpretationen.* Berlin, 1914.

Winnington-Ingram, R. P. "Aeschylus' *Agamemnon 1343–1371*" CQ 4 (1954) 23–30.

INDEX